THE MOST BEAU
POP BALLADS

ISBN 1-57560-738-7

Cherry Lane Music Company
Director of Publications/Project Editor: Mark Phillips

Visit our website at www.cherrylane.com

CONTENTS

4	All My Life	*Linda Ronstadt & Aaron Neville*
7	Amanda	*Boston*
12	Amazed	*Lonestar*
17	Annie's Song	*John Denver*
20	Don't Know Much	*Linda Ronstadt & Aaron Neville*
32	Dulcinea	*from* Man of La Mancha
34	Feel Like Makin' Love	*Roberta Flack*
36	Follow Me	*John Denver*
27	For Always	*Josh Groban & Lara Fabian*
40	From a Distance	*Bette Midler*
52	Give Me Forever (I Do)	*John Tesh & James Ingram*
47	Goodbye My Friend	*Karla Bonoff*
58	Here I Am	*Bryan Adams*
62	Hero	*Mariah Carey*
67	I Want to Know What Love Is	*Foreigner*
72	If Ever You're in My Arms Again	*Peabo Bryson*
82	The Impossible Dream	*from* Man of La Mancha
86	In My Daughter's Eyes	*Martina McBride*
77	Just Once	*Quincy Jones & James Ingram*
90	May You Always	*The McGuire Sisters*
93	Misty	*Johnny Mathis*
96	My Cherie Amour	*Stevie Wonder*
99	On My Own	*from* Les Misérables
104	Only the Lonely	*The Motels*
112	Perhaps Love	*Plácido Domingo & John Denver*
107	She's Always a Woman	*Billy Joel*
116	Someone Like You	*from* Jekyll & Hyde
120	Superstar	*The Carpenters*
126	This Is the Moment	*from* Jekyll & Hyde
123	This Masquerade	*George Benson*
130	Through the Years	*Kenny Rogers*
140	Time After Time	*Cyndi Lauper*
144	Unchained Melody	*The Righteous Brothers*
135	Unusual Way	*from* Nine
148	Up Where We Belong	*Joe Cocker & Jennifer Warnes*
152	Waiting for a Girl Like You	*Foreigner*
159	What a Wonderful World	*Louis Armstrong*
162	When You Believe (from *The Prince of Egypt*)	*Whitney Houston & Mariah Carey*
169	Where Is the Love?	*Roberta Flack*
172	Your Song	*Elton John*

All My Life

Words and Music by
Karla Bonoff

Moderately

Am I real - ly here in your arms?
And I nev - er real - ly knew how to love.

It's just like I dreamed it would be.
I just hoped some - how I'd see.

I feel like we're fro - zen in time,
asked for a lit - tle help from a - bove.

and you're the on - ly one I can see.
Send an an - gel down to me.

Lyrics below the staves:

Hey, ___ I've ___ looked all ___ my life ___ for you. ___

___ Now, you're here. ___

Hey, ___ I'll ___ spend all ___ my life ___ with you. ___

___ All my life.

Nev - er thought that I could feel a love so ten - der.

Nev - er thought I could let those feel - ings show. _____ But now my

heart is on my sleeve, and this love will nev - er leave, I _____

D.S. and fade

know, I know. _____

Amanda

Words and Music by
Tom Scholz

Slowly, in 2

1. Babe, _____ to - mor - row's so far _____ a - way. _____ There's
2.3.4. (See additional lyrics)

some - thin' I just have to say. _____ I don't

think I could hide ___ what I'm feel - in' in - side ___ an - oth - er day

know - in' I love ___ you.

2. And ___ you?

7

Chorus

take you by sur-prise and make you re-al-ize, A-man-da.___

I'm gon-na tell you right a-way; I can't wait an-oth-er day, A-

man-da.___ I'm gon-na say it like a man and

I'm gon-na

make you un-der-stand, A - man - da. ____ I

love _____ you.

I know that we ___ can't wait. ___ And I swear, ___

I swear it's not a lie,___ girl.___ To - mor - row may be too late.___

___ You, you and I,___ girl, we can

share a life ___ to - geth - er. It's now or nev - er, and to-

mor - row may be too late. ___ Oh. ___

Tag

And

feel - in' the way — I do, — I don't wan - na wait my whole life

through _____ to say

I'm in love with you. _____

Additional Lyrics

2. And I, I'm gettin' too close again.
   I don't wanna see it end.
   If I tell you tonight, will you turn out the light
   And walk away knowin' I love you?

   Chorus

3. And I feel like today's the day.
   I'm lookin' for the words to say.
   Do you wanna be free? Are you ready for me
   To feel this way? I don't wanna lose ya.

4. So, it may be too soon, I know.
   The feelin' takes so long to grow.
   If I tell you today, will you turn me away
   And let me go? I don't wanna lose you.

   Chorus

   Bridge

   Tag

Amazed

Words and Music by
Chris Lindsey, Marv Green
and Aimee Mayo

Moderately slow Country Ballad

Ev - 'ry time our eyes meet this feel - in' in - side me
The smell of your skin

is al - most more than I can take.
the way you whis - per in the dark.

Ba - by, when you touch me, I can feel how much you love me,
Your hair all a - round me; ba - by you sur - round me.

and it just blows me a - way.
You touch ev - 'ry place in my ____ heart.

I've nev - er been this close to an - y - one or an - y - thing.
Oh, it feels this close like the first time ev - 'ry time.

I can hear your thoughts. I can see your dreams.
I wan - na spend the whole night in your eyes.

I don't know how you do what you do. ____ I'm so in love with you. It just keeps get - ting bet - ter. _____

I wan - na spend the rest of my life _____ with you by my side _____

_____ for - ev - er and ev - er. _____

Ev - 'ry lit - tle thing that you do, _____ ba - by, I'm a - mazed _____ by you.

2.

B♭ · C

ba - by, I'm a - mazed ___ by you.

E♭ · F · C

E♭ · B♭ · Fsus4 · F · B♭

Ev - 'ry lit - tle thing that you do. ___

C · Dm

I'm so in love with you. It just keeps get - tin'

B♭ · F

bet - ter. ___ I wan - na spend the rest of my life ___

with you by my side ___ for - ev - er and ___

ev - er. ___ Ev - 'ry lit - tle thing that you do, ___

___ ev - 'ry lit - tle thing that you ___

Freely   **Tempo I**

do,   ba-by, I'm a-mazed __ by __ you.   *mp*   *rit.*

Annie's Song

Words and Music by
John Denver

Lyrics below the staves:

rain. _____
arms. _____
Like a storm in the
Let me lay down be -

des - ert,
side you,
like a sleep - y blue
let me al - ways be

o - cean,
with you; _____
you fill up my
come let me

sens - es,
love you,
come fill me a -
come love me a -

Don't Know Much

Words and Music by
Barry Mann, Cynthia Weil
and Tom Snow

Look at this face,

I know the years are show - ing.

Look at this life, ___ I

still don't know where it's go - ing.

I don't know much,

but I know I love you, _____ and that may be _____ all I need to know.

Look at these eyes, they've nev - er seen what mat - ters.

Look at these dreams, _ so beat - en and so bat - tered. _____

Lyrics under the staff:

I don't know much,   but I know I love you,   and that may be ____ all I need to know. So man-y ques-tions still left un-an-swered. So much I've nev-er bro-ken through.

And when I feel you near me

some-times I see so clear-ly

the on-ly truth I've ev-er

known is me and you.

Look at this man

so blessed with in-spi-ra-tion. Look at this soul, __ still

search-ing for sal-va-tion. __ I don't know much,

but I know I love you, _____ and

that may be _____ all I need to know.

Lyrics:

I don't know much,

but I know I love you,

and that may be all I need to

know.

I don't know much,

but I know I love you.

and

that may be ___ all there is to know. ___

For Always

from the Motion Picture A.I. ARTIFICIAL INTELLIGENCE

Lyric by Cynthia Weil

Music by John Williams

Moderately slow, in 4

I close _____ my eyes, _____ and

there in the shad-ows I see _____ your light. _____ You

come to me out of my dreams a - cross _____ the

night. You

take _____ my hand _____ though

you may be so man-y stars a - way. _____ I

know that our spir-its and souls are one. _____ We've

cir-cled the moon and we've touched _____ the sun; so

here _____ we'll stay. For

al - ways, for - ev - er, be -

yond here and on to e - ter - ni - ty. _____ For

al - ways, for - ev - er; for

us, there's no time or no space. _____ No bar - ri - er love won't e - rase. _____ Wher -

ev - er you go, I still know in my heart you will be with

me. From this _____ day

on, _____ I'm cer-tain that I'll nev-er be a-

lone. _____ I know what my heart must have al - ways

known, _____ that love has the pow-er that's all its

Dulcinea

from MAN OF LA MANCHA

Lyric by Joe Darion

Music by Mitch Leigh

Dul - ci - ne - a, _____ I see heav - en when I see thee, Dul - ci - ne - a. _____ And thy name is like a pray'r an an - gel whis - pers, _____ Dul - ci - ne - a, _____ Dul - ci - ne - a.

rit.

a tempo

Feel Like Makin' Love

Words and Music by
Eugene McDaniels

Moderately

Stroll - in' in the park, ___ watch - in'
When you talk to me, ___ when you're
In a res - tau - rant, ___ hold - in'

win - ter turn to spring. ___
moan - in' sweet and low. ___
hands by can - dle - light. ___

Walk - in' in the dark ___ see - in'
When you're touch - in' me ___ and my
While I'm touch - in' you, ___ want - in'

lov - ers do their thing.
feel - in's start to show.
you with all my might.

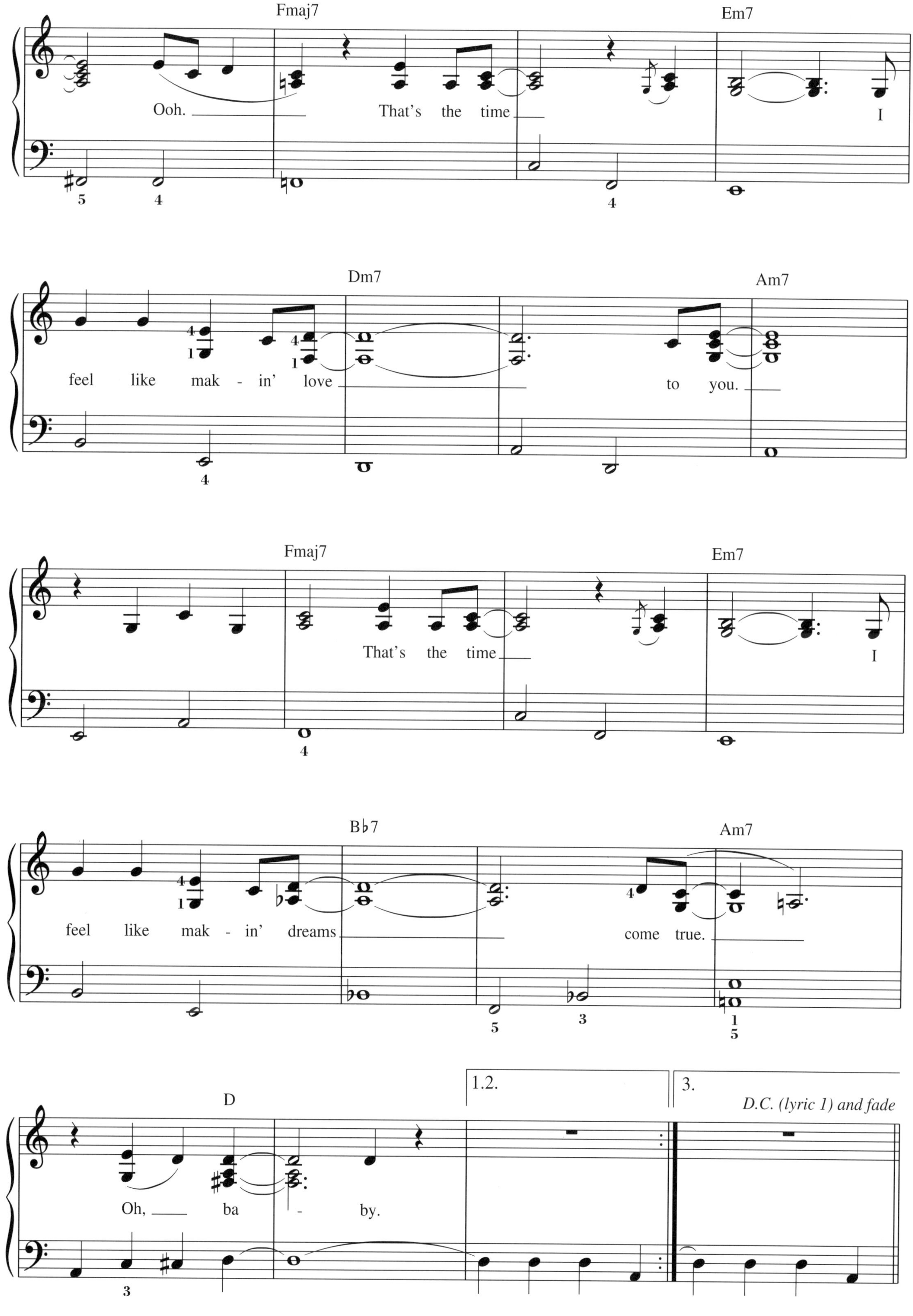

Follow Me

Words and Music by
John Denver

Moderately fast

It's by far the hard-est thing I've ev-er done,_____ to be so in love with you and so a-lone._____ Fol-low me where I go, what I do and who I know._____ Make it part of you_____ to be a part of

me._____ Fol - low me up and

down, all____ the way and all a - round.

Take my hand_____ and say you'll fol - low

It's long been on my
You see, I'd like to share my

mind. You know it's been a long, long
life with you and show you things I've

time. I'll try to find the way that I can
seen, places that I'm going to,

make you un-der-stand the way I feel a-
places where I've been, to have you there be-

bout you and just how much I need you_____ to be
side me and nev - er be a - lone, and

there where I can talk to you when
all the time that you're with me, then

there's no one else a - round._____ Fol - low
we will be at

1.
A

mf

2.
A

home._____ Fol - low
mf

D.S. al Coda

Coda
D

me._____

From a Distance

Words and Music by
Julie Gold

Lyrics:

From a dis-tance the world ___ looks blue and ___ green, ___ and the snow-capped moun-tains white. From a dis-tance the o-cean ___ meets the stream, and the ea - gle

takes to flight. From a

dis - tance there is har - mo - ny, and it

ech - oes through the land. It's the

voice of _____ hope, _____ it's the voice of _____

peace, _____ it's the voice of ev - 'ry

man.

From a dis - tance we _____ all
dis - tance you _____ look

songs of ___ peace, ___ they're the songs of ev - 'ry
love of ___ loves, ___ it's the

man. God __ is watch - ing us, ___ God __ is

watch - ing us, ___ God __ is watch - ing us from a dis - tance. ___

From a

Coda

heart _____ of ev - 'ry ____ man. It's the

hope of ____ hopes, ____ it's the love of ____ loves, ____ it's the

song of ev - 'ry man.

Goodbye My Friend

Words and Music by
Karla Bonoff

Moderately slow, in 2

Oh, we nev - er know things where that life make
I see a lot of

will take us.
me cra - zy.

We know it's just a
And I guess I

ride on the wheel.
held on to you.

And we nev - er know when death will
I could - 've run a - way when and left. Well,

shake us,
may - be,

and we won - der how it will
but it was - n't time, and we will both

feel.
knew.

So

good - bye, my ____ friend. ____

I know I'll nev - er see you a - gain.

But the time to - geth - er through all ____
But the love you gave me through all ____

Bb/C ... the _____ years will / the _____ years will

F take / take

C6/E a - way these _____ tears. _____ / a - way my _____ tears. _____

D7

Cadd2/G It's o - kay now. / I'm o - kay now.

C/G   Cmaj7/G

F/G

N.C. Good - bye, _____ my

1. Cadd2 friend.

Am7add4

Fadd2

Dm7 Em7 Fmaj7   F/G   G7

Lyrics:

friend.

A life so fragile, a love so pure; we can't hold on but we try.

We watch how quickly it disappears, and we'll never know why.

But I'm okay now.

Good - bye, _____ my

friend.

You can go _____ now. _____

Good - bye, _____ my

friend. _____

rit.

Give Me Forever

(I Do)

Words and Music by
Carter Cathcart, John Tesh,
Juni Morrison and James Ingram

Look - ing out I
With this ring I'm

Lyrics beneath the staves:

make you my / give you my
wife. / love.
Won't you

give me for - ev - er to show

all of the love I have here for

you. _____ And if you give me my

rea - son   for   liv -   ing, _____   to
love   you,   I   love   you,   I   do.
(melody)

Here I Am

from the Motion Picture SPIRIT: STALLION OF THE CIMARRON

Words and Music by Bryan Adams,
Gretchen Peters and Hans Zimmer

Lyrics:

Here I am,
Here we are, we've

this is me.
just be-gun.

There's
And

no-where else on earth I'd rath-
af-ter all this time our time

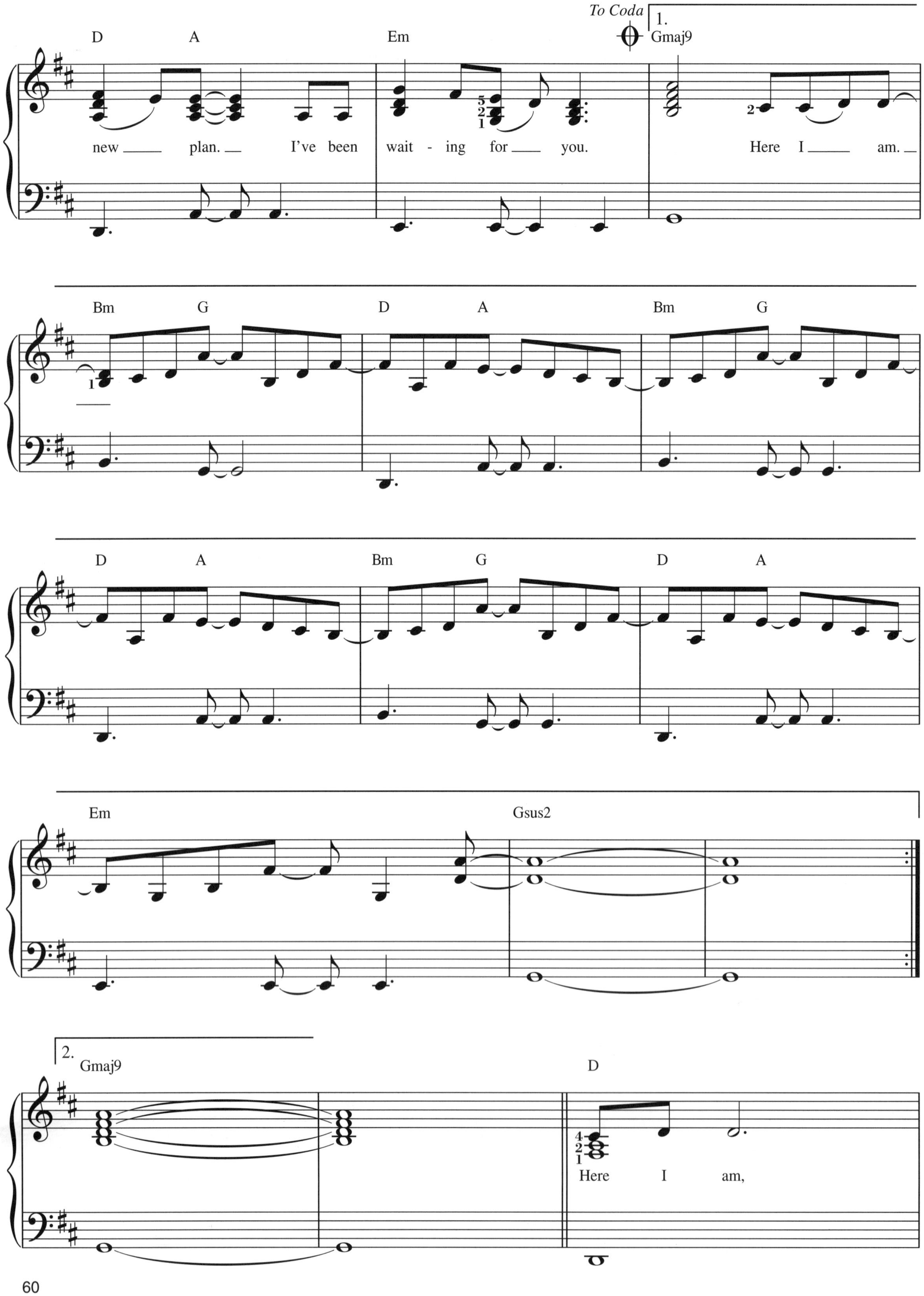

Lyrics under the staves:

new ____ plan. __ I've been wait - ing for ___ you. Here I _____ am.

Here I am,

this is me. _____ There's no - where else on earth I'd rath -

er be. _____ Here I am, _____ just me and you. _____ To -

night we'll make our dreams _ come true. Oh, it's a

Oh, _____ here I am. _____

(Spoken:) This is me.

Hero

Words and Music by
Mariah Carey and Walter Afanasieff

There's a he - ro if you look in - side __ your
long __ road __ when you face the world __ a -

heart. You don't have to be __ a - fraid of what you are. __
lone. No one reach - es out __ a hand for you to hold. __

There's an an - swer if you reach in - to ___ your soul ___
You can find love if you search with - in ___ your - self ___

and the sor - row that ___ you know will melt a -
and the emp - ti - ness ___ you felt will dis - ap -

way. ___
pear. ___

And then a he - ro comes ___ a

long with the strength to car - ry on and you cast your fears ___ a -

side, and you know you can — sur - vive. So when you feel like hope — is

gone look in - side you and — be strong and you'll fi - n'lly see — the

truth that a he - ro lies — in you.

It's a you.

Lord knows _____ dreams are

hard to fol - low, but don't let an - y - one

tear them a - way. _____ Hold ____ on, _____

there will be to - mor - row. In _____

That a he - ro lies in you.

I Want to Know What Love Is

Words and Music by
Mick Jones

Lyrics: I've got-ta take a lit-tle time, a lit-tle time to think ___ things

Em
o - ver.
D
G
I bet - ter read be - tween the lines,
C
Em
in case I need it when I'm old - er.
D
Em

Now, this moun- tain I _____ must climb
I'm gon- na take a lit- tle time, _____

feels like the world up- on _____ my shoul-
a lit- tle time to look _____ a- round _____

ders. _____ Through the clouds I see love
me. _____ I've got no- where left to

shine. _____ It keeps me warm as life grows
hide. _____ It looks like love has fi- n'lly

cold- er. _____ In my life _____
found me. _____

there's been heart-ache and pain. I don't know

if I can face it a-gain.

Can't stop now. I've trav-eled so far to

change this lone-ly life.

I want to know what love is.

I want you to show ___ me.

I want to feel what love ___ is. ___

I know you can show ___ me. ___

___ me.

D.S. and fade

If Ever You're in My Arms Again

Words and Music by
Michael Masser, Tom Snow
and Cynthia Weil

Moderately slow

It all came so eas-y, all the lov-in' you gave __ me; the
I'm see-in' clear-ly how I still need you near __ me. I

feel-ings we shared.
still love you so. __

And I still can re-mem-ber how you
There's some-thing be-tween __ us that

F/C

touched me so ten - der. It told me you care. ___
won't ev - er leave _ us. There's no let - ting go. ___

Bb   Ebmaj7   Eb6   Cm   Gm

We had a once in a life - time, ___ but I just could - n't see ___ un -
We had a once in a life - time, ___ but I just did - n't know _ it till my

Bb   F   Bb   Ebmaj7   Eb6

til it was gone. ___ A sec - ond once in a life - time _ may be
life fell a - part. ___ A sec - ond once in a life - time ___ is - n't

Cm   Gm   Bb   F   G

too much to ask, ___ but I swear from now on ___
too much to ask, ___ 'cause I swear from now on ___

73

if ev - er you're in my arms a - gain, _____ this time _____ I'll love

_____ you much bet - ter. If ev - er you're in my arms a - gain,

_____ this time _____ I'll hold _____ you for - ev - er. This time will nev - er

Now

74

Coda

This time we'll nev - - er end, nev - er

end. _____ The best of ro - manc - in' de -

serves sec - ond chanc - es. I'll get to you some - how, 'cause I prom - ise now. _____

(end.) If ev - er you're in my arms a - gain, _____ this time _____ I'll love

Em7   G   A   D   D/F#   Gmaj7   A

___ you much bet - ter.   If ev - er you're in my arms a - gain,

F#m7   Bm7   Em7

___ this time ___ I'll hold ___ you for - ev - er.

Em7   Bm

This time we'll nev - er end.

D/A   Em7   G/A   A   D

rit.

Just Once

Words by Cynthia Weil

Music by Barry Mann

Slowly

I did my best, but I
I gave my all, but I

guess my best was-n't good e - nough, 'cause
think my all may have been too much, 'cause,

here we are back where we were be -
Lord knows, we're not get - ting an - y

fore.   Seems
where.   It

noth - ing ev - er chang - es, we're
seems we're al - ways blow - in' what

back to be - ing stran - gers,
ev - er we've got go - in', and it

Dm7 · C/E · F · F/G · G · F/G · G

won-d'ring if we ought to stay or head on out the door.
seems at times with all we've got we have-n't got a prayer.

C · G/C · Gm7/C · C7/E

Just once, ___ can't we fig - ure out what we've been do - ing
Just once, ___ can't we fig - ure out what we've been do - ing

Fmaj7 · C/E · Dm7 · G/F

wrong? Why we nev - er last for ver - y
wrong? Why the good times nev - er last for

Em7 · Am7 · Dm7 · F/G · G · C · G/C

long? What are we do - ing wrong? Just once, _ can't we
long? Where are we go - ing wrong? Just once, _ can't we

why it al-ways comes back to good-bye.

Why can't we get our-

selves in hand

and ad-mit to one an-oth-er

we're no good with-out each oth-er.

Take the best and make it bet-ter,

find a way to stay to-geth-er.

Just once,__ can't we

Lyrics:
find a way to fin-'lly make it right? To make the mag-ic last for more than

just one night?___ I know we could break through it if

we could just get to it just ___ once.
rit. *a tempo*

rit.

The Impossible Dream

(The Quest)

from MAN OF LA MANCHA

Lyric by Joe Darion

Music by Mitch Leigh

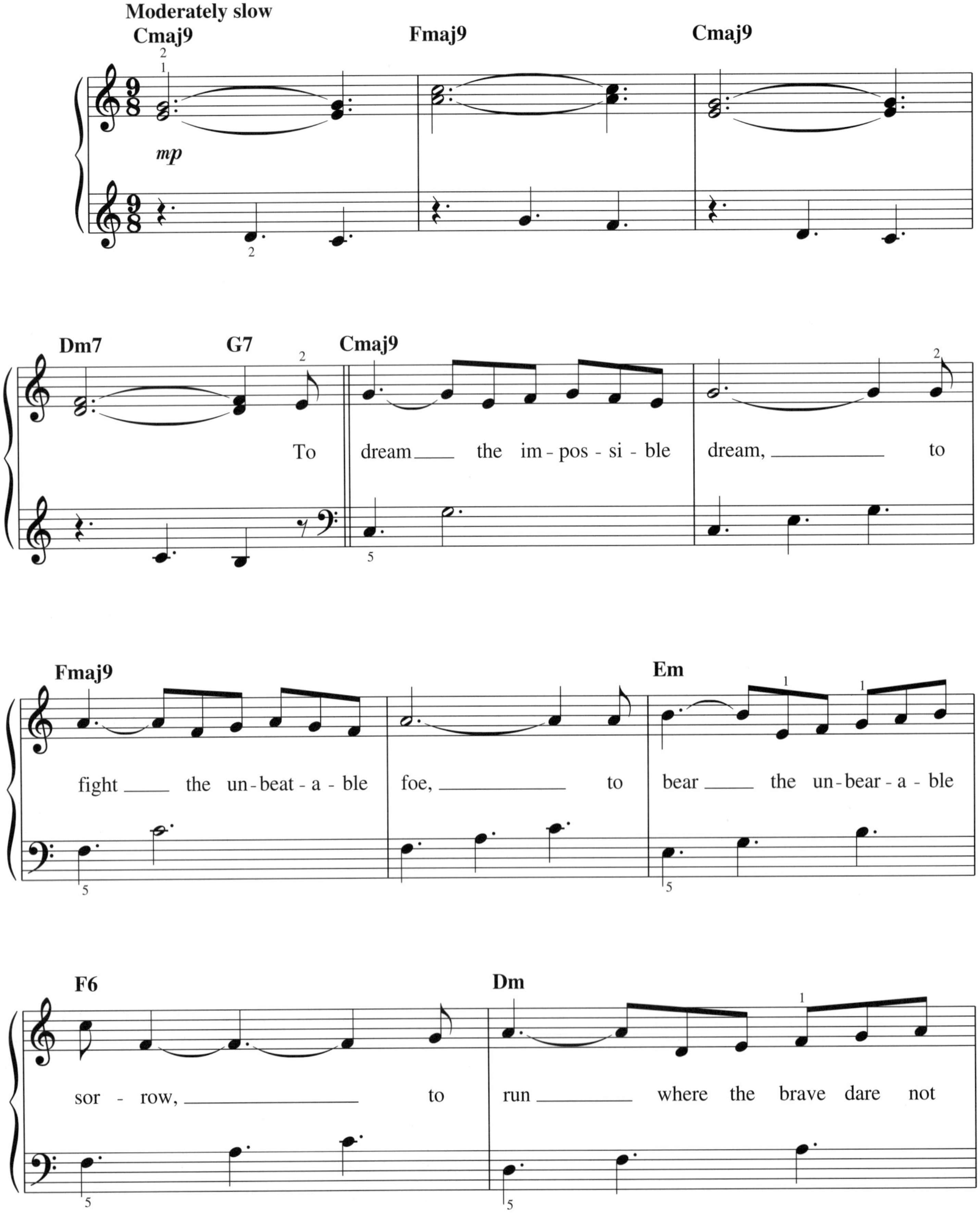

Lyrics under the staves:

To dream___ the im - pos - si - ble dream, _____ to

fight ___ the un - beat - a - ble foe, _____ to bear ___ the un-bear - a - ble

sor - row, _____ to run _____ where the brave dare not

G7
Cmaj9
go. To right the un-right-a-ble wrong, to
Fmaj9
Em
love pure and chaste from a-far, to try when your arms are too
F6
Dm
G7
Dm7
wea-ry, to reach the un-reach-a-ble star! This is my
C
Am
quest to fol-low that star, no mat-ter how

Em   **F6**   **Am**

hope-less, ____ no mat-ter how far; _____ to fight for the right ___ with-out ques-tion or

A♭   **A♭+**   **C**   **C+**   **Am**   **B♭**

pause, __ to be will-ing to march in - to hell for a heav-en - ly cause! _____ And I

Dm   **B♭**   **E**

know _____ if I'll on-ly be true _____ to this glo-ri-ous quest _____ that my

F6   **B7**

heart _____ will lie peace-ful and calm _____ when I'm laid to my

Fm   **G**   **Cmaj9**

rest.   And the   world ___ will be bet - ter for   this: _____ that one

Fmaj9   **Em**

man, ___ scorned and cov-ered with   scars, _____ still ___ strove ___ with his last ounce of

F6   **C/G**   **Dm7/G**   **C**

cour - age _____ to   reach ___ the un-reach-a - ble   stars. _____

Am   **Fmaj9**   **Dm7**   **C**

In My Daughter's Eyes

Words and Music by
James Slater

Lyrics:

In my daugh-ter's eyes

eyes
eyes
I am a he - ro. ____ I am
ev - 'ry-one is e - qual. ____ Dark - ness

strong and wise, ____ and I know no fear. But the truth is
turns to light ____ and the world is at peace. This mir - a - cle God

plain to see, she was sent to res - cue me. I see who I
gave to me gives me strength when I am weak. I find rea - son

wan - na   be   in my daugh - ter's eyes.
to be - lieve   in my daugh - ter's

In my daugh - ter's   eyes.   And when she wraps her

hand   a - round my fin - ger,   al - ways puts a   smile ____ in my heart.   Ev - 'ry - thing be -

comes   a lit - tle clear - er.   I re - al - ize what   life is all a - bout.   It's hang - ing on when your heart has had e-nough. It's giv-ing more when you feel like giv-ing up. _____ I've

seen the light. It's in my daugh-ter's eyes.

In my daugh-ter's

eyes I can see the fu-ture, _____ a reflec - tion of who I am and what will be. And though she'll grow and

some - day leave, may - be raise a fam - i - ly, when I'm gone I

hope you'll see how hap - py she made me, for I'll be

there in my daugh - ter's eyes. *a tempo*
rit.

rit.

May You Always

Words and Music by
Larry Markes and Dick Charles

Moderately slow

This spe - cial time, this spe - cial place is bright - ened by your
though we go our sep - 'rate ways, we'll share the mem - 'ry

spe - cial face. The gang will soon sing "Auld Lang Syne" and
of this day. I wish I may, I wish I might

touch this sen - ti - men - tal heart of mine. Al -
have this wish I wish for you to - night.

rit.

May you al - ways walk in sun - shine, slum - ber warm when

night winds blow. May you al - ways live with laugh - ter,

for a smile be - comes you so. May good for - tune

find your door - way, may the blue - bird sing your song.

May no trou - ble trav - el your way, may no wor - ry

stay too long. May your heart - aches be for - got - ten,

may no tears be spilled. May old ac - quaint - ance

be re - mem - bered and your cup of kind - ness filled. And

may you al - ways be a dream - er, may your wild - est

dream come true. May you find some - one to love as

much as I love you.

Misty

Words by Johnny Burke

Music by Erroll Garner

near. You can say that you're
cresc.

lead-ing me on, but it's just what I

want you to do. Don't you no-tice how hope-less-ly I'm lost?

That's why I'm fol-low-ing you. On my
f *dim.*

own, as I wan - der through this won - der - land a -

lone, nev - er know-ing my right foot from my left, my

hat from my glove. I get mist - y and too much in

love. You can say that you're

My Cherie Amour

Words and Music by
Stevie Wonder, Sylvia Moy
and Henry Cosby

La la la la la la, La la la la la la. My Che - rie A - mour,

rie A - mour, _
ca - fé _ or
some _ day _ you'll

love - ly as a sum - mer day, My Che -
some-times on a crowd - ed street, I've been
see my face a - mong the crowd, May - be

Gmaj7   **B♭/C**   **Fmaj7**

rie   A - mour, _   dis - tant   as   the   Milk - y   Way.
near ____ you ___ but you   nev - er   no - ticed   me.
some ____ day ___ I'll   share your   lit - tle   dis - tant   cloud.

C/D   **Cmaj7**   **C/D**

My   Che - rie   A - mour, _   pret - ty   lit - tle   one   that
My   Che - rie   A - mour, _   won't you   tell   me   how   could
Oh,   Che - rie   A - mour, _   Pret - ty   lit - tle   one   that

F7   **E7**

I   a - dore, ____   You're   the   on - ly   girl   my
you   ig - nore, ____   That   be - hind   that   lit - tle
I   a - dore, ____   You're   the   on - ly   girl   my

A7   **D7**   **To Coda** ⊕

heart   beats   for, ____   How   I   wish   that   you   were
smile   I   wore, ___   How   I   wish   that   you   were
heart   beats   for, ____   How   I   wish   that   you   were

On My Own

from LES MISÉRABLES

Lyrics by
Alain Boublil, John Caird, Trevor Nunn,
Jean-Marc Natel and Herbert Kretzmer

Music by
Claude-Michel Schönberg

Slowly

With pedal

EPONINE:

On my own, pre- tend- ing he's be- side me. ___ All a-

lone I walk with him 'til morn- ing. With- out him I feel his arms a-

Bm

round me. And

Em

when I lose my way I close my eyes and he has

A

found me. In the

D   Em/D

rain, the pave-ment shines like

D   D/C#

sil - ver. All the

Bm   E7/B

lights are mis-ty in the

A   A/G#

ri - ver In the

G   F#7

dark-ness the trees are full of

Bm

star - light. And

Em

all I see is him and me for-ev-er and for

ev - er. And I know it's on - ly in my mind that I'm talk - ing to my - self and not to him. And al - though I know that he is blind, Still I say there's a way for us. I love him, but when the night is o - ver, ____ he is gone, the riv - er's just a

ri - ver. With - out him the world a - round me chang - es. The

trees are bare and ev - 'ry - where the streets are full of strang - ers. I

love him but ev - 'ry day I'm learn - ing all my life I've on - ly been pretend - ing.___ With - out me his world will go on turn - ing. The world is full of hap-pi-ness that I have nev - er known. I love him, I love him, I love him, but on - ly on my own.

rall.

Only the Lonely

Words and Music by
Martha Davis

lied ___ a - bout each oth - er's dreams; ___ we
men - tioned ___ the time we were to - geth - er

Am7

lived ___ with - out each oth - er think - ing what
so ___ long a - go. ___ Well, I

F

an - y - one ___ would do ___ with - out
don't re - mem - ber. All I know is it

Cmaj7   **Gsus4**   **G**

me and you. ___ 1. 2. It's like I told ___ you,
makes me feel good now. 3. On - ly the lone - ly,
...Instrumental ends

Fsus2   **1.**
                                          Cmaj7

on - ly the lone - ly can play. ___
on - ly the lone - ly can   So

She's Always a Woman

Words and Music by
Billy Joel

Moderately

She can kill with a | smile. She can wound with her
love, She can take you or

eyes. _____ She can ru - in your | faith with her cas - u - al
leave you, _ She can ask for the | truth but she'll nev - er be -

lies. And she on - ly re | - veals what she wants you to | see. She
lieve you, And she'll take what you | give her as long as it's | free yeah, she

Am · Am/G · F · G7 · 1. C · Csus

hides like a child but she's al-ways a wom-an to me.
steals like a thief but she's al-ways a wom-an to

C · G · 2. C · Csus · C · %Am · Am/G

She can lead you to me. Oh,

Add pedal

D7/F# · D7 · G · G/F# · Em · C

she takes care of her-self she can wait if she

F · F/E · Dm · G7 · C · Csus

wants, she's a-head of her time.

Oh, and she nev-er gives out and she nev-er gives in, she just chang-es her mind.

And she'll prom-ise you more than the gar-den of
She is fre-quent-ly kind and she's sud-den-ly

no pedal

E - den. ___ Then she'll care-less-ly
cru - el. ___ She can do as she

cut you and laugh while you're
pleas-es she's no - bo-dy's

bleed - in'____ But she brings out the best and the worst you can

fool _____ But she can't be con - vict - ed she's earned her de -

be. Blame it all on your - self 'cause she's al - ways a wom - an to

gree. And the

me. _____ (Hum) _____

most she will do is throw

sha-dows at you But she's al-ways a wom-an to me.

(Hum)

Perhaps Love

Words and Music by
John Denver

Lyrics (line 3):
love is like a rest-ing place, a shel-ter from the storm. It ex-
love is like a win-dow, per- haps an o-pen door. It in-

Lyrics (line 4):
ists to give you com-fort, it is there to keep you warm. And
vites you to come clos-er, it wants to show you more. And

in those times of trou - ble, when you are most a - lone, the
e - ven if you lose your - self and don't know what to do, the

mem-o - ry of love will bring you home. Per-haps
mem-o - ry of love will see you

1.

2.
through. Oh, love to some is like a cloud, to
Instrumental
mf

some as strong as steel; for some a way of liv - ing, for

113

some a way to feel. And some say love is hold-ing on and

some say let-ting go. And some say love is ev-'ry-thing,

some say they don't know. Perhaps
dim. *rit.* *mp*

love is like the o-cean, full of con-flict, full of pain, like a
a tempo

fire_____ when it's cold out-side, thun-der when it rains. If

I should live for-ev-er and all my dreams come true, my

mem-o-ries of love will be of you.

rit.

you.

115

Someone Like You

from JEKYLL & HYDE

Words by Leslie Bricusse

Music by Frank Wildhorn

Slowly and freely

Lyrics under the staves:

I peer through win-dows, watch life go by,

dream of to-mor-row, and won-der "why?"

The past is hold-ing me, keep-ing life at bay.

I wan-der, lost in yes-ter-day, want-ing to

B♭   **Gm7**   **B♭/C**

fly,   but scared to try.   But if

F   **Gm7**

some - one like you found   some - one like me, then

F   **B♭**   **Gm7♭5**

sud - den - ly noth - ing would ev - er be the same! My

F   **Gm**   **F/A**   **Gm7**

heart would take wing—— and I'd feel so a - live,—— if

To Coda

F   **Dm7**   **Gm7**   **D♭/E♭**   **Fadd2**   **Em7**   **G/A**

some - one like you—— found me!

rit.   *a tempo*

117

So man-y se-crets I long to share! All I have need-ed

is some-one there to help me see a world

I've nev-er seen be-fore, a love to o-pen ev-'ry

D.S. al Coda

door, to set me free so I can soar! If

cresc.

mf

Coda

me! Oh, if some-one like you found

rit.

f a tempo

Lyrics under the staves:

some - one like me, then sud - den - ly_____ noth - ing would

ev - er be the same! My heart would take wing,___ and I'd

feel so a - live,____ if some - one like

you loved me, loved_

me, loved_ me!

Superstar

Words and Music by
Leon Russell and Bonnie Sheridan

Medium Rock Ballad

Long a-go and, oh, so far a-way,
Lone - li - ness is such a sad af - fair,

I fell in love with you
and I can hard-ly wait

be - fore the sec - ond show.
to be with you a - gain.

Your gui - tar, it sounds so
What to say, to make you

sweet and clear, but you're not
come a - gain, come back to

real - ly here; it's just the ra - di - o.
me a - gain and play your sad gui - tar?

Don't you re - mem - ber you told me you loved me, ba -

Lyrics beneath the staves:

by? _____ You said you'd be com - in' back _ this way _ a - gain,

ba - by. Ba - by, ba - by, ba - by, ba - by, oh

ba - by. _____ I love _____ you. _____

I real - ly do.

I real - ly do. _____

I real - ly do.

This Masquerade

Words and Music by
Leon Russell

Am7   D7

stand - ing an - y - way, ___ we're
car - ry on this way, ___ we're

To Coda

F7   Bm7/E   E7#5

lost _____ in a mas - quer -
lost _____ in a mas -

Am   Abm7   Db9   Gm7

rade. _____   Both a - fraid to

C7b9   Fmaj9   D7#5   D7b9

say we're just ___ too far a - way ___

Gm7   C7b9   Fmaj7

from be - ing close to - geth - er from ___ the start. ___

124

We tried to talk it o - ver, but the words got in the way. We're lost in - side this lone - ly game we play. quer - ade.

This Is the Moment

from JEKYLL & HYDE

Words by Leslie Bricusse

Music by Frank Wildhorn

Lyrics:

This is the mo - ment! This is the day when I send
mo - ment, this is the time when the mo -

all my doubts and de - mons on their way! Ev - 'ry en -
men - tum and the mo - ment are in rhyme! Give me this

deav - our I have made ev - er is com - ing in - to play, is
mo - ment, this pre - cious chance. I'll gath - er up my past and

here and now to - day! This is the

make some sense at

Bb/C   F   Gm/F

last!   This is the mo - ment   when all I've
                          mo - ment,   my fi - nal

F   Gm7b5/F   F   Dm

done,   all of the dream - ing, schem - ing and scream - ing be - come
test.   Des - ti - ny beck - oned, I nev - er reck - oned sec - ond

Bbmaj7   C/Bb   Gm   C/Bb

one!   This is the day,_____ see it spar - kle and
best!   I won't look down,_____ I must not

To Coda

Am   Dm   Gm   Bb/C

shine,   when all I've lived for be - comes
fall!   This is the

F   C/Bb   Bb   Am7   F/A

mine!   For   all these years I've

C/B♭   F/A   Gm   F/A

faced   the   world   a - lone,   and   now   the   time   has   come   to

D.S. al Coda
𝄋

B♭m   Csus4   B♭/C

prove   to   them   I   made   it   on   my   own!   This   is   the

Coda   Gm   F/A   Gm   B♭/C
⊕

mo - ment,   the   sweet - est   mo - ment   of   them

F   D7   G   Am/G

all!   This   is   the   mo - ment!   Damn   all   the

f

G   Am7♭5/G   G   Em

odds!   This   day   or   nev - er,   I'll   set   for - ev - er   with   the gods! When I look back,_____ I will al - ways re -

call mo - ment for mo - ment, this was the

mo - ment, the great - est mo - ment of them

all!

Through the Years

Words and Music by
Steve Dorff and Marty Panzer

With tenderness

Lyrics:

I can't re-mem-ber when you were-n't there,
can't re-mem-ber what I used to do,

when I did-n't care for an-y-one but you,
who I trust-ed, who I lis-tened to be-fore.

swear____ we've been through
swear____ you've taught me

ev'-ry-thing there is. Can't i-mag-ine an-y-thing we've
ev'-ry-thing I know. Can't i-mag-ine need-ing some-one

Bb | F | Gm7

missed, Can't i-mag-ine an - y - thing the two of us can't
so, but through the years it seems to ___ me I need you more and

C7 | F | D7

do. Through the years, you've nev - er let me
more. Through the years, you've through all the good and

Gm | C7 | Am7

down, you've turned my life a - round. The
bad I knew how much I had. I've

Dm7 | Gm7 | C7

sweet - est days I've found I've found with you. Through ___ the
al - ways been so glad to be with you. Through ___ the

years, / years,
I've / It's
nev - er been a - / bet - ter ev' - ry
fraid, / day.
I've / You've

loved the life we've / kissed my life tears a -
made, / way,
And / As
I'm _____ so glad I've / long _____ as it's o -

stayed _____ / kay _____
right here with / I'll stay with
you _____ / you _____

through the / through the
years.

years.

Through the

years when you've
years

ev' - ry thing went wrong _____ to - geth - er we were _____
nev - er let me down _____ you turned my life a -

strong. I
round; The

know that I be - longed right here with
sweet - est days I've found I've found with

you. Through _ the years, I nev - er had a
you. Through _ the years, It's bet - ter ev' - ry

doubt / day, ____ we'd / you've al-ways / kissed work / my things ____ / tears a- out / way way / I've As

learned / long what / as love's / it's a- / o- bout ____ / kay ____ by / I'll lov- / stay ing / with

you ____ / you ____ through / through the / the years. Through ___ the

years.

Unusual Way

(In a Very Unusual Way)
from NINE

Words and Music by
Maury Yeston

Moderately, flowing

with pedal

In a ver - y un - u - su - al way

ver - y un - u - su - al way

one time I need - ed you.

I think I'm in love with you.

In a

In a

ver - y un - u - su - al way

ver - y un - u - su - al way

you were___ my___

I want___ to___

Lyrics under the staves:

friend.
cry.

Maybe it lasted a
Something inside me goes

day,
weak,

maybe it lasted an
something inside me sur -

hour,
ren - ders,

but some-how it will never - er

end...

In a

and you're the rea - son

Lyrics under the staves:

I can hard-ly speak. In a

ver-y un-u-su-al way I owe__ what I am to you.

Though · at times it ap-pears__ I won't stay, I won't stay,

I nev-er__ go.

Spe-cial to me in my life since the first day__ that I

met— you, how could I ev - er for - get you once you had touched my soul?— In a

ver - y un - u - su - al way— you've made me whole.

Time After Time

Words and Music by
Cyndi Lauper and Rob Hyman

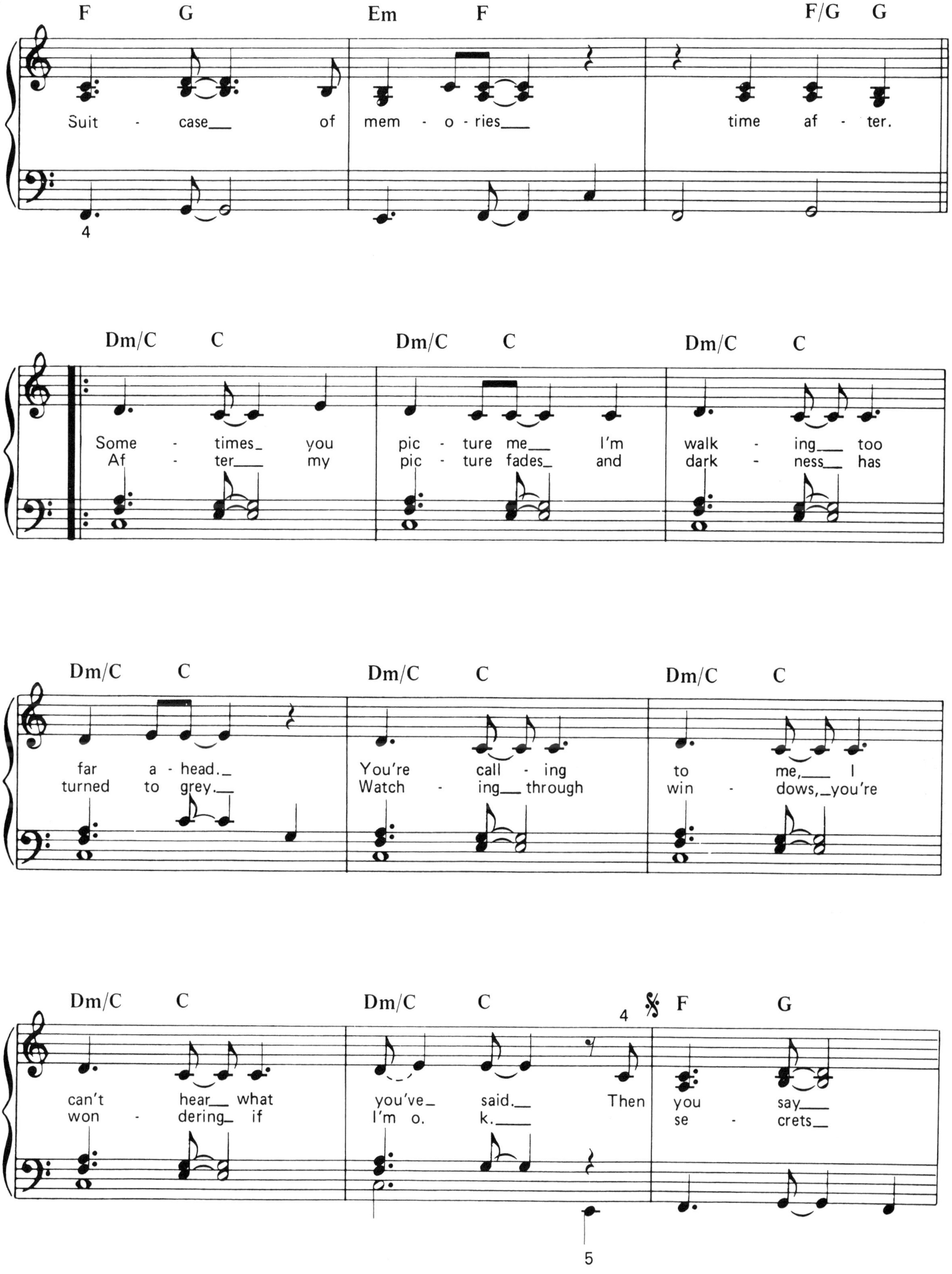

Lyrics under the staves:

If you're lost___ you can look___ and you will___ find me___

time af - ter time.___ If you fall___ I will catch___ you I'll be___

___ wait - ing___ time af - ter time.___

To Coda ⊕

D.S. al Coda
(verse 1)

⊕ **CODA**

Repeat and Fade

Time af - ter time.

Unchained Melody

Lyric by Hy Zaret

Music by Alex North

Oh, my love, my dar-ling, I've hun-gered for your touch a long, lone-ly time.

Time — goes by — so slow - ly and
time can do so much. Are you still
mine? _____ I
need your love, _____
_____ I need your love, _____ God

Am ... **D7** ... **G**

speed your love ... to ... me!

Slightly faster

To Coda ⊕ **C** ... **D**

Lone - ly riv - ers flow to the
Lone - ly moun - tains gaze at the

mf

C ... **D** ... **C**

sea, to the sea, to the o - pen
stars, at the stars, wait - ing for the

D ... **G**

arms of the sea. _____
dawn of the day. _____

146

C
D
C
Lone - ly riv - ers sigh, "Wait for me, wait for
All a - lone, I gaze at the stars, at the
D
C
1 2 1
D
me!" I'll be com - ing home, wait for
stars, dream - ing of my love far a -
1.
G
R.H.
L.H.
2.
G
me!
way.
R.H.
D.S. al Coda
L.H.
CODA
R.H.
L.H.

Up Where We Belong

from the Paramount Picture AN OFFICER AND A GENTLEMAN

Words by Will Jennings

Music by
Buffy Sainte-Marie and Jack Nitzsche

Slow and soulful

mp

Who knows what to - mor - row brings; _ in a
Some hang on to "used - to - be", ___ live their

world, few hearts sur - vive? All I know is the
lives look - ing be - hind. All we have is

way I feel; _ when it's real, I keep it a - live.
here and now; _ all our life, out there to find.

The

Em   **A**   **D**   **D/F♯**

road   is ____ long.   There are   moun - tains in our

G   **G/B**   **C**   **A**   **A7**

way,   but we   climb a step ev - 'ry day.

D   **D/F♯**   **G**   **Bm/F♯**   **Em**   **D/F♯**

mf

Love lift us up where we be - long,   where the ea - gles cry ____ on a

C   **G**   **A**   **D**   **D/F♯**

moun - tain high.   Love lift us up where we be -

long, far from the world we know, up where the

clear winds blow. _

clear winds blow. _ Time goes by, _

no time to cry, _ life's you and I, _ a -

live to - day. _____ Love lift us up where we be -

long, where the ea - gles cry, __ on a moun - tain high.

Love lift us up where we be - long, far from the world we know, __ where the

1.
clear winds blow. _

2.
clear winds blow. _

rit.

mp

Waiting for a Girl Like You

Words and Music by
Mick Jones and Lou Gramm

Moderately

So _____ long _____ I've been

wait - ing too hard, _____ I've been wait - ing too long. _____

Some - times I don't ___ know what ___ I will find. _____

I on - ly know ___ it's a mat - ter of time. _____ When you

love some - one, ___ when you love some - one, ___

it feels so right, _____ so warm ___ and true. ___

This time I wan-na be sure. I've been waiting for a girl like you to come in-to my life.
I've been wait - ing for a girl like you, a
love that will sur - vive. I've been wait - ing for
some - one new to make me feel a - live.

Yeah, wait - ing   for a   girl like you ___ to

come in - to ___   my life.

You're so   good. _____ When

we make love ___ it's un - der - stood. _____ It's

ment I wake ___ up till deep ___ in the night. ___ There's

no - where on earth ___ that I'd rath - er be ___ than hold-ing

D.S. al Coda

you ten - der - ly. ___ I've been wait -

Coda

Repeat and fade

What a Wonderful World

Words and Music by
George David Weiss and Bob Thiele

Slowly, but with a lilt

F   Am   B♭   Am   Gm   F

mp I see trees of green, red ros - es too, I see them bloom

A7   Dm   D♭   C7sus   C7

for me and you, and I think to my - self What a won - der - ful

F   F+   Gm7   C7   F   Am   B♭   Am

world. I see skies of blue and clouds of white, the

Gm   F   A7   Dm   D♭

bright bless-ed day, the dark sa - cred night, and I think to my - self

C7sus   C7   F   B♭   F

What a won - der - ful world.   The

C   F   C

col - ors of the rain - bow, so pret - ty in the sky are al - so on the fac - es of

F   Dm   C/E   Dm/F   C/E

peo - ple go - in' by. I see friends shak - in' hands, say - in', "How do you do?"

They're real-ly say-in', "I love you." I hear ba - bies cry, I

watch them grow; They'll learn much more than I'll ev - er know. And I

think to my - self, what a won-der-ful world, _____ Yes, I

think to my - self what a won-der-ful world.

When You Believe

(From The Prince of Egypt)

from THE PRINCE OF EGYPT

Words and Music Composed by
Stephen Schwartz
with Additional Music by
Babyface

Slowly

Man - y nights we've prayed, with no proof an - y - one could hear.

In our hearts a hope - ful song we bare - ly un - der - stood. Now

we are not a - fraid, al - though we know there's much to fear.

We were mov - ing moun - tains long be - fore we knew we could.

There can be mir - a - cles | when you be - lieve. | Though hope is frail, it's

hard to kill. | Who knows what mir - a - cles | you can a - chieve?

When you be - lieve, some - how you will. | You will when you be -

lieve. | In this time of fear, when

prayer so of-ten proves in vain, hope seems like the sum-mer birds, too __

swift-ly flown a-way. __ Yet now I'm stand-ing here, my

heart so full __ I can't ex-plain, __ seek-ing faith and speak-ing words __ I

nev-er thought I'd say: __ There can be mir-a-cles

when you be - lieve. ____
(When you be - lieve)

Though hope is frail, it's hard to kill.

Who knows what mir - a - cles ____ you _ can a - chieve? _____
(You can a -

When you be - lieve, _____ some - how you will. _____
chieve?)

You _____ will _ when _ you _____ be - lieve. _____

poco rit.

a tempo

There can be mir - a - cles when you be - lieve. Though hope is frail, it's

hard to kill. Who knows what mir - a - cles

you can a - chieve? When you be - lieve, some -

how you will, now you will.

Am7　　　　　　D　　　　　Em　　　　　D6

You will when you be - lieve. _____

decresc.

Cmaj7　Tacet

_____ You ___ will ___ when you, you will when you ___ be -

mf

expressively

G　　　　　　　Em　　　　　　G

lieve, just be - lieve, just be -

mp p　　　*mp*　　　　　　*p*　　　　　*mp*

Em　　　　　　　　　G

lieve. You will when you be - lieve. _____

poco rit.

p _____　　　*pp*

Where Is the Love?

Words and Music by
Ralph MacDonald and William Salter

Moderately

Abmaj7 ... F/G

Where is the love?
Where is the love?

Cmaj7 ... Eb6

You told me that you did - n't love him,
If you had had a sud - den change of heart,
Oh, how I wish I'd nev - er met you.

Abmaj7 ... F/G

and you were gon - na say good - bye.
I wish that you would tell me so.
I guess it must have been my fate

Cmaj7 ... Eb6 ... Abmaj7

But if you real - ly did - n't mean it,
Don't leave me hang - ing on - to prom - is - es.
to fall in love with some - one else - 's love.

To Coda

F/G

why did you have to ___ lie? ___
You've got to let me ___ know. ___
All I can do is ___ wait.

Cmaj7

D.S. al Coda

C7   F6   Bb7

Coda

Cmaj7

Where is the love? ___

Repeat and fade

C7   F6   Bb7

Where is the love? ___   Where is the love? ___   Where is the love?

171

Your Song

Words and Music by
Elton John and Bernie Taupin

It's a lit-tle bit fun-ny this feel-ing in-side, _____
If I were a sculp-tor but then a-gain no, _____
I sat on a roof _____ and kicked off the moss _____

I'm not one of those who can eas-i-ly hide, _____
or a man who makes potions in a trav-el-in' show, _____
a few of the verses well they've got me quite cross, _____

I don't have much mon-ey, but boy if I
I know it's not much _ but it's the best I can
but the sun's been quite kind _____ while I wrote this

did, _____
do. _____
song. _____

I'd buy a big house where _____
My gift is my song and _____
It's for peo-ple like you that _____

1.
we both _ could live. _____

this one's _ for
keep it _____ turned

you.
on.

cresc.

mf And you can tell

ev - 'ry-bod - y

this is your

song. _____

It may be quite simple, but now that it's done,____ I hope you don't mind, I hope you don't mind what I put down in __ words. How won-der-ful life is __ while you're__ in the world. ____

C/E   Dm   Gm7

B♭   **To Coda** Dm   Dm/C

cresc.

Dm/B   B♭   F/A   B♭

C   Csus   C

D.S. al Coda (with repeats)

dim.

174

CODA

Dm I hope you don't mind, *cresc.*

Dm/C I hope you don't mind

Dm/B what I put down in __ words.

B♭ words. How

F/A won - der - ful *f*

B♭ life is __ while

you're __ in the

F world.

B♭ *dim.*

F *p*

B♭/F

C/F

B♭/F *rit.*

F

175

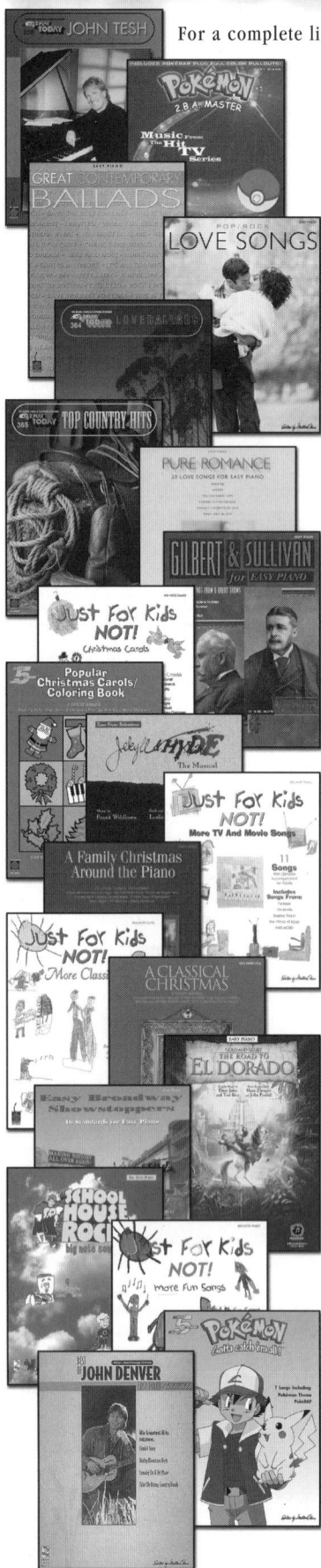

hot california graphics

hot california graphics

MADISON SQUARE PRESS / NEW YORK

Madison Square Pres
10 East 23rd Street
New York, NY 10010

Distributors to the trade in the United States and Canada
BHB
108 East North First Street
Seneca, SC 29678
Phone (212) 505-0950
Fax (212) 979-2207

Distributors outside the United States and Canada
HarperCollins International
10 East 53rd Street
New York, NY 10022-5299

Library of Congress Cataloging in Publication Data:
Entertainment Destinations

Printed in Hong Kong
ISBN 0-942604-76-8

Jacket Design: Morla Design, San Francisco

contents

Introduction..7

Patrick SooHoo Design...........................9

Landor Associates................................17

Fuse...25

Hunt Design..33

Profile Design/Cymbic Interactive...........41

KBDA Kimberly Bear..............................49

Michael Brock Design............................57

Evenson Design Group.........................65

Curry Design Associates.........................73

Warren Group..81

Mires Design...89

Point Zero...97

James Robie Design Associates.............105

Hershey Associates..............................113

Sargent & Berman................................121

Huerta Design......................................129

Steven Morris Design, Inc....................137

Tharp Did It...145

Vigon/Ellis...153

Mike Salisbury.....................................161

Laura Coe Design.................................169

Michael Osborne Design.......................177

Morla Design..185

Miriello Grafico, Inc.............................193

Shimokochi/Reeves...............................201

Baker Design..209

Ph.D..217

Bright Strategic Design.........................225

Yashi Okita Design...............................233

Sackett Design Associates....................241

Cahan & Associates.............................249

Sussman Prejza & Co...........................257

Curtis Design.......................................265

Louey/Rubino Design............................273

Groupe 22..281

Sapient Corp..289

Libera Design.......................................297

Madeleine Corson Design......................305

Follis Design..313

INTRODUCTION

Whilst looking at this edition a thought occurred to me.

Once upon a time, I'm talking 1950s, I would see a job and be able to conclude with some certainty: that's Dutch, or American, or Swiss, or from wherever. Furthermore, I'd be able to say: that's a Wim Crouwel, that's Max Huber, that's Giovanni Pintori, that's Karl Gerstner, a Herb Lubalin, or whoever.

A couple of decades passed. The patterns changed. I found myself noting: that's from Texas, this by a Swiss in Milan, this one from Toronto via Yale, that obviously from Basle rather than Zurich, from California rather than Boston-a Sussman, a Greiman, a Cross, and so on. Come the 1990s and the spectrum shifts again, particularly with the population explosion in the design fraternity and the new technologies. Individuality and quirky local styles are being replaced by international conformity of styles-layering, superimposing, blurring and all the other mannerisms of the times. Today, between Los Angeles and Warsaw, I still see an evident difference. Between Amsterdam and Rhode Island less so. Electronics is beginning to morph graphic cultures.

Teetering on the edge of yet another era, my impression is that we're entering a decade of anodyne globalisation-individuality, regionalisation and ideologies are not too apparent on this menu. Furthermore, today there are thousands upon thousands more designers than there were fifty years ago. And soon, with newer, more accessible technologies, everyone will be a designer. So, looking through this edition you will see a range of skills and graphic expertise on a scale which was inconceivable in the 1950s. At the time it would not have been possible to have produced such a book for the States as a whole-let alone California in particular. I guess it is a reflection of the parallel increase in the range, variety and quantity of corporations and businesses who commission design. Nothing altruistic about this-it took a long, long time, but business eventually discovered that design pays.

Looking closely, I try to determine whether I can tell that this work is from California rather than Texas or Chicago. I can't. I guess the reason is the international lingua franca of graphics has tended to supplant regional accents. Perhaps the distinguishing feature of the next decade is something else. Maybe design will seem to be a way of imposing meaning on the chaos of the marketplace, of adding value to eyesight and grey cells, as much as the bottom line. An understanding that good designers want to change ugly and inappropriate objects, signs and environments. That they want to make their clients more beautiful, their customers happier, themselves more satisfied. And what more likely place for this to happen-than California?

Alan Fletcher

Alan Fletcher's international design reputation is reflected by his commissions from major corporations and cultural institutions around the world. He began his career in New York where he worked for Fortune magazine, the Container Corporation and IBM. He moved back to London and co-founded Fletcher/Forbes/Gill, which served such clients as Pirelli, Cunard, Penguin Books, BP and Olivetti. He co-founded Pentagram and created design programmes for Reuters, Lucas Industries, The Mandarin Oriental Hotel Group, The Victoria & Albert Museum, Lloyd's of London, Daimler Benz, Arthur Andersen & Co and ABB. Later, Fletcher left Pentagram to establish his own studio and to work directly with his clients. He has received numerous awards from the most prestigious organizations and societies worldwide and was elected to the Hall of Fame of the New York Art Directors Club. In his career he has served many outstanding societies in various capacities with great distinction.

Alan Fletcher trained at the Central School of Arts & Crafts, the Royal College of Art in London and the School of Architecture and Design at Yale University.

1424 Marcelina Avenue
Torrance, CA 90501
Phone: 310. 381. 0170
Fax: 310. 381. 0169
www.soohoodesign.com

SOOHOO DESIGNERS

An ancient Chinese puzzle—the Tangram—is comprised of five triangles, one square and one rhomboid. The Tangram challenges the creative thinker to design distinct forms using all seven pieces. The puzzle concept is simple and only one's imagination and creativity limit the many possible solutions to the Tangram.

At SooHoo Designers, we use the Tangram as a metaphor for how we develop solutions to the varied communication challenges faced by our Clients. Our methodology of listening, probing and thinking enables SooHoo Designers to solve creative, marketing and communication problems simply, imaginatively and effectively.

Each year, SooHoo Designers produces award-winning, strategic and creative solutions for companies in a broad range of industries, covering regional, national and international markets. Our experience, combined with our multilingual capabilities, gives us a global approach to design.

SooHoo Designers' solutions are strategic, unique and encompass a variety of media. We combine our collective expertise to bring forth results that enable our Clients to build brand equity, communicate effectively, evoke positive responses, and motivate consumers to action.

SooHoo Designers

PROMOTIONS

1. Identity and stationery for sales
   incentive program.

2. Portion of a sales incentive program: itinerary
   booklet, embroidered patches, luggage tags
   and announcement brochure.

3. Announcement posters for sales
   incentive program.

1

2

TREASURES OF
RUSSIA

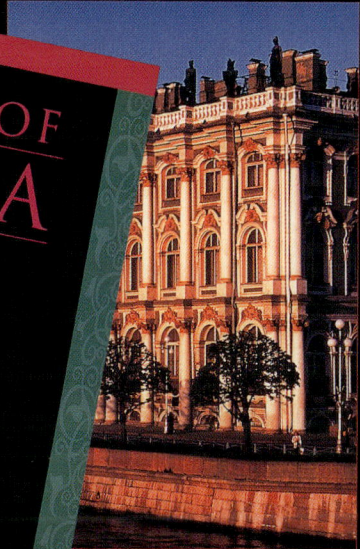

Fabergé

TREASURES OF
RUSSIA

Hermitage

TREASURES OF
RUSSIA

Ballet

BRAND IDENTITIES

1. Technology identity for Epson America, Inc.
2. Identity for Rokenbok Toy Company.
3. Identity program for L.A. Care Health Plan.
4. Identity refresh for California Federal Bank.
5. Identity program for Hacienda del Mar Resorts Cabo San Lucas, Mexico.
6. Identity for a sales incentive program.
7. Posters to launch L.A. Care Health Plan.
8. Corporate identity program for California Federal Bank.

1

2

3

7

4

5

6

8

SooHoo Designers

PACKAGING

1. Frozen food package for Overhill Farm's
   Chicken Chili casserole.
2. Digital camera packaging for Epson America, Inc.
3. Fruit beverage packaging concept.

COLLATERAL

4. Ink jet printer brochure for Epson America, Inc.
5. Financial product brochure for
   California Federal Bank.
6. Scanner brochure for Epson America, Inc.

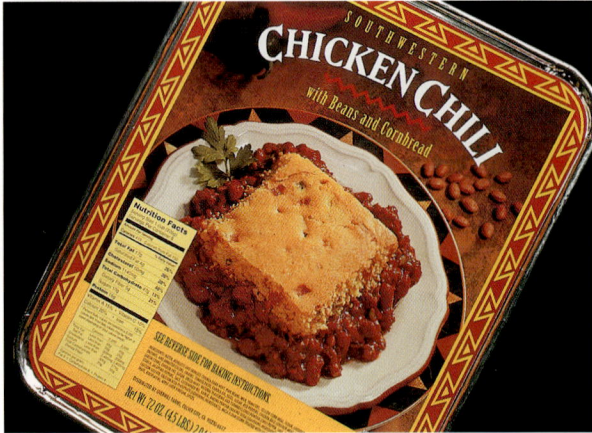

1

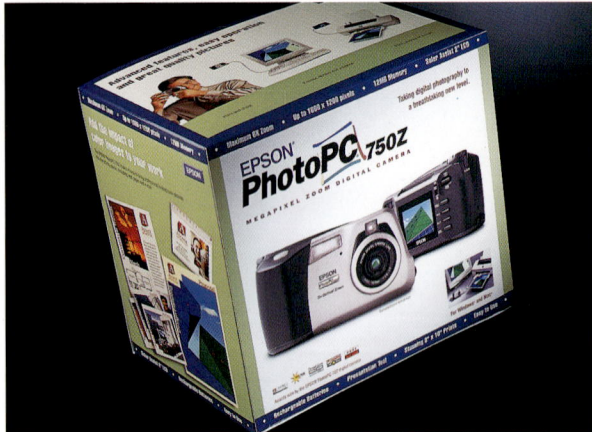

2

3

4

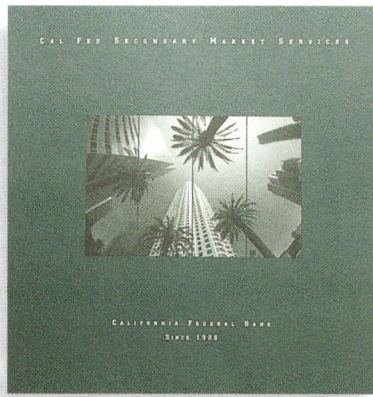

CAL FED SECONDARY MARKET SERVICES

CALIFORNIA FEDERAL BANK
SINCE 1926

5

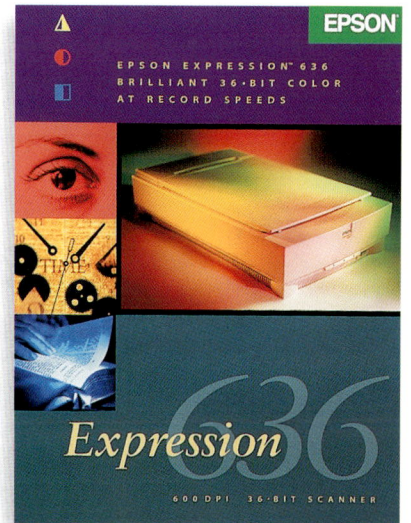

EPSON

EPSON EXPRESSION™ 636
BRILLIANT 36·BIT COLOR
AT RECORD SPEEDS

Expression 636
600 DPI · 36·BIT SCANNER

6

Believe It.

EPSON

EPSON STYLUS PRO 5000

EPSON
Stylus
Pro 5000

digital color
technology and an EFI Fiery
dependency on expensive analog pr
process. Whether you are a print
or fine a
imag
Pr

Print It. Proof It. Belie

7

SooHoo Designers

NEW MEDIA
1. Web site design for GSC organizational consulting group.
2. Web site design for Good Samaritan Hospital.
3. Web site development for Kovert Design.

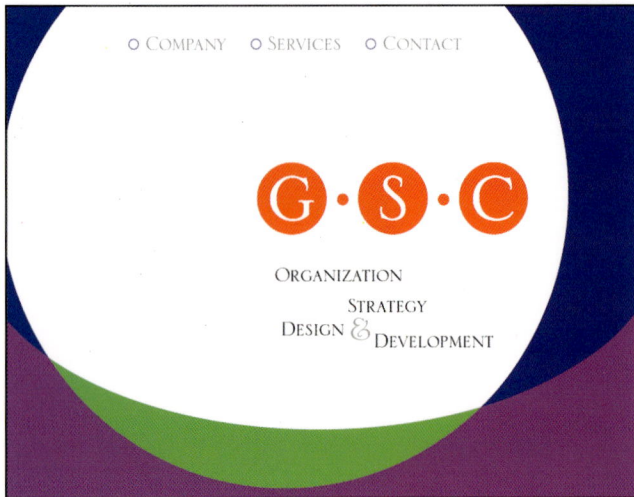

1

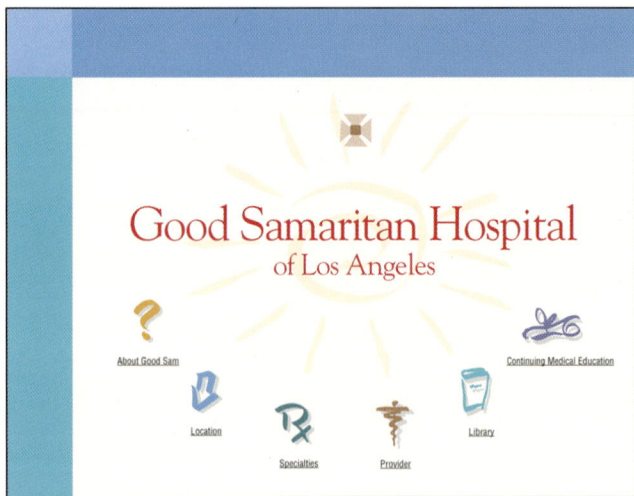

2

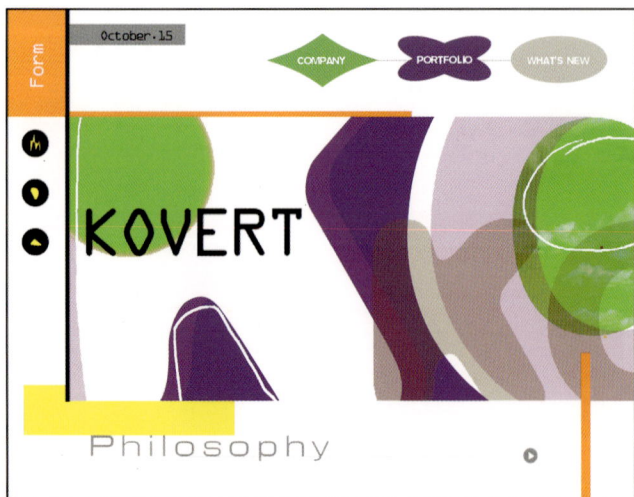

3

"At SooHoo Designers, we do more than create work that is visually stimulating, we design solutions that accomplish the Client's objectives and exceed their expectations."

Patrick SooHoo

1

Klamath House
1001 Front Street
San Francisco, California 94111
415.365.1700
www.landor.com

2

LANDOR ASSOCIATES

From airplanes and wine bottles to Web sites and corporate literature, the work of Landor Associates touches the lives of consumers day in and day out. Since its establishment in 1941 by legendary German designer Walter Landor, the company has created many of the world's best loved and most enduring brands.

Landor believes that successful brands are built by creating experiences that engage consumers and influence brand preference. To that end, Landor offers a broad and expanding spectrum of consulting and design services world-wide for corporate, service and consumer brands, including research, naming, corporate identity, brand identity, inter-active branding and branded environments.

Partnering globally with clients, Landor's network includes 20 offices in the Americas, Asia and Europe with full-service consulting and design studios located in San Francisco (international headquarters), New York, Seattle, Irvine, Cincinnati, Mexico City, London, Paris, Hamburg, Sydney, Tokyo and Hong Kong, and market-ing offices based in Bangkok, Madrid, Miami, Milan, Sâo Paulo, Seoul, Stockholm and Taipei.

1. Landor SF office design front.
2. Landor SF interior office.

17

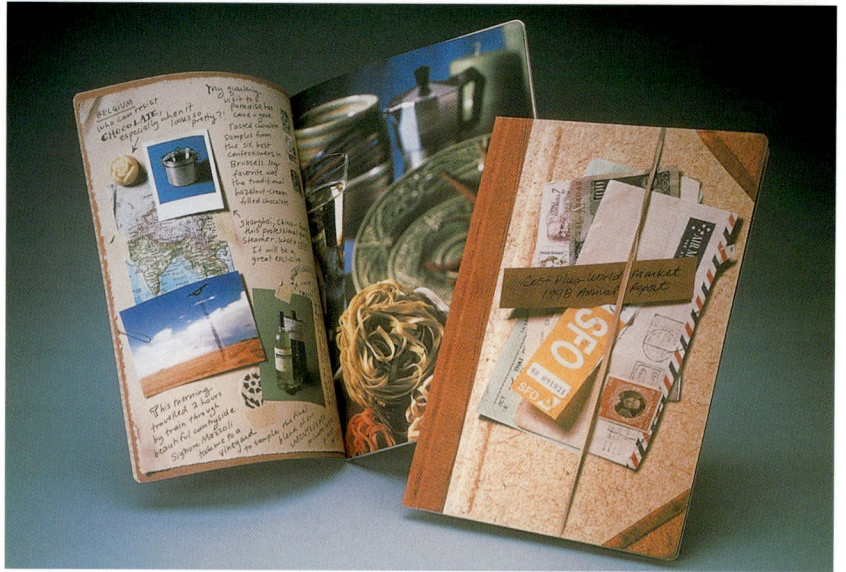

1

2

1. 1998 Annual Report for Cost Plus World Market.
2. Lincoln Model Year 2000 Brochure for Lincoln Mercury.
3. Spread from Embark–New Employee Orientation Program.

3

Agilent Technologies
Innovating the HP Way

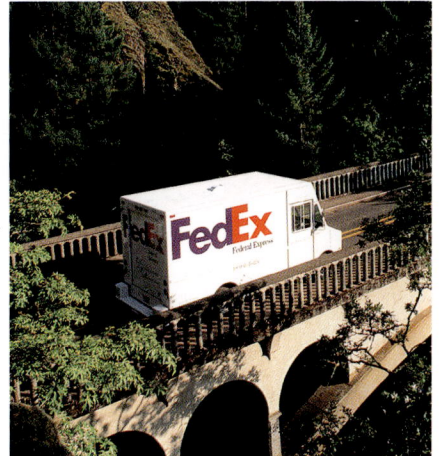

2

3

4

ex*O*ratorium

1

1. Identity for Exploratorium.
2. Identity for Agilent Technology.
3. Identity for Federal Express.
4. Identity for San Francisco Zoo.
5. Identity for Xerox.

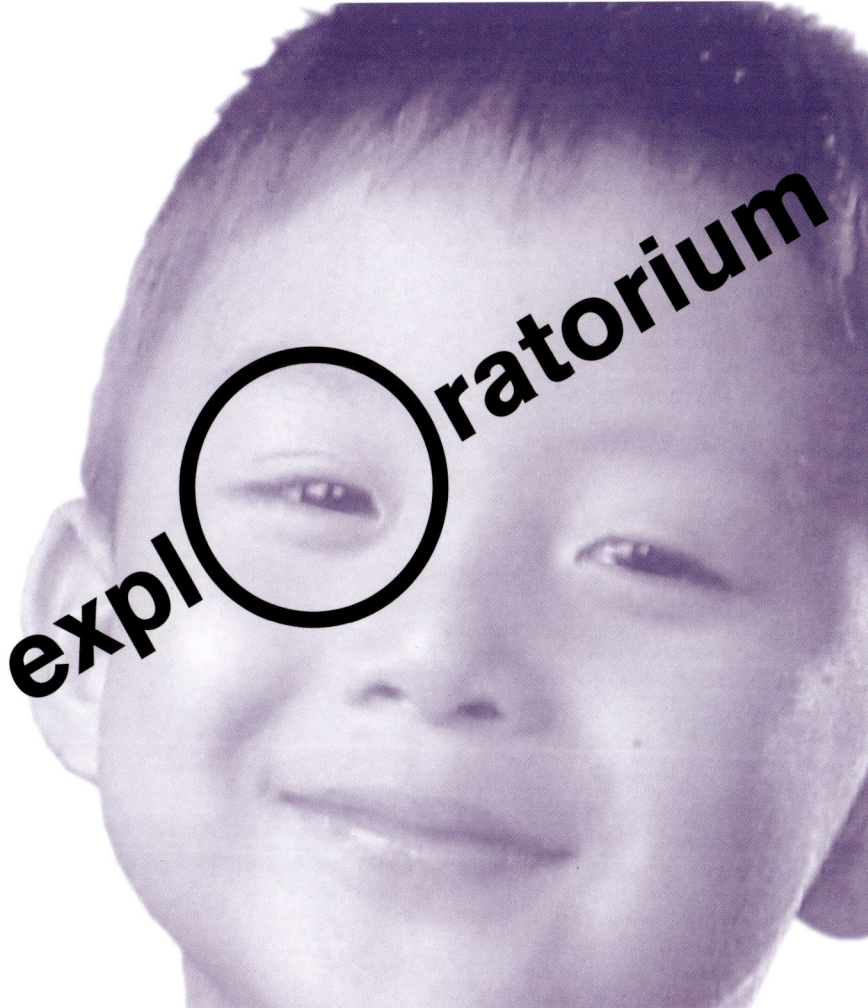

5

NETSCAPE

1

1. Identity for Netscape.
2-3. Brand Manual and Identity for ITT Industries.
4-5. Identity and Signing for Canadian Airlines.

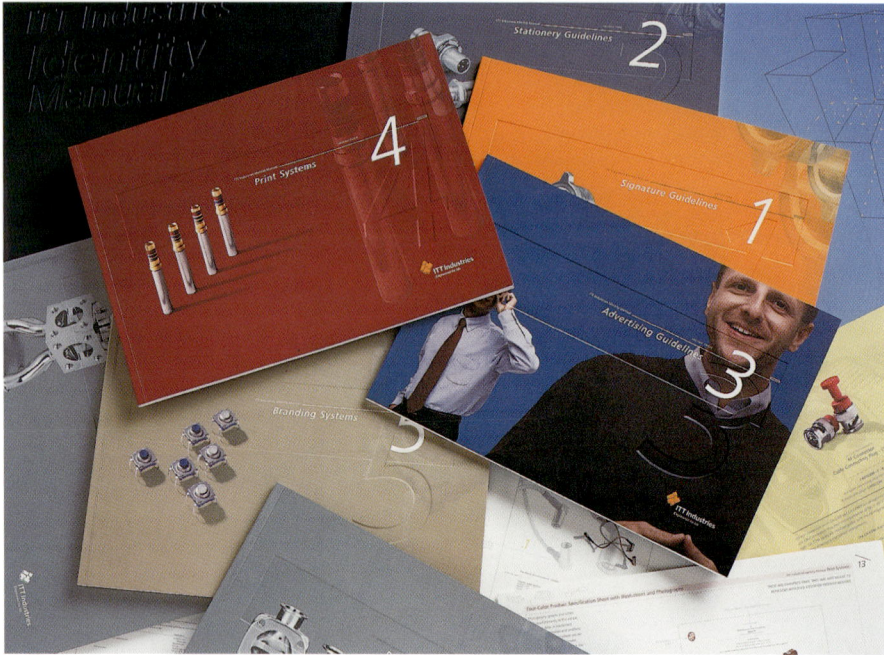

2

ITT Industries
Engineered for life

3

4

5

GeoCities

1

Lucent Technologies

2

SALT LAKE 2002

3

4

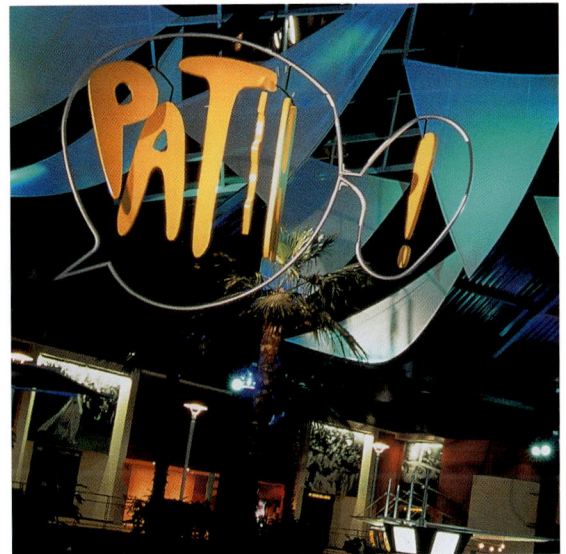

5

6

1. Identity for Geocities.
2. Identity for Lucent Technologies.
3. Identity for 2002 Salt Lake Olympic Games.
4-5. Identity for Pathé.
6. Identity for SeaWorld Adventure Parks.

1

2

3

4

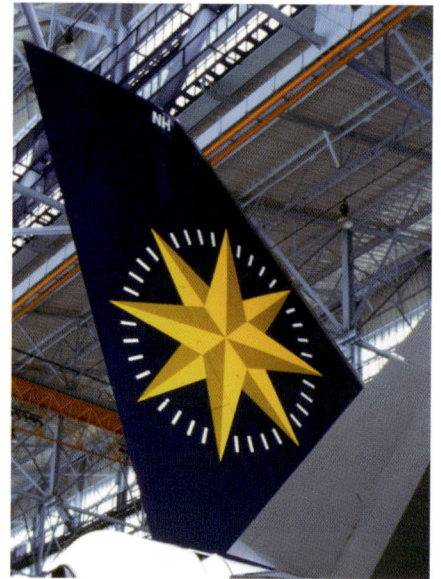

5

1. Identity for Gifts.com.
2. Identity for Pizza Hut.
3. Identity for Saba.
4. Packaging for Frito-Lays.
5. Identity for Varig Airlines.

1. Packaging for Gerber Tender Harvest.
2. Packaging for Chandon.
3. Packaging for Killian's Irish Red.
4. Packaging for Helmac Evercare.
5. Pacakaging for Health Valley Granola.

1

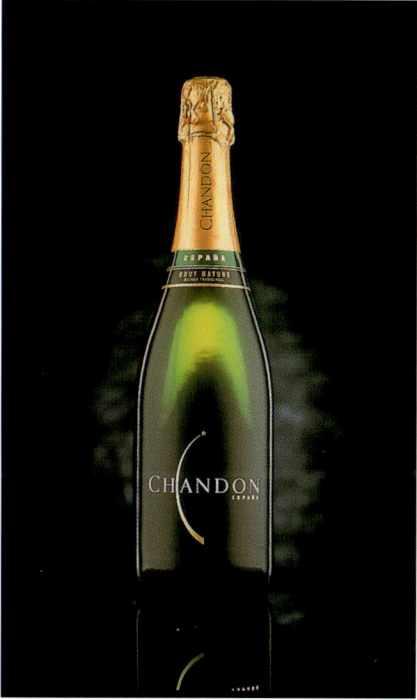

2

3

4

5

1

2

3

4

5

1. AG Ferrari Store.
2. Trade Show Booth for SGI.
3-4. Packaging for AG Ferrari.
5. Identification Signing for Visteon.

FUSE, Inc.
775 Laguna Canyon Road
Laguna Beach, CA 92651
949 376 0438
www.gofuse.com
info@gofuse.com

FUSE, INC.

The quality of the idea. The ability to think, strategically. That's what we're selling. Pretty pictures are cool, so are fancy words, but without a substantial conceptual framework they amount to sugar coating. We're not into artificial sweeteners. What we are into is conceptual purity ... Ideas that work on multiple levels ... And using the power of the computer to turbo-charge traditional thought processes.

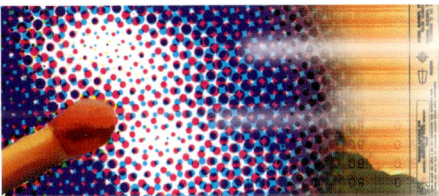

At Fuse, there's no limit to the implementation of those ideas - Graphical brand development or web marketing; integrated advertising or computerized selling tools; point-of-sale stuff or multimedia presentations – we specialize in bringing ideas to life using the ideal balance of communications, intelligence and technology.

As the name implies, our charter follows a fairly elementary concept. We're the genesis for explosive creativity. Our ideas are sparked from combustible thinking. And our reputation for innovation is blowing up.

1

3

1. Brand development
2. Integrated web marketing – Yamaha Drums
3. Internet innovation – Yamaha Guitars

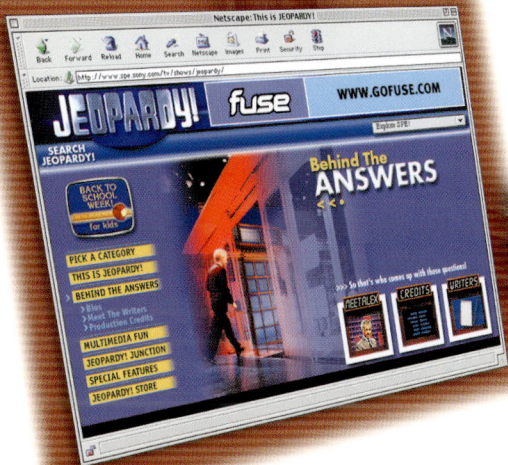

1

2

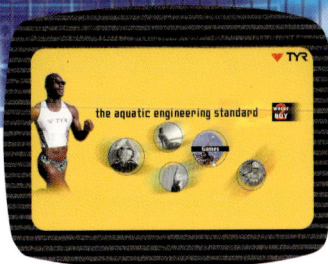

3

1. Online design and development – Columbia TriStar Interactive

2. Interactive online design – Columbia TriStar Interactive

3. Internet brand reinforcement – TYR Sport

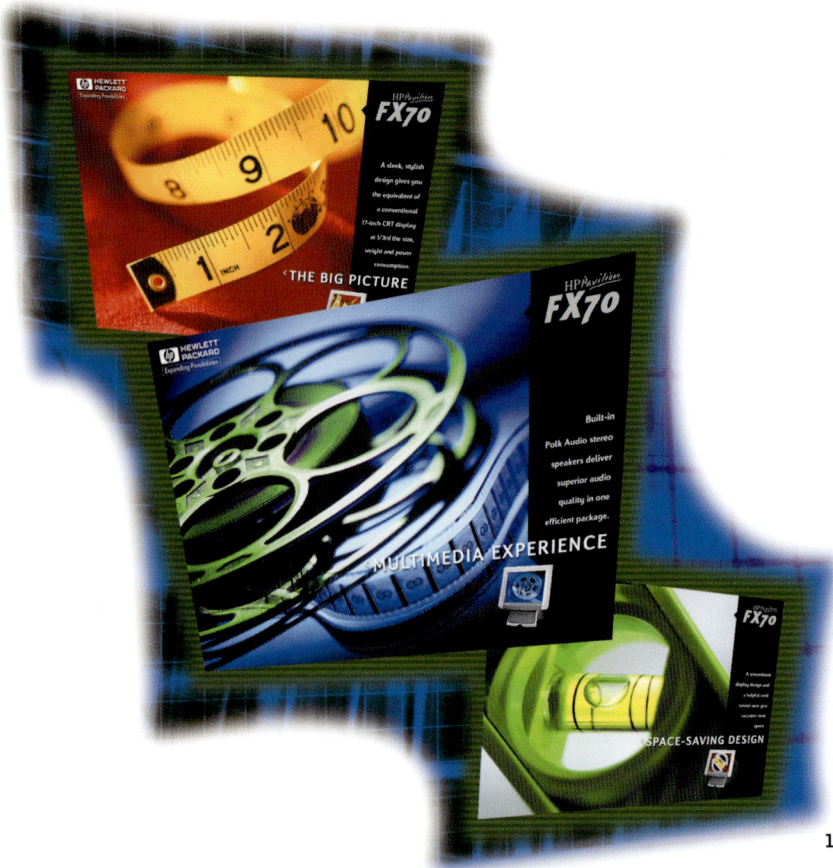

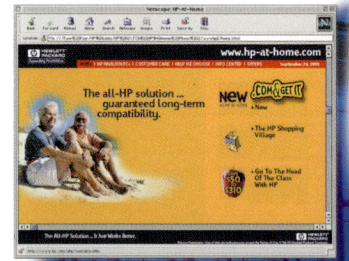

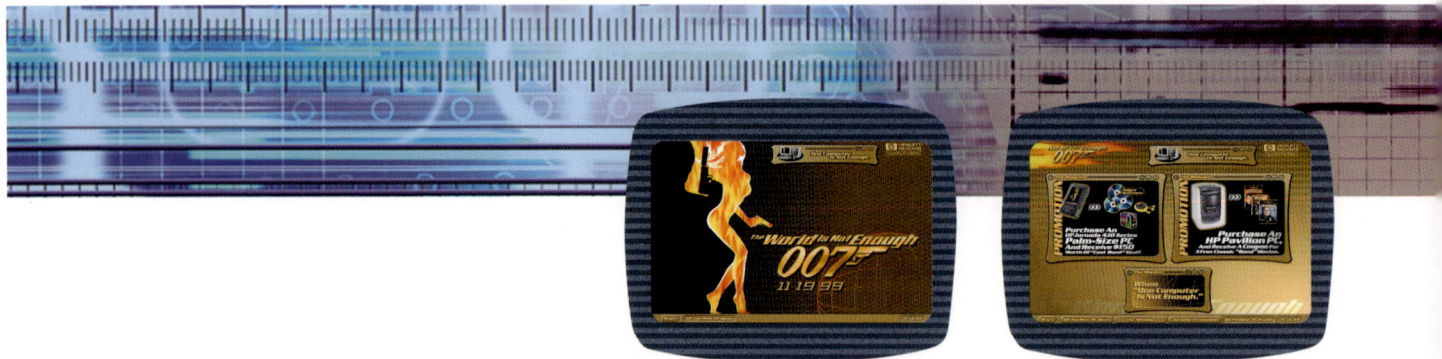

1. In-store digital advertising – Hewlett-Packard

2. Ecommerce/Internet development – Hewlett-Packard

3. Integrated campaign advertising – Hewlett-Packard

4. Point-of-sale visual marketing – Hewlett-Packard

1

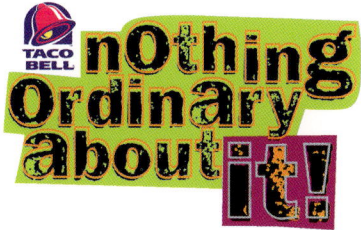

1A

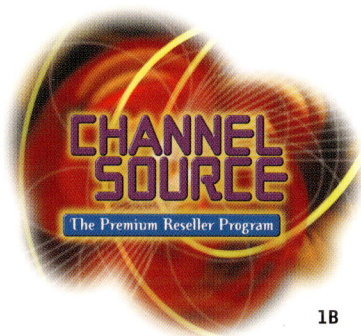

1B

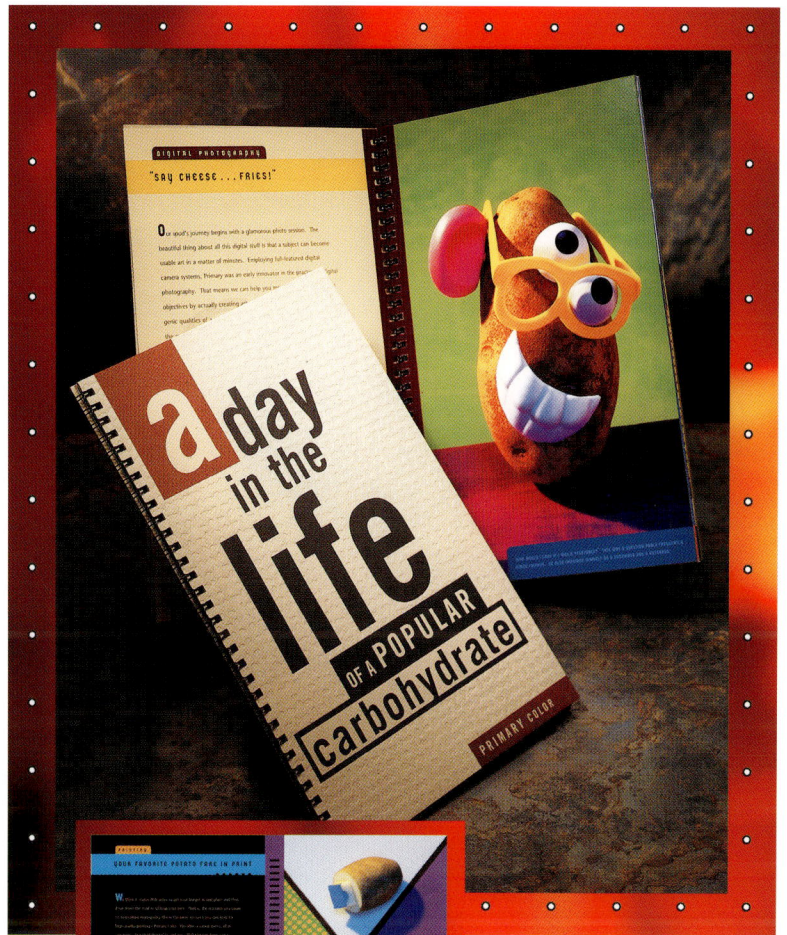

2

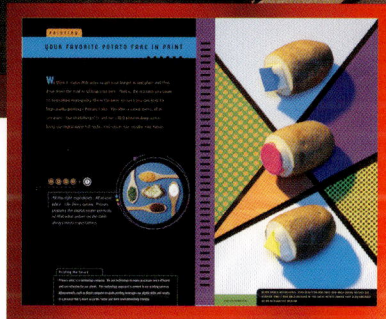

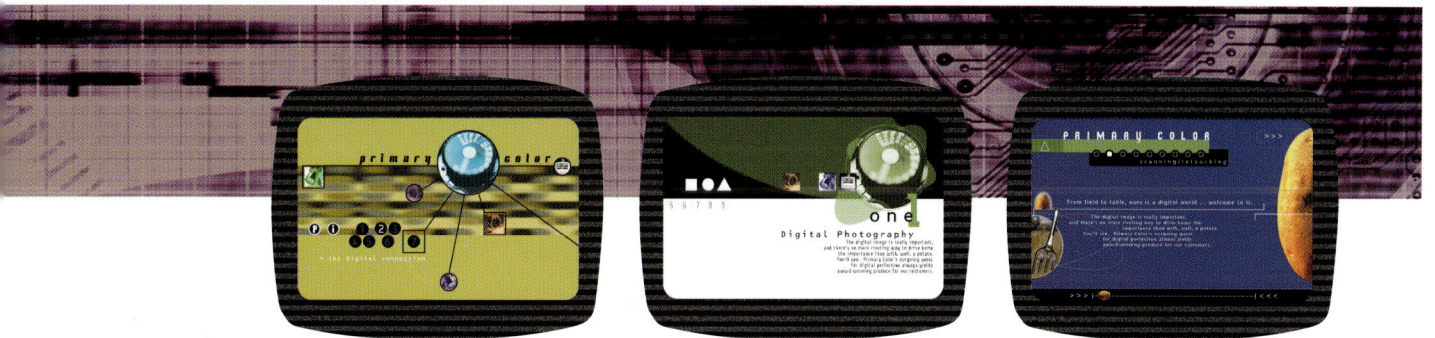

3

1. Product and brand signatures – PairGain Technologies, Taco Bell, Fujitsu PC
2. Collateral story telling – Primary Color
3. Visual Internet marketing – Primary Color

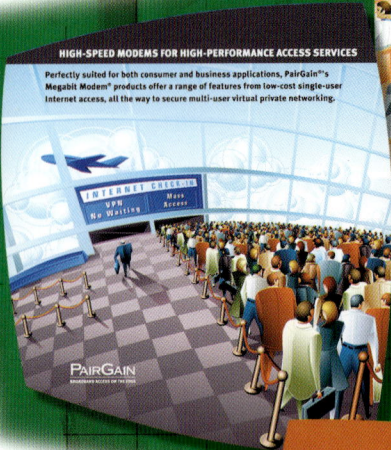

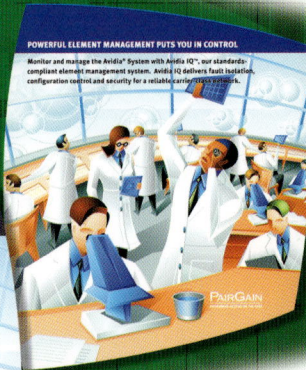

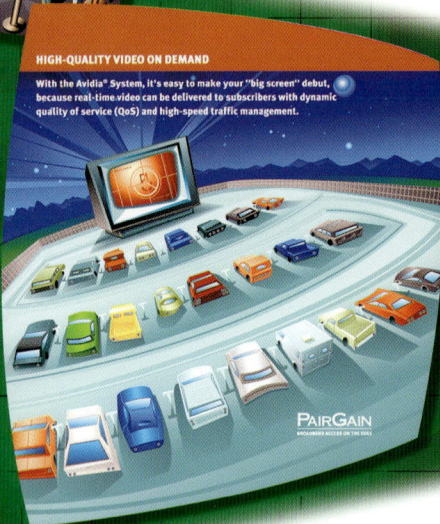

1

2

2A

2B

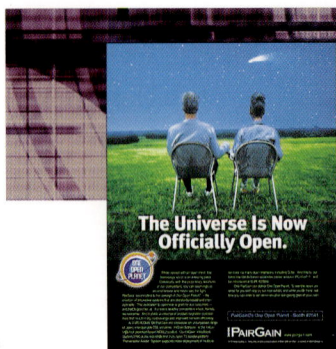

3

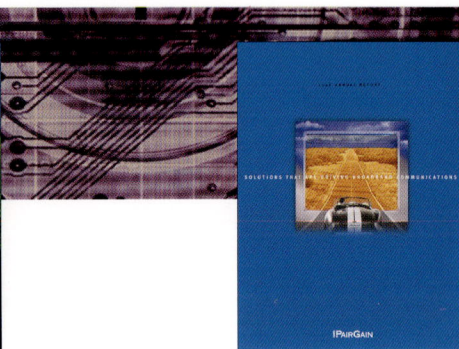

4

1. Event marketing – PairGain Technologies

2. Product identities – PairGain Technologies

3. Print advertising – PairGain Technologies

4. Annual shareholder communications – PairGain Technologies

1. Interactive product marketing – Fujitsu PC
2. CD-based advertising tools – Qualcomm
3. Tasty Internet design – Ruby's Restaurants

1

2

3

1. Multimedia product marketing – Experian
2. Interactive selling tool – Experian
3. Detonate your current agency and hire FUSE

Hunt Design Associates
25 North Mentor Avenue
Pasadena, California 91106-1709
626.793.7847
fax 626.793.2549
nnette@huntdesign.com
www.huntdesign.com

HUNT DESIGN ASSOCIATES

Housed in their own historic brick building in the culturally aware city of Pasadena, Hunt Design Associates is a leading firm in the emerging design field Environmental Graphics. "We do graphic design for buildings, places and spaces," says company principal Wayne Hunt. Hunt Design combines the classic principles of two dimensional graphic design with processes and techniques of architecture and industrial design.

The firm's sixteen full-time staff are comprised of designers, drafts persons and programmers. Each has an interest in the built environment — how places are designed and constructed, and how people interact with physical space. "We pride ourselves in being active participants in the real world, not the virtual world," states Hunt, a veteran of thirty years in design — he started Hunt Design in 1977 after a few critical years in a well-known signage-oriented design firm.

Hunt Design has built an enviable reputation in the exciting people-based industries of entertainment, retail, gaming and hospitality, executing major projects for the Walt Disney Company, MGM Grand, Universal, Warner Bros., and Park Place Entertainment. In addition, the firm extends its reach to exhibition design and visitor destinations of all kinds, including Kennedy Space Center, The New Jersey Aquarium and New York's World Trade Center. "We like to work on and be part of the places people want to go to," concludes Hunt.

1

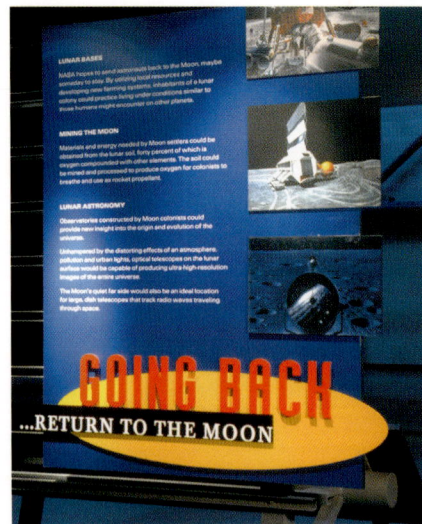

2

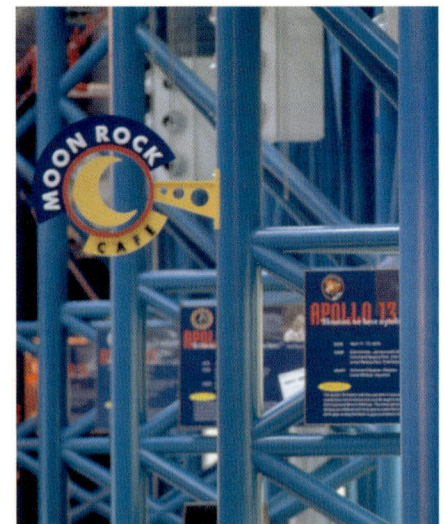

3

1. – 3. 28,000 sq. ft. Apollo Saturn V exhibit at Kennedy Space Center presents the story of Americas journey to the moon

4. – 5. Top of the World visitor center at New York's World Trade Center

4

5

6

7

8

9

6. – 9. Comprehensive signage program for Las Vegas' McCarran International Airport

1

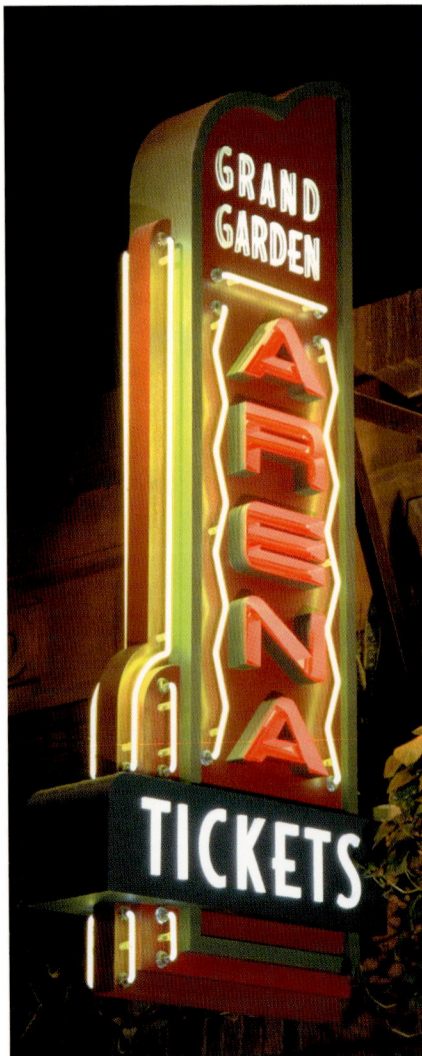

4

2

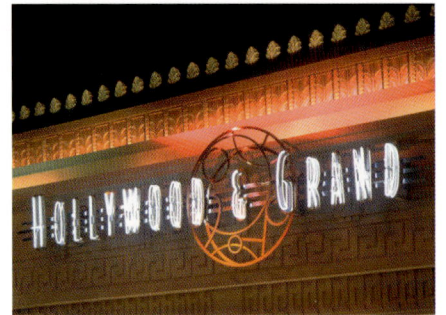

3

5

6

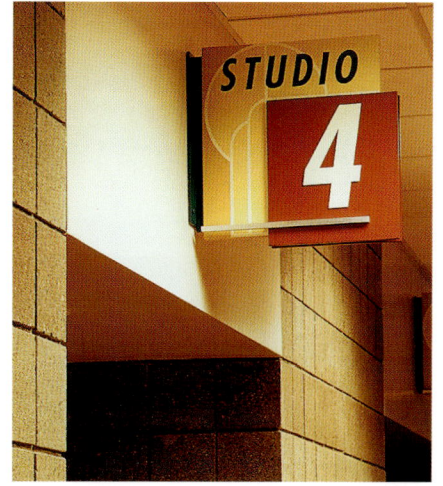

7

8

9

1. – 4. Themed graphics for the Studio Walk shopping experience at the MGM Grand Hotel and Casino, Las Vegas

5. Custom floor design for Studio Walk

6. – 7. Signage at MGM Grand Garden Arena

8. – 11. Comprehensive signage program for the MGM Grand, over 300 signs

10

11

1. – 6. Colorful, period-style graphics designed for the innovative Paris Las Vegas

1

2

3

4

5

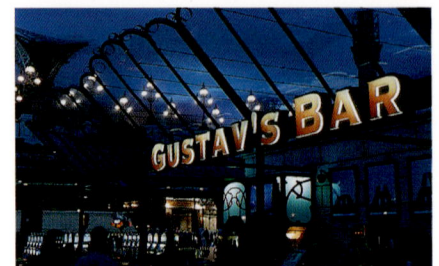

6

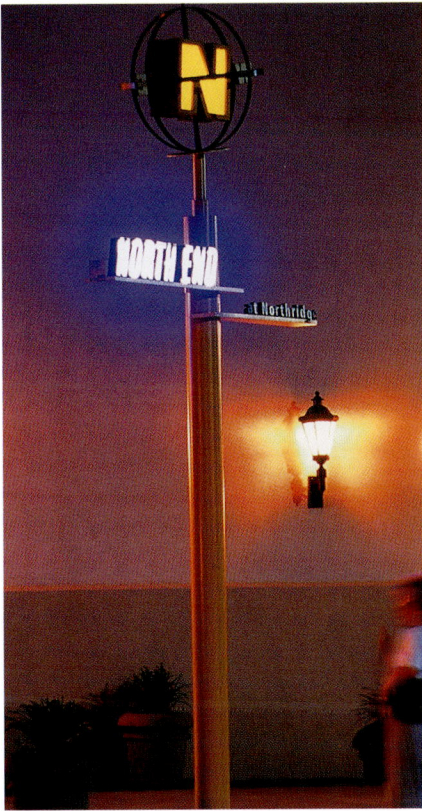

7

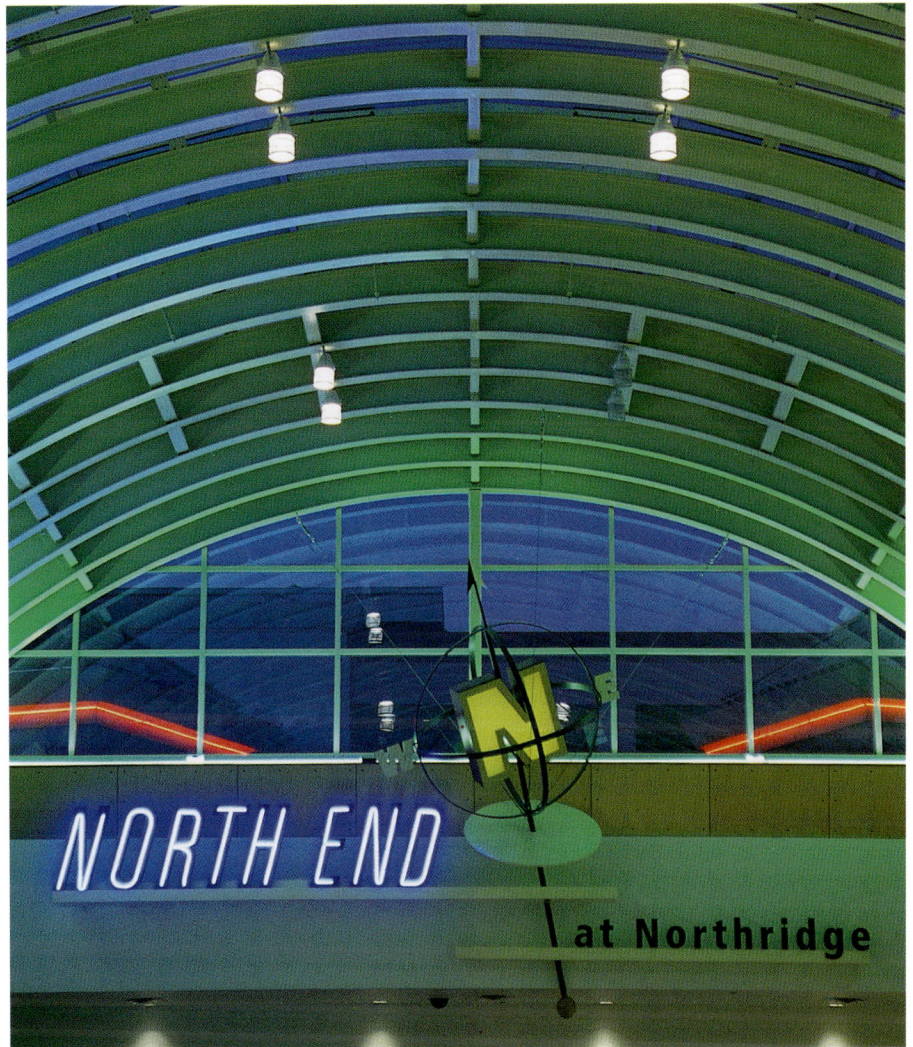

8

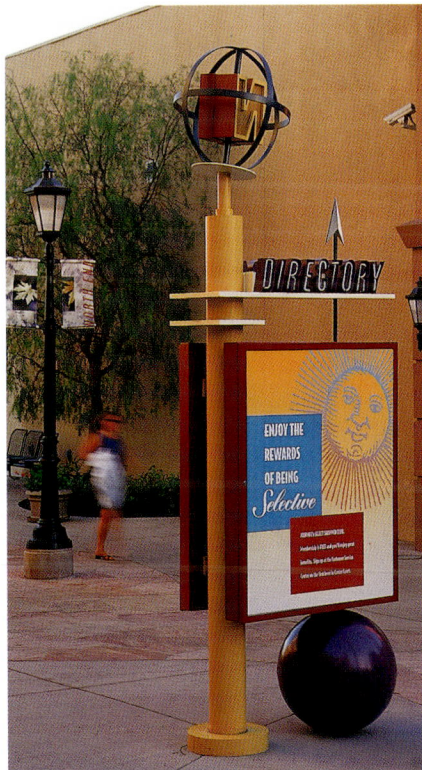

9

9

7. – 9. Retail identity expressed through
dimensional signage at Northridge
Fashion Center, California

1

2

3

4

5

1. – 2. Branding and interior graphics for a new chain of cook-to-order fast food restaurants

3. New image for the Southwest Museum, Los Angeles

4. Logo for a space center in Germany

5. Identity for a Pasadena realtor

6. Typographic logo for an upscale Las Vegas restaurant

7. Branding statement for a science and learning park in California

6

7

Profile Design
835 5th Avenue
San Rafael, CA 94901
415.485.1492
www.profiledesign.com

Cymbic Interactive
835 5th Avenue
San Rafael, CA 94901
415.485.5760
www.cymbic.com

PROFILE DESIGN & CYMBIC INTERACTIVE

PROFILE:

cymbic INTERACTIVE

Profile Design and Cymbic Interactive provide integrated branding and design solutions. Profile creates brand identity. Cymbic creates brand experience.

PROFILE

As a hands-on team, Profile Design is dedicated to creating strategic, innovative and effective design that reflects and reinforces our client's values and vision in the marketplace. We strive to achieve this goal with integrity and imagination.

Profile Design is a strategic design firm specializing in brand and corporate identity programs, print collateral, and packaging systems. Since Profile's launch in 1989, we've focused our creative energy on translating marketing objectives into effective designs that position our clients in the forefront of their industry.

CYMBIC

Cymbic Interactive began as the web services arm of Profile Design. In the chaos of early Internet growth, Profile began building a web team on a foundation grounded in design fundamentals—a team that could balance the principles of design, the power of technology, and the discipline of marketing with a passion for innovation.

Cymbic emerged in 1998 as an independent subsidiary—free enough to follow its own path in the marketplace, but close enough to share the same business values and creative inspiration. Cymbic provides Internet consulting, digital design and web development services to highly competitive businesses. On many projects Cymbic and Profile work in concert to provide cross-channel print and digital design.

41

SENDMAIL®

1.

Sendmail, Inc. delivers the Internet's mail—literally. Sendmail's Mail Transfer Agent software is responsible for routing and delivering as much as 85% of all email. Built on the foundation of an Open Source community, Sendmail, Inc. was formed in 1997 to market a commercial version of its successful software. Sendmail asked Profile and Cymbic to create a strong branding program to communicate the value of their software and services to their highly technical audience.

2.

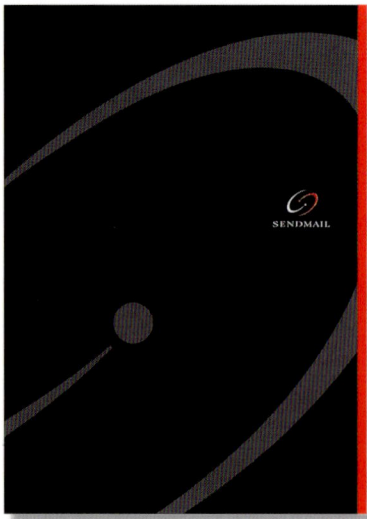

3.

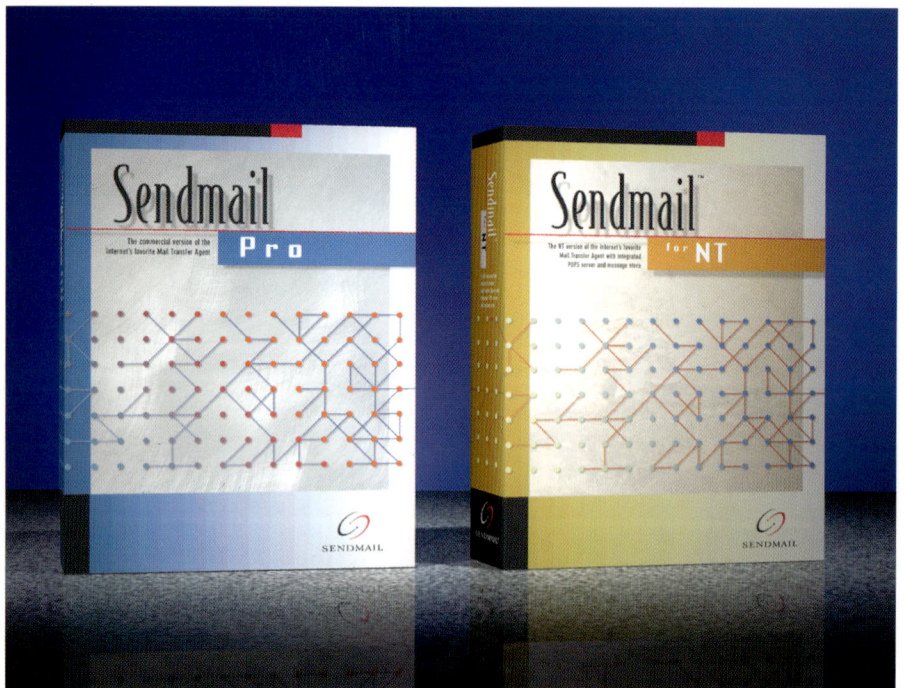

4.

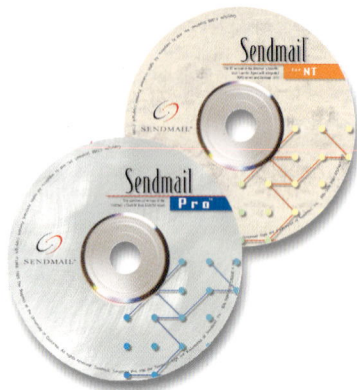

5.

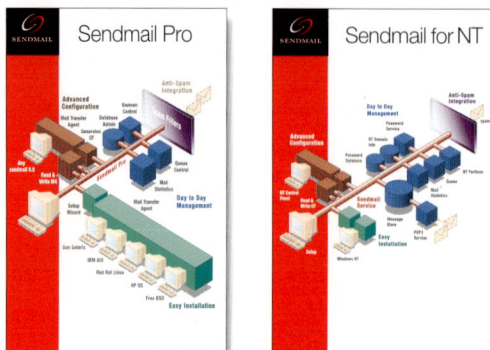

6.

1. Corporate Identity
2. Business Collateral
3. Presentation Folder
4. Product Packaging
5. CD Labels
6. Tradeshow Signage

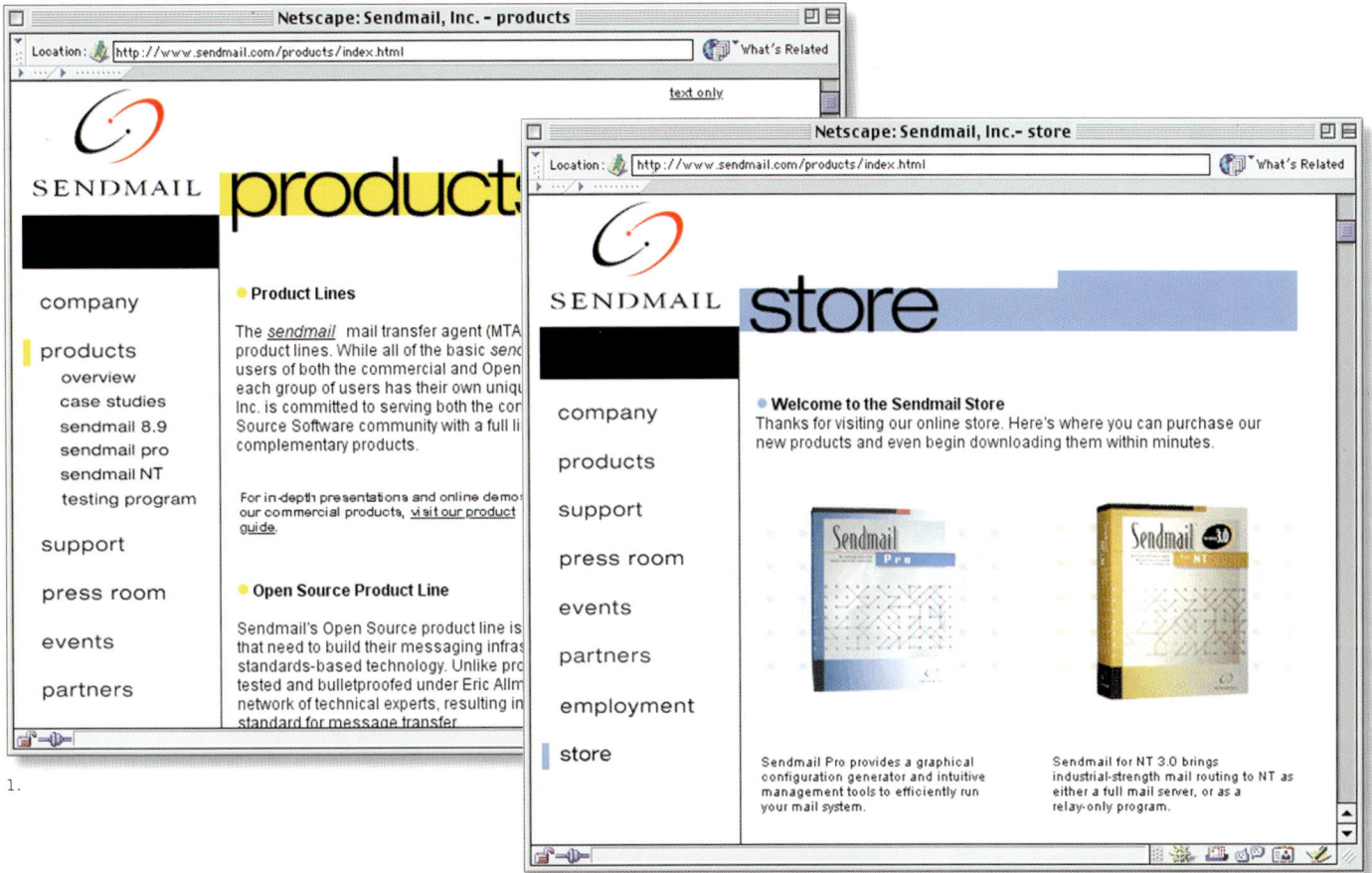

1.

In addition to the general marketing requirements, Sendmail's Web site and product demonstration needed to conform to highly specialized technical standards. The site was required to support Unix and Linux platforms, using 3rd generation browsers, and text viewers. In order to meet Sendmail's standards, we used a combination of pure HTML, animated gifs, and Flash.

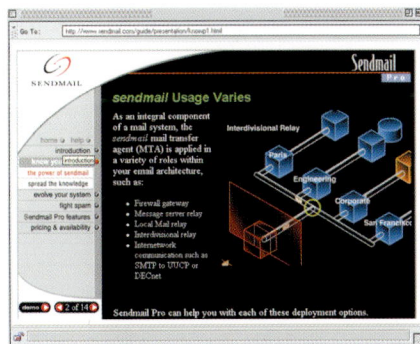 

2.

1. Corporate Web site
2. Interactive Product Guide
3. Software User Interface

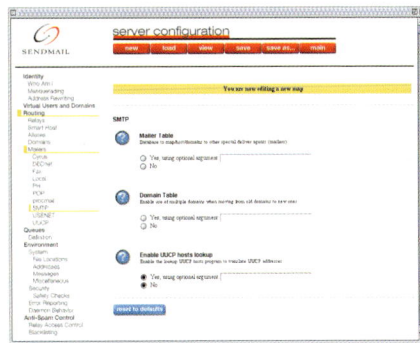 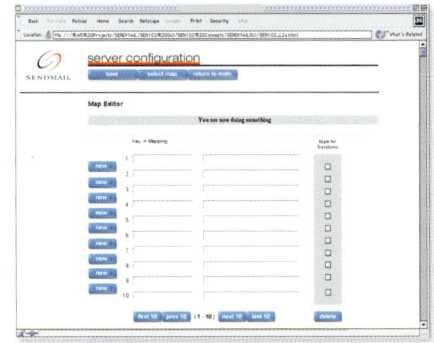

3.

COPPER MOUNTAIN

1.

2.

3.

4.

5.

6.

7.

Copper Mountain Networks develops and markets a comprehensive family of Digital Subscriber Line (DSL) solutions that enable high-speed internetworking through existing copper facilities. Transmitting data through copper wiring at broadband speeds, DSL has revolutionized access to the Internet. Profile created a brand identity that would clearly differentiate Copper Mountain from the flavor-of-the-month technology brands, and establish a strong corporate and customer culture.

1. Corporate Identity
2. Copper Compatible Logo
3. FastStart DSL Logo
4. Business Collateral
5. Datasheets
6. Product Packaging
7. Tradeshow Booth Graphics
8. Solution Packs

8.

Cymbic Interactive created an information architecture to support Copper Mountain's highly segmented audience. By breaking the audience into zones and using color for differentiation, Cymbic incorporated hundreds of pages of marketing and technical information into a unique and intuitive interface.

1. Corporate Web site
2. Document Level Page
3. Virtual Press Room

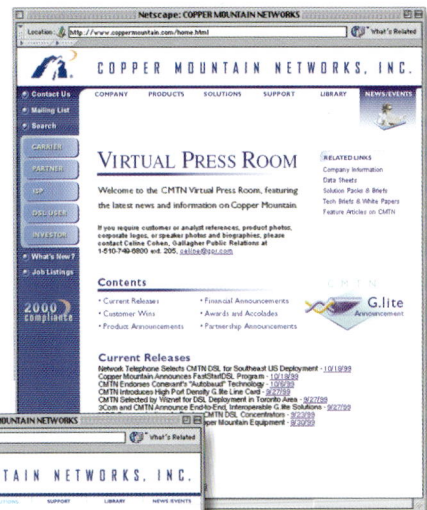

1.

2.

3.

1. Sony Electronics Vaio Product Datasheet
2. Sony Electronics Direct Mail Campaign
3. Hemptech, Nutiva Packaging
4. Hemptech, Nutiva Brand Hempseed Bars
5. Hemptech, Nutiva Brand Mark
6. ZA Zenchu, Kumai Harvest Packaging
7. ZA Zenchu, Kumai Harvest Brand Mark

1.

2.

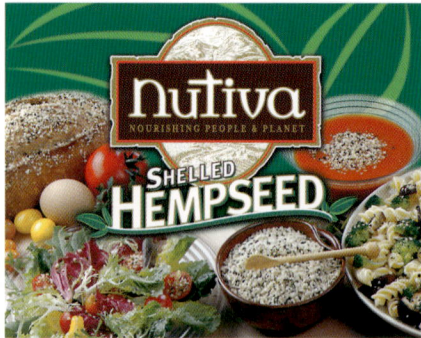

3.

4.

5.

6.

7.

1.

2.

ZHONE

3.

4.

5.

6.

1. Fujitsu Systems Corporate Brochure
2. AtComm Corporate Identity
3. Zhone Corporate Identity
4. Website Pros Corporate Identity
5. Validigm Corporate Business System
6. Vertical Networks Software Packaging
7. Vertical Networks Corporate Brochure
8. Validigm Corporate Identity
9. InterActive Corporate Identity

Validigm

8.

InterActive
PUBLIC RELATIONS

9.

7.

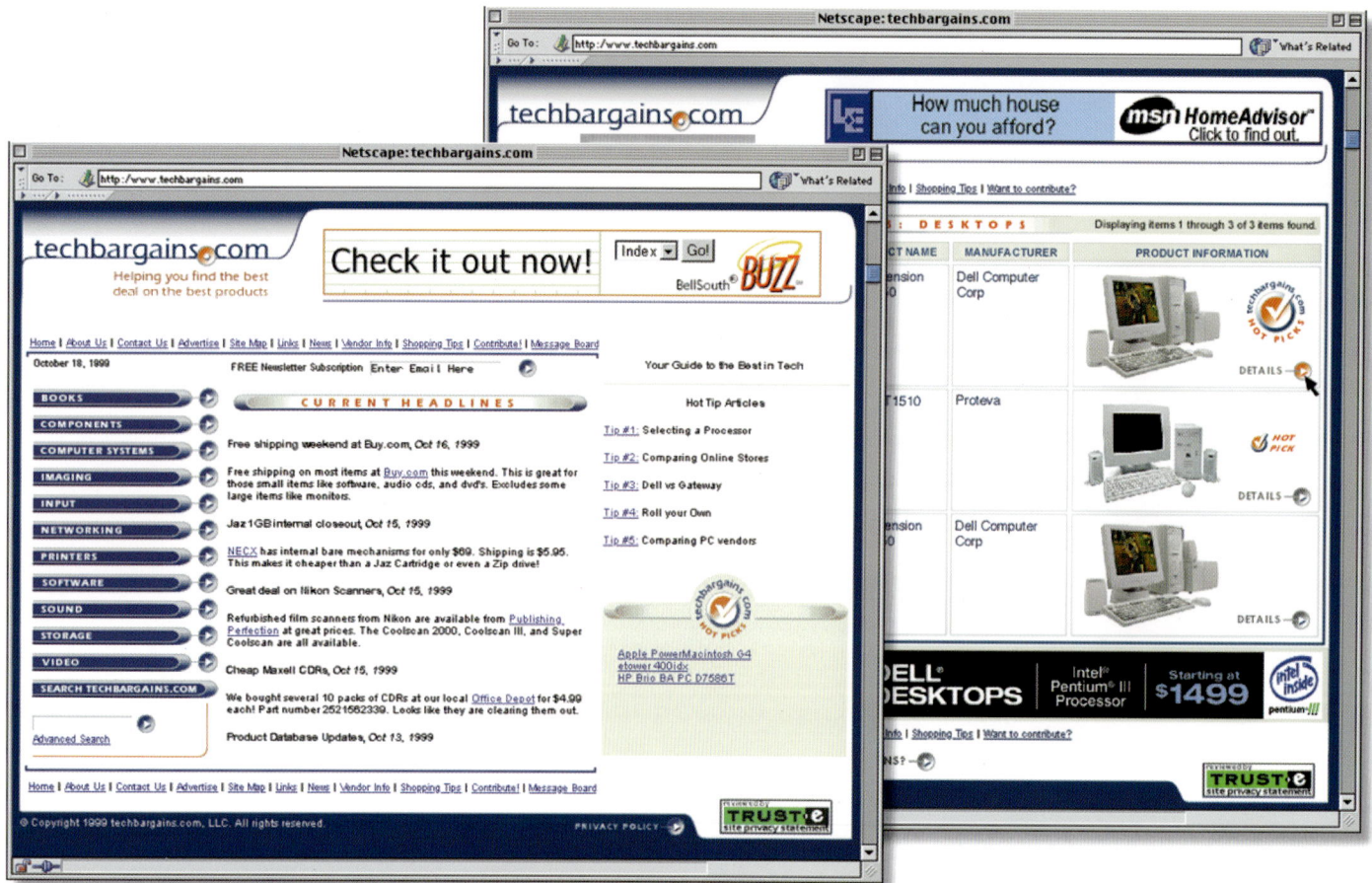

1.

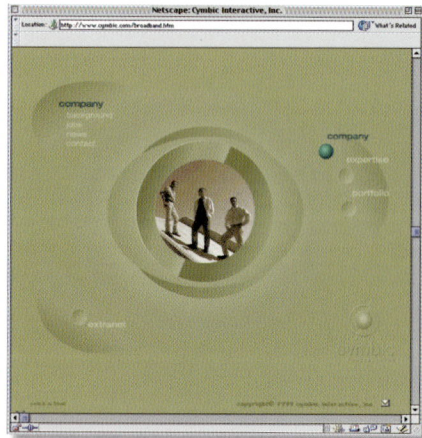 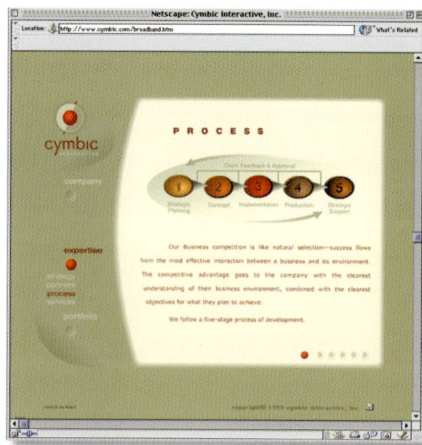 

2.

1. Techbargains Web site
2. Cymbic Interactive Web site
3. Website Pros Web site home page
4. Website Pros' online Web building application

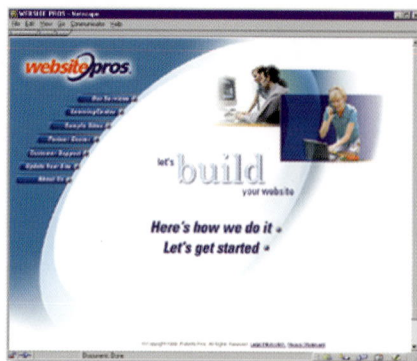 

3.

4.

Kim Baer Design Associates
Santa Monica, California
Telephone: 310 399 3295
Fax: 310 399 7964
www.kbda.com

KIM BAER DESIGN ASSOCIATES

The folks at KBDA love a good story. Storytelling is a touchstone of the studio's work, informing their polished and pragmatic design solutions. "We always gravitate towards the story as a way to speak to people" says the firm's founder, Kim Baer.

Baer began her career more than 20 years ago, and quickly learned that the real challenge lay not only in designing a beautiful piece, but also in holding onto the audience. KBDA's approach to each project begins with copious research and in-depth client conversation. This acquired understanding leads to the development of a strong concept and a compelling story to tell. "We've found the process to work for all of our varied projects, from logos and packaging to websites and corporate collateral – even the renaming of a company or product" adds Baer.

The studio doesn't espouse a "house style", but a look at their work reveals a definitive clarity. Simplicity finds a partner in beauty, with more than an occasional dash of wit. The combination draws a reader in.

The studio's success lies in finding a voice that goes deeper than reader cynicism and short attention spans. It's the voice of each client, their business, and their goals, translated with care and attention to detail. "Every project is really a unique story waiting to be told," Baer tells us. "Once we've found it, then the real fun begins."

KBDA's clients have included 3Com, Nike, Carl's Jr., IBM, UCLA, Acura, Ask Jeeves, Blue Cross and The Getty Center.

1

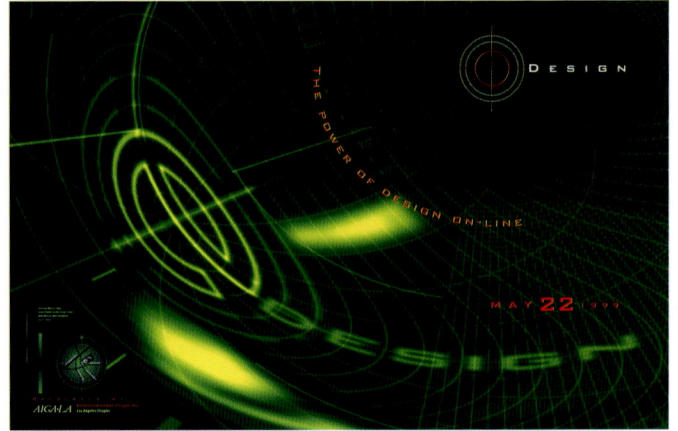

2

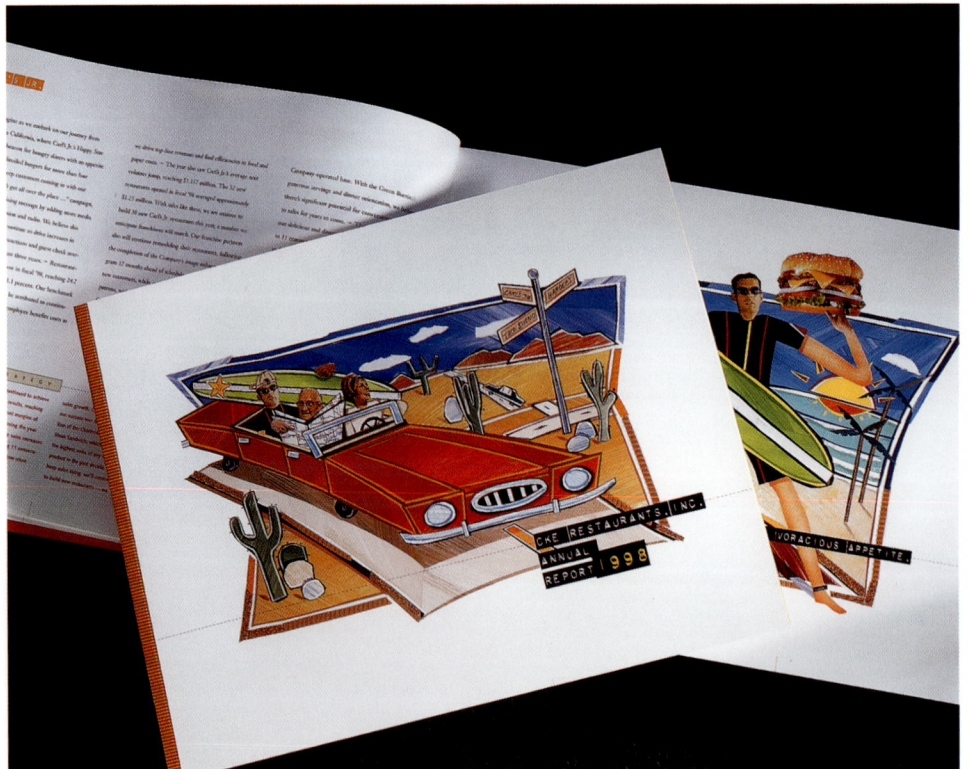

3

1. Networking company logo
2. Design symposium poster *(with M. Wilken)*
3. Restaurant corporation annual report

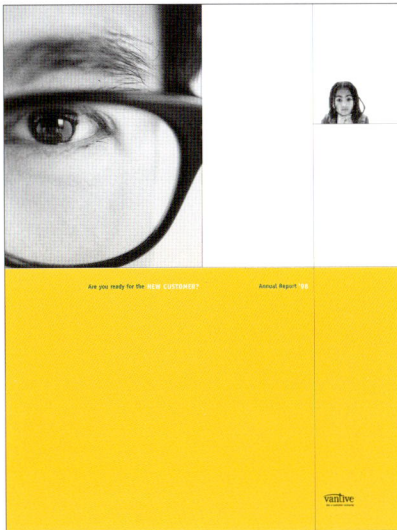

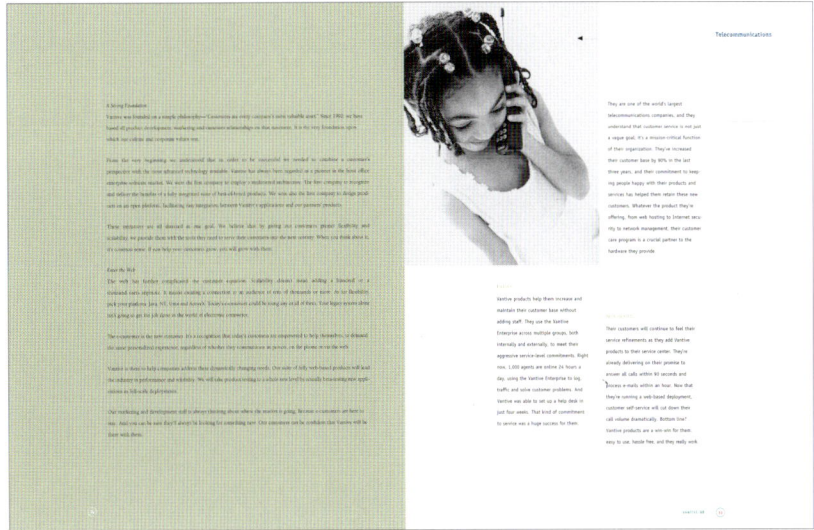

1

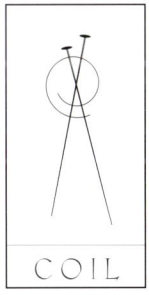

3

2

1. Annual report for customer relationship
software company
2. University recruitment brochure
3. Logo for designer knitwear company

Valley
Community
Clinic

1

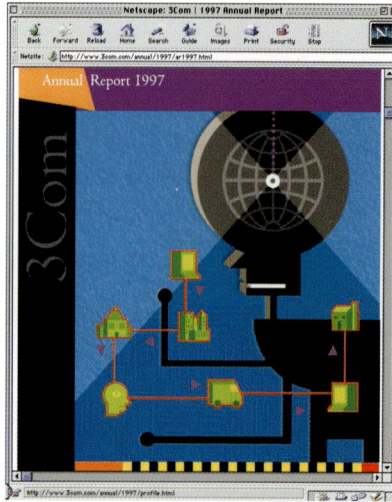

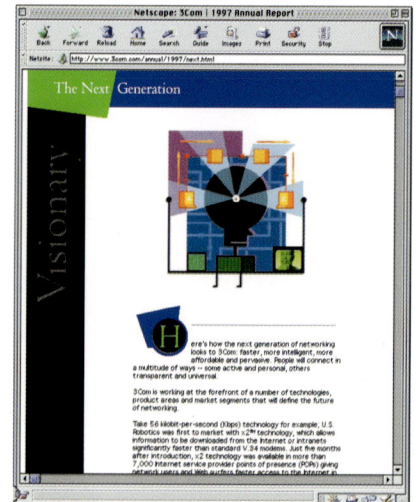

3

1. Community clinic logo
2. Technology company website
3. Suite of collateral materials for
   music programming company

1

3

3

1. Gift bags for cultural center
2. Restaurant logo
3. Signage and environment for restaurant *(with S. Karten)*
4. Toy and promotions company annual report

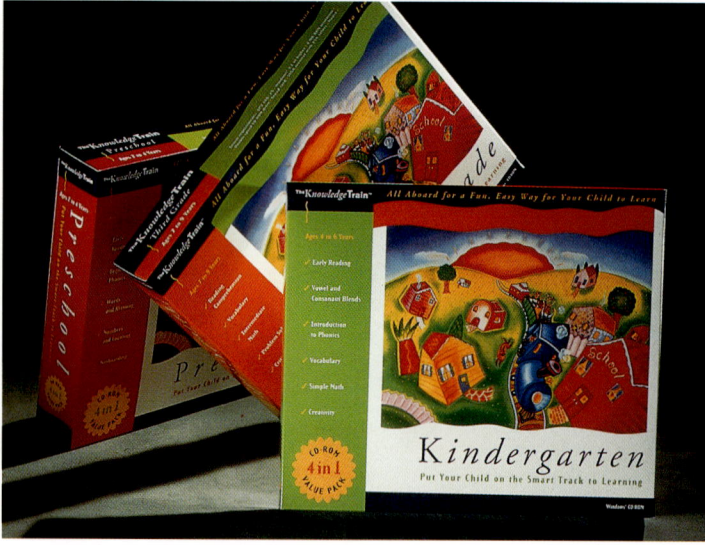

1

2

3

1. Packaging for educational software
2. Logo for satellite broadcast company
3. Logo for web portal
4. Annual report for healthcare company

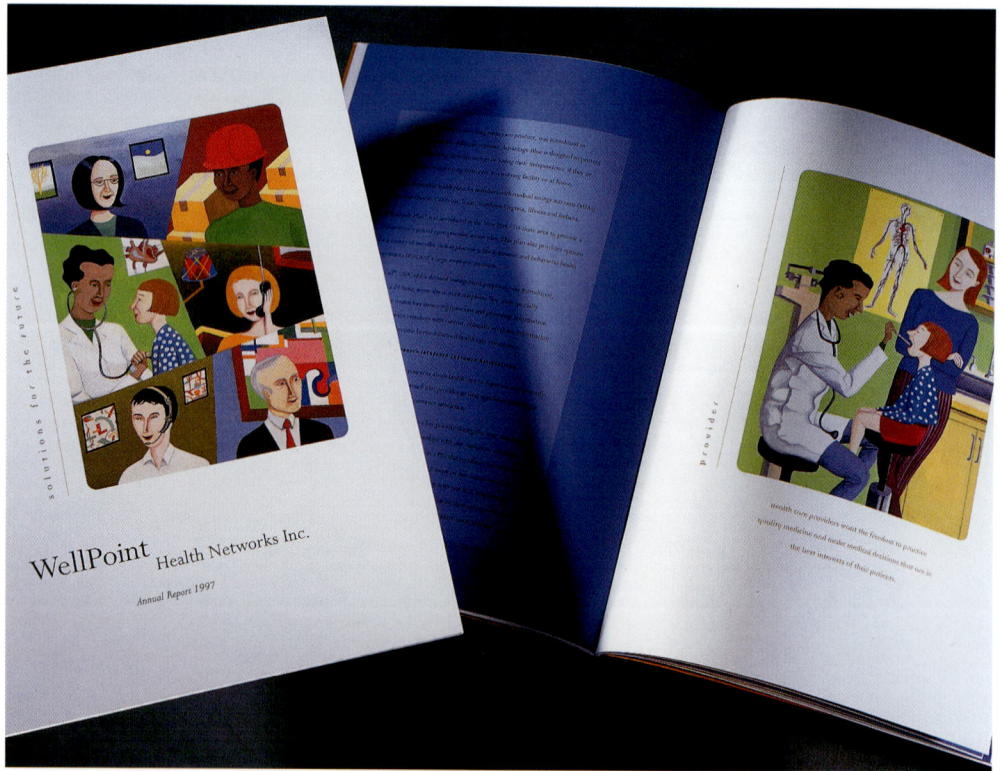

4

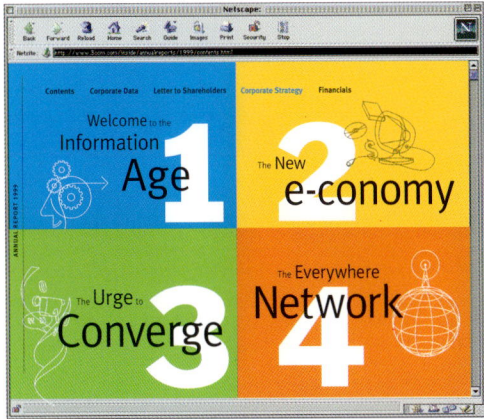

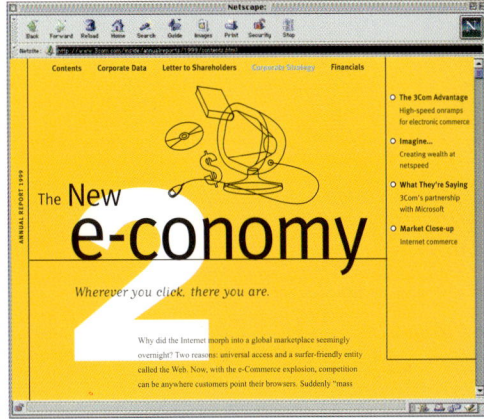

1. Technology firm website
2. KBDA self-promotion
3. Annual report for supply chain
   management software company

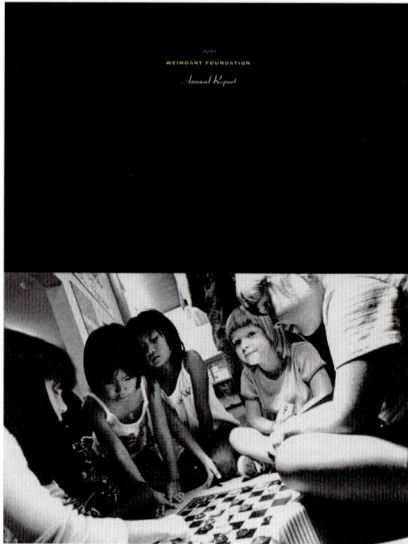

1

2

1. Annual report for philanthropic foundation
2. Logo for university school of arts and architecture
3. Annual report for retail real estate company

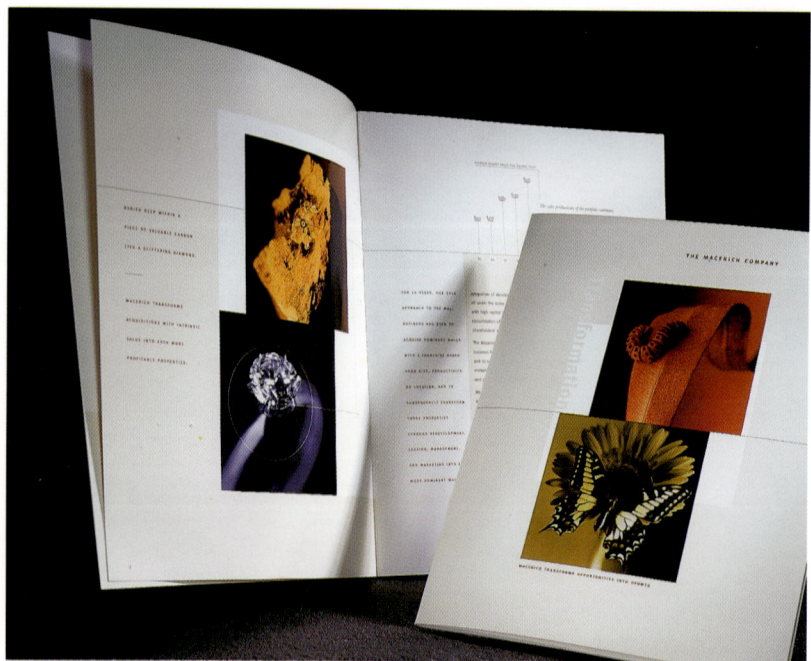

3

Michael Brock Design
8075 West Third Street, Suite 300
Los Angeles, California 90048-4318
Tel. 323.932.0283
Fax. 323.932.8165
E-mail. MBDes1@aol.com

MICHAEL BROCK DESIGN

If you have mailed or received a letter in the last six years, you've been exposed to the graphic design influence of Michael Brock. Appointed by the Postmaster General of the United States to the United States Postal Service Citizens Stamp Advisory Committee, Michael meets regularly in Washington, D.C. with the 12-member commission to determine the subjects and designs of all United States postal issues. Michael Brock is the principal behind Michael Brock Design (MBD), a Los Angeles design firm which provides strategic design, corporate identity, consulting, publication and art direction services to a variety of regional, national, and international clients.

Increasingly, the emphasis is on the development of design solutions which span a variety of media and work on both a regional and global basis.
"Design today must have the capability of working at a global level, even if it originates as a regional assignment. New and emerging markets and the increased value and importance of branding, requires solutions which are both fluid and definitive, capable of extending a brand or marketing message across the city, country, or globe. The DVD project is a perfect example."

MBD created the international brand identity for DVD. Developed in America, presented in Japan, the logo is now seen on DVD discs, hardware, and packaging released throughout the globe.
DVD is-in form and reach-the prototype of today's modern graphic identity. Brock notes that long term relationships like the one his firm has with Warner Home Video, who proposed MBD as their design firm in the worldwide DVD logo competition, provide an optimum working situation for both client and designer, as each assignment can build on previous experience and proprietary knowledge.

Convergence and working in very modern "virtual firm" relationships are two emerging themes at MBD.
"Clients may start with a need for a graphic identity program and then desire to extend the brand into three-dimensions or electronic media. This provides an opportunity to develop design solutions that span media and perceptions. Executing these programs often requires building 'virtual firms', developed specifically to meet the needs of one client and composed of other specialists and consultants. Modern technology and communications make this way of working seamless and incredibly productive, and we know from experience it works internationally as well as locally."
While working increasingly for the media, entertainment, electronics, real estate, and communications industries, MBD today continues the firm's heritage of innovative publication design. Recent assignments include a new publication in London; past projects have included the innovative *L.A. Style* and the Los Angeles Olympic Program.

"The goal at MBD is to develop solutions which meet client needs, not just for today and for one application, but for tomorrow and the expanding marketplace of opportunity all clients seek. This requires research, a broad and innovative range of solution options, and the ability to move quickly to seize strategic design initiatives. The range of design applications has multiplied in the last decade as more companies realize the strategic value of design as a marketing initiative. There's never been a better time to be a client-or a designer."

1

2

1. DVD worldwide brand logo

2. Warner Home Video DVD In-store product launch poster, part of a comprehensive marketing program

3 & 5. Warner Home Video Campaigns: Continuing DVD marketing materials including initial launch monthly publications (immediate right) and the latest campaign created which includes brochures, in-store posters and other point-of-purchase materials (far right)

4. DVD Display Case: A custom-designed case premiered to the media and communications industry was filled with DVD movies, and market and technical information

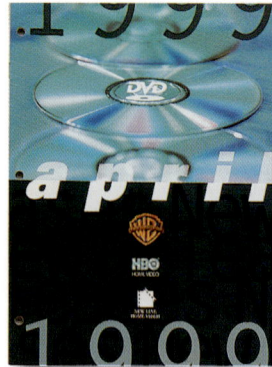
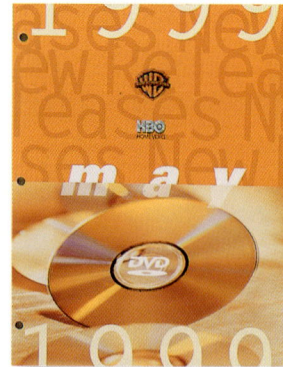
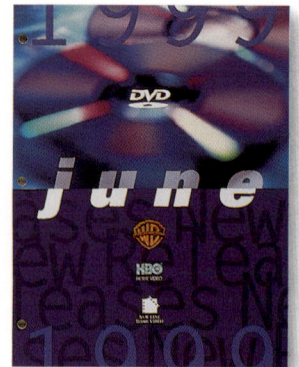

3

4

 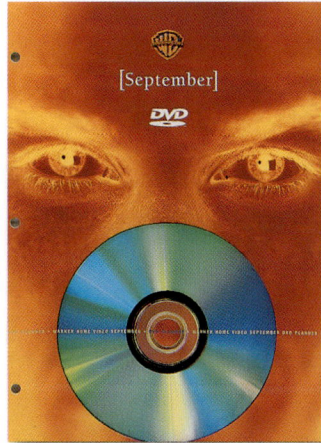 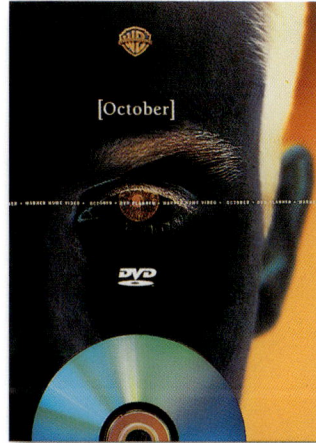 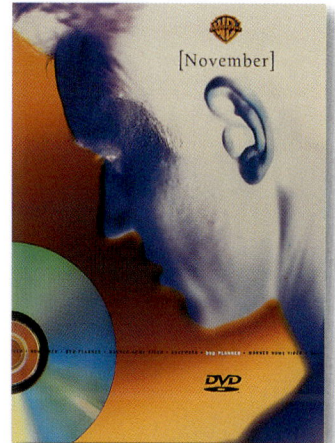

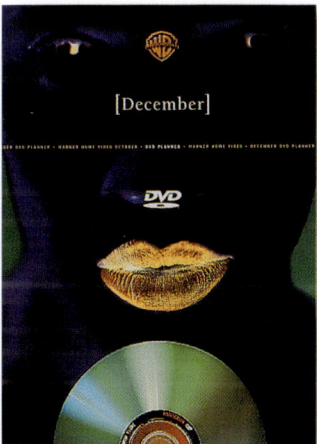 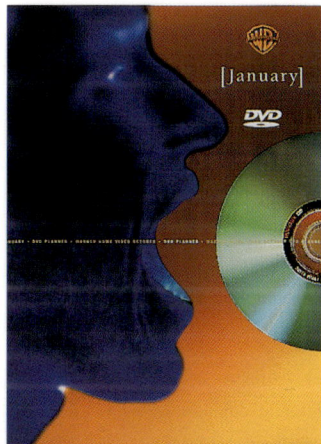

5

1

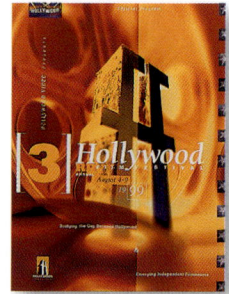

3

2

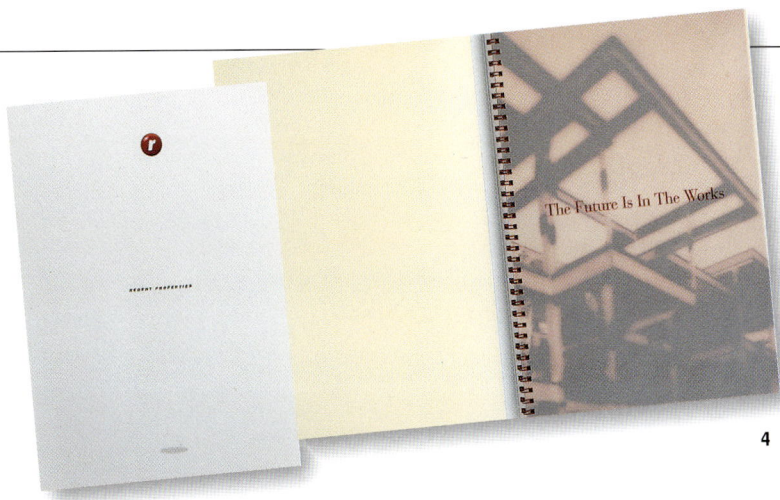

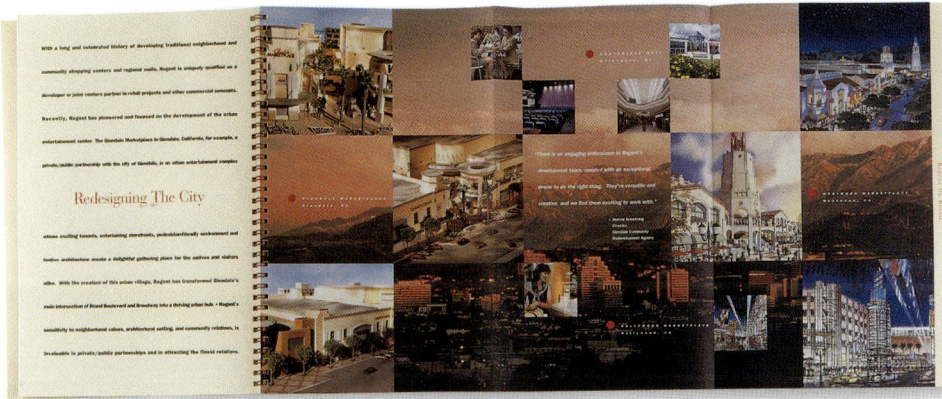

REGENT PROPERTIES

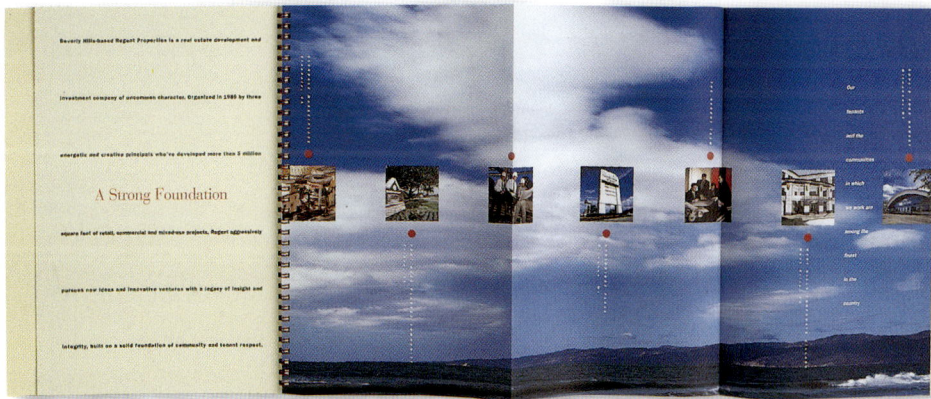

1. Garden of Eatin' organic tortilla chips packaging
2. 3rd Annual Hollywood Film Festival poster
3. Hollywood Film Festival magazine cover and various spreads
4. Regent Properties corporate capabilities brochure
5. Regent Properties logo/identity

1

2

3

4

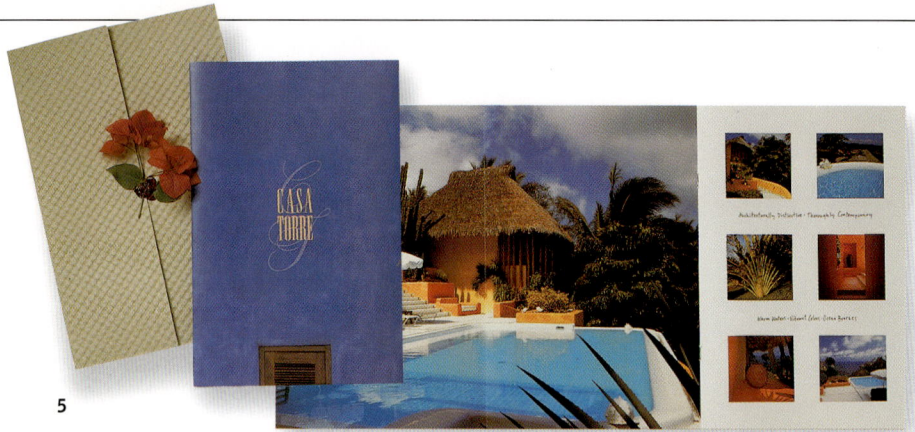

5

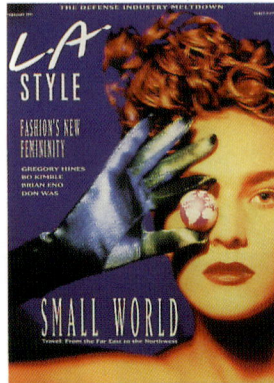

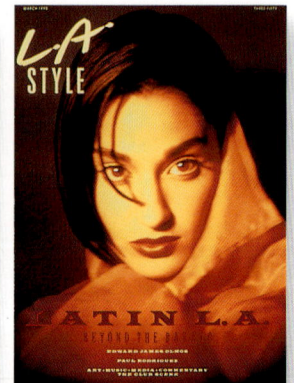

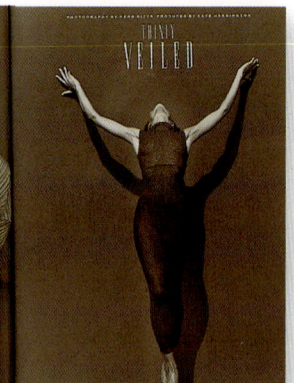

6

7

1. Select Syndication, a film syndication company logo/identity

2. Interscope Communications & Pictures logo

3. Tumbleweed Restaurant logo

4. The Complex logo, a Japanese owned sound studio

5. Custom sales package for Fred Sands Realty

6. *L.A. Style* magazine covers and interior pages

7. The Official Olympic magazine for the Los Angeles Olympic Committee

8. *Welcome to the World* brochure for The Blind Children's Center

9. Covers and representative pages from *Auto Gallery* magazine

10. Publication design for FTD *Florist* magazine

11. *ANIMA*, book design, Arts Alternative Press

12. *American Film* magazine, American Film Institute

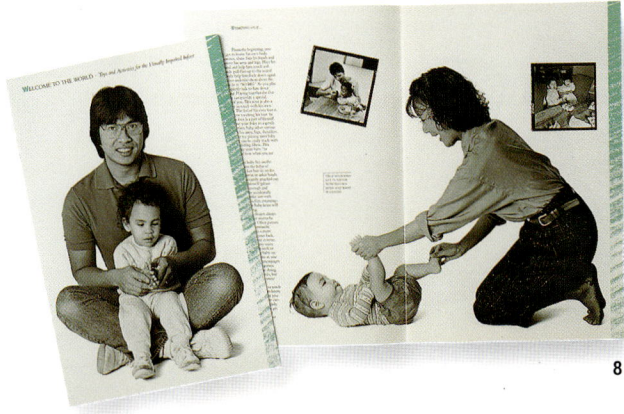

8

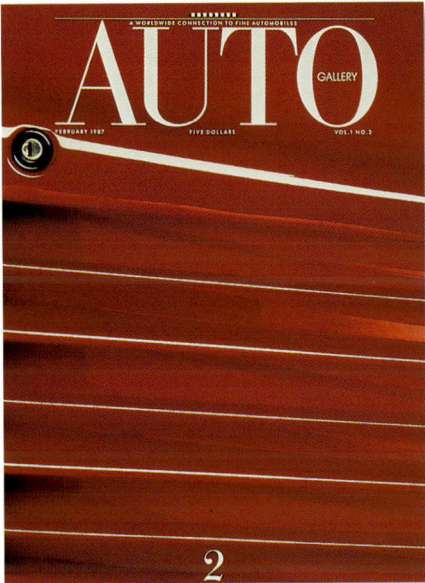

2

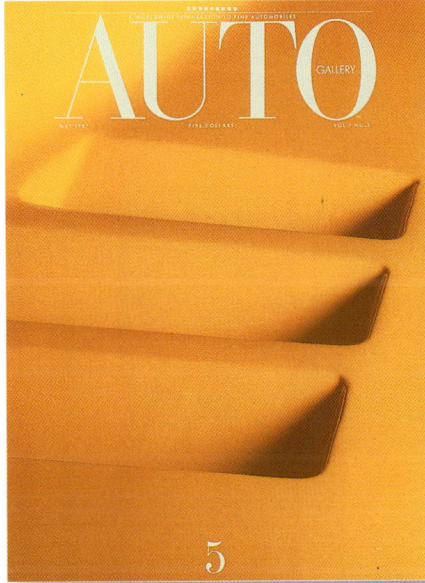

5

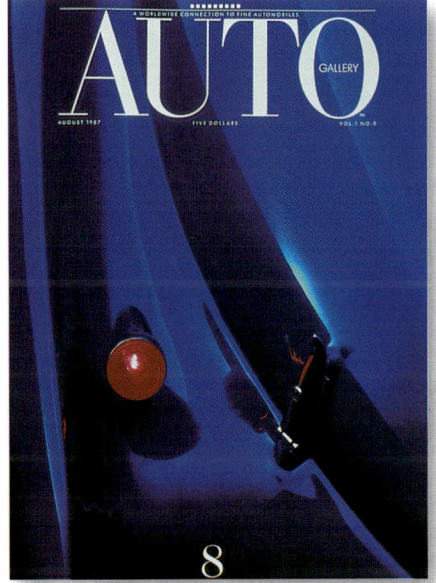

8

9

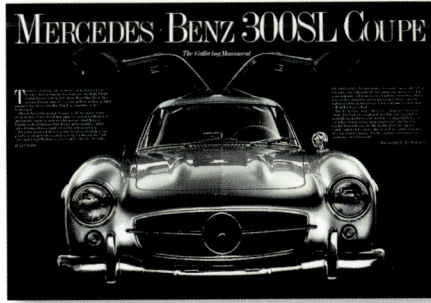

10

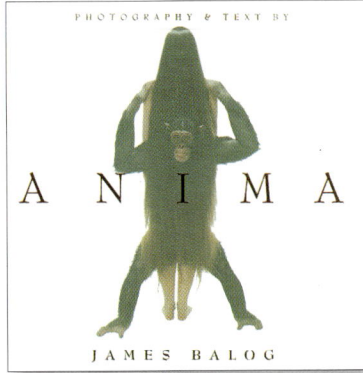

11

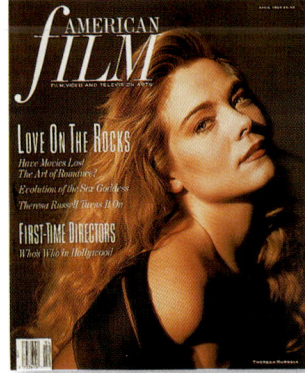

12

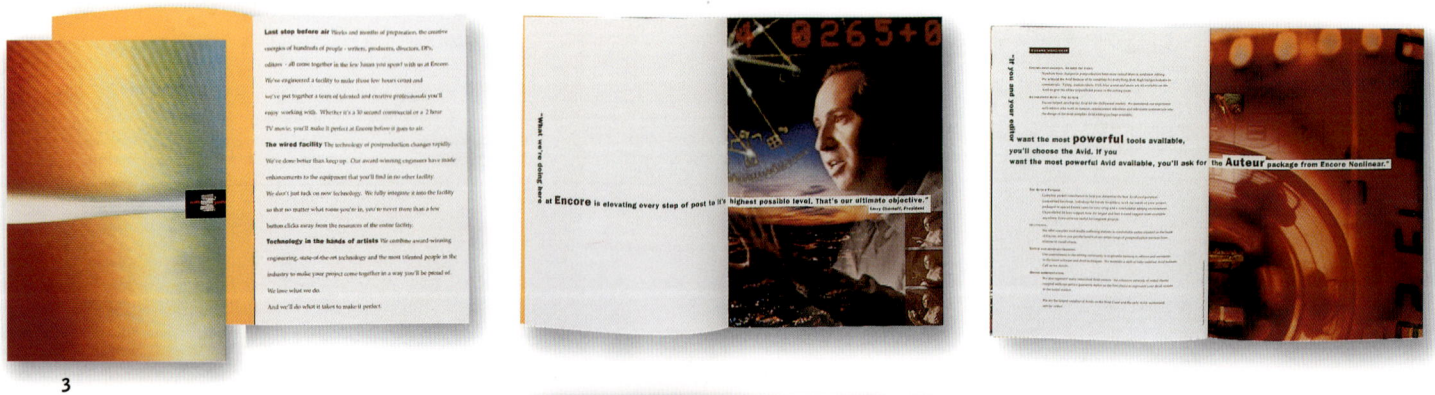

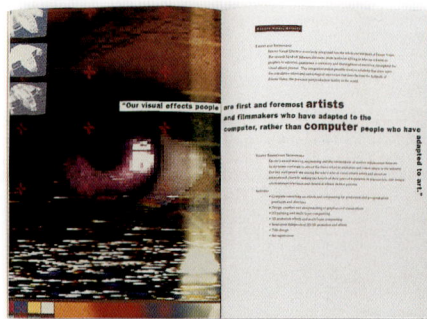

1. On the Scene Productions, Inc.
Electronic Publicity brand logo, media kit
and capabilities brochures

2. Roberto Santo, gallery brochure for an
American sculptor living in Italy

3. Encore Video Post Production corporate
facility brochure

Evenson Design Group
4445 Overland Avenue
Culver City, California
310.204.1995
www.evensondesign.com

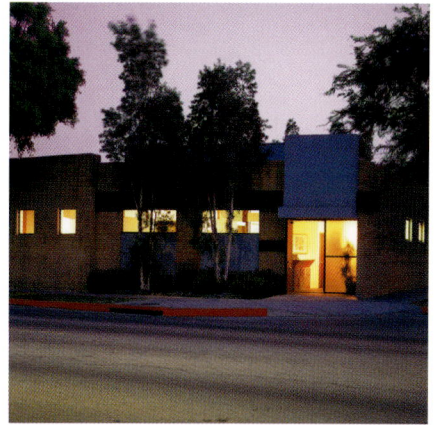

EVENSON DESIGN GROUP

If there's value in attracting a target market to achieve the desired results, and a reason for quality and performance to be perceived, we at Evenson Design Group (EDG) go the extra mile to deliver. With over twenty three years of dedication to our craft, we believe that our design team widens the gap between "competence" and "excellence." At EDG, we include you in on every level of the design process. In essence, you become an integral part of the effort to achieve the goals you set forth. We understand that you know your product, competition, and market better than anyone else, and it's our responsibility to listen carefully, interpret, and translate your message in a clear, succinct, and powerful way. Our goal is not only to help you win new business, influence a tough crowd, or be on the cutting edge, but to establish a lasting relationship and show you what remarkably positive things happen when you team up with EDG.

1

5

2

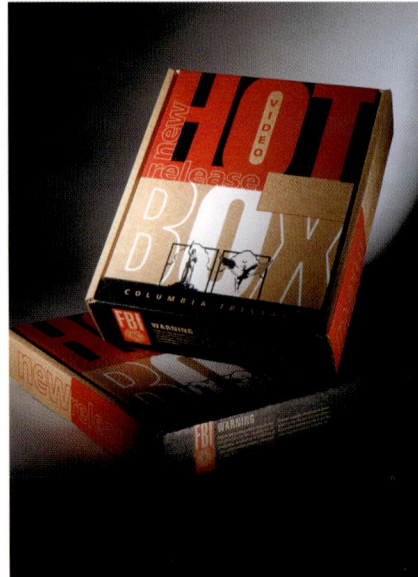

6

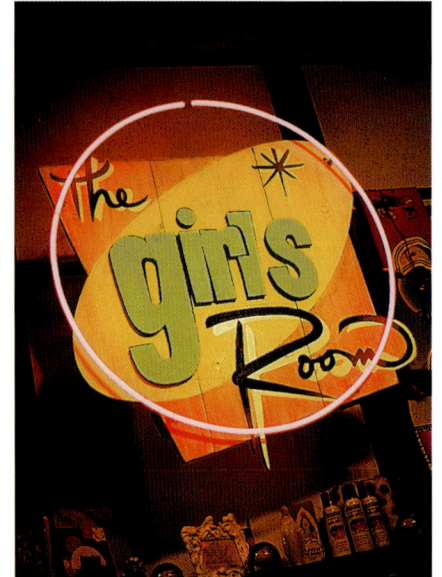

7

3

4

1. **Reading Entertainment:** This historic railroad company now owns several theatre complexes worldwide.

2. **Felbro:** A leader in the design/creation of POP displays.

3. **Niq Naq:** A whimsical yet sophisticated identity for this new line of upscale apparel for girls.

4. **CityWeb:** Warner Bros. online local news service.

5. **Honda Racing:** One of several merchandising logos created for a variety of racing apparel and products.

6. **Hot Box:** This attractive package housed Columbia TriStar International's hot new video releases.

7. **The Girls Room:** Wet Seal's hip in-store signage.

8. **Idyllwild Jazz in the Pines:** This promotion attracted media, sponsors and fans alike. The poster is now in the permanent collection of the Library of Congress!

8

1

2

1. **Marina Physical Therapy:** A sales and marketing brochure featuring the talents and commitment of the entire Marina Physical Therapy team.

2. **Deluxe Fruitcake:** This package housed interactive disks in a handsome tin to entertain unsuspecting clients and friends with zany graphics and sounds effects from our bizarre fruitcake-making machine.

3. **Apple iBook icon:** One of several icons developed for TBWA/Chiat Day for the new national Apple iBook advertising campaign.

3

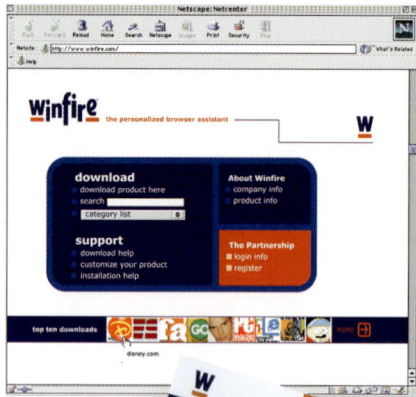

1

2

1-3. WinFire: This company provides a personalized browser assistant that shortens the distance between internet users and information. EDG provided this successful start-up company with a complete identity system, collateral, website, and even the paint job graphics for the CEO's classic Scout.

3

1

2

3

4

CULVER CITY
UNIFIED SCHOOL DISTRICT

5

6

7

1-3. **California Coffee House:** An appealing new image from exterior graphics, to signage and packaging.

4. **California Fire Station:** A sizzling new logo for a retail store featuring hot sauces from around the world.

5. **Culver City Unified School District:** This new identity represents all Culver City public schools.

6. **Warner Bros. Studio Store:** This new identity brings back the historic and classic WB image.

7. **Waldorf and Crawford Communications:** This logo represents a marketing/communications firm.

1-5. Universal Studios Escape (USE) Branding Guides: This assignment included designing five individual branding guides and a case for USE properties: Universal Studios Escape, Universal Studios Florida, Universal Studios Islands of Adventure, Universal Studios Citywalk and Universal Studios Escape Resorts.

6-9. Seuss Landing: EDG created several pieces of merchandise for one of the five destinations at Universal Islands of Adventure: Shown here are, Thing One and Thing Two Silk Pajamas, Water Pistols, a full line of candy product, and the development of Baby Seuss products and apparel line.

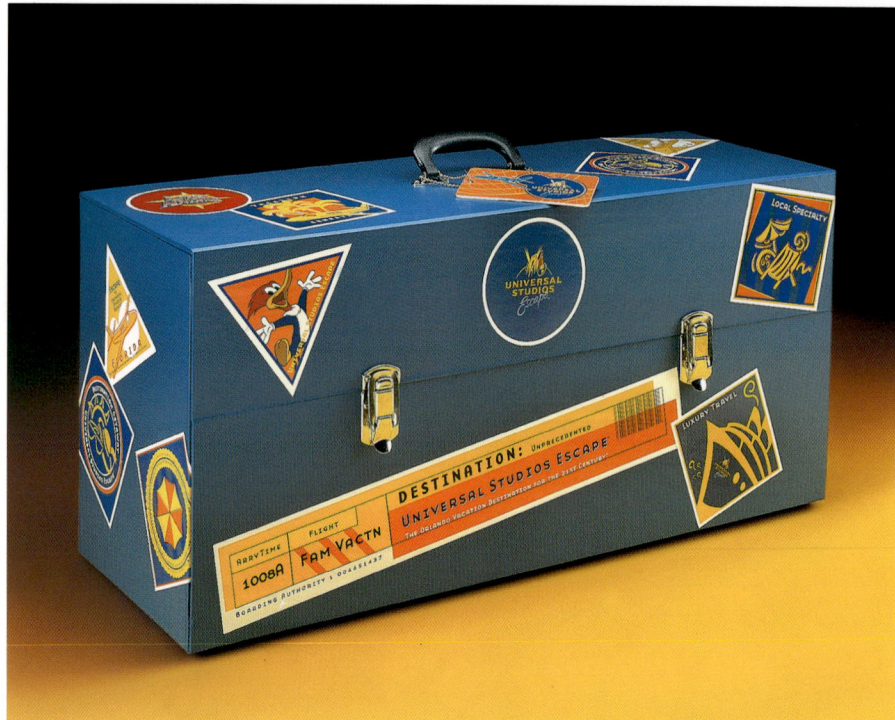

1

2

3

4

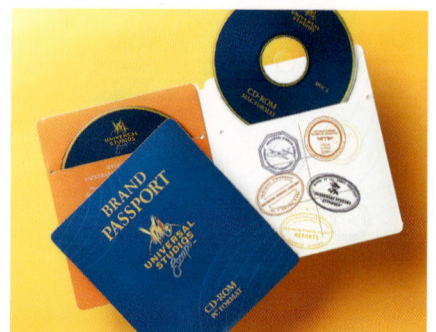

5

6

7

8

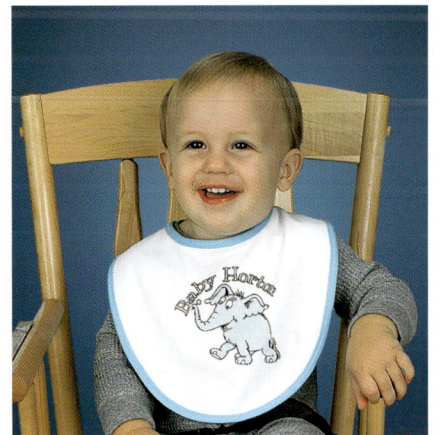

9

Evenson Design Group

1. Day Runner: EDG developed a multimedia presentation that simplified a complicated and often confusing strategic branding concept. This friendly animation with a humorous western theme utilized sound effects, customized music, and animated charts and graphs to round out the message.

2. EDG Case Study Promotion: This series of individual mailers were sent to potential clients to highlight a variety of successfully completed projects.

1

2

Curry Design Associates
1501 S. Main Street,
On Windward Circle
Venice, California 90291
310.399.4626
www.currydesign.com

CURRY DESIGN ASSOCIATES

Curry Design was founded in 1988, out of a subterranean studio with two phone lines, two art tables, one photostat machine and one designer. In the beginning, clients were fairly slim, and primarily included small fashion accounts, corporate banking, NASA's Jet Propulsion Lab and a lot self-promotion.

As the roster of clients grew, so did the company, adding personnel and taking on a new space above a wine store in West LA. The new location provided more space, an invigorated attitude, and a great buzz. At this location, the first computers were purchased, and quickly rendered the old comping methods of photocopied type and cut Pantone paper obsolete.

In the early 90s the company moved to its present location in Venice Beach, California. The sea breeze, sunshine and colorful population of locals has provided inspiration and a constant source of entertainment for the growing creative team.

Both the move and subsequent increase in size made it possible to service new and larger corporate software, entertainment, automotive, health and beauty, and telecommunications accounts.

Aside from all the self-professing accolades, awards and published work, the current office team consists of a basketball player, a gardener, a father, a fitness junkie, a Tarot card reader, a black-belt, a fisherman, a Niner fan, a modern-day hippie and a bilingual shop-a-holic.

Curry Design's full-service, tightly-knit interdisciplinary team draws upon a combination of insight and experience yield solutions that are both dynamic and refreshingly unique.

1.

2.

3.

4.

1. Curioso: Logo for a specialty boutique store.
2. Great Ink: Logo for an animation art gallery.
3. Nissan Motor Corp: Sales Guides for an automobile manufacturer.
4. Nissan Motor Corp: Corporate Training and Sales Certification Collateral System.

1.

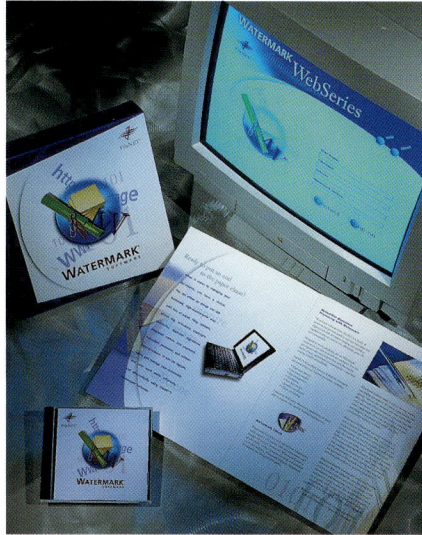

2.

Timeless in celebration of THE HUMAN SPIRIT.

3.

USERNET99

4.

V VANSCOY ∞

5.

1. Telemundo Network: Launch materials and housing system for the rebranding of a Sony owned network.

2. Watermark Software: Identity, packaging and web development for a suite of software products.

3. KX2 Network: Tabloid size launch brochure introducing a new network for the millennium.

4. UserNet: Logo for a software industry convention.

5. VanScoy: Letterform logo design for a multi-disciplined photographer.

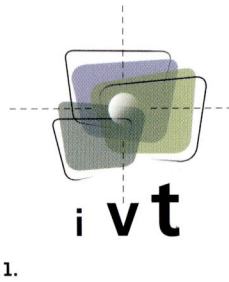

1.

3.

2.

1. IVT: Interactive Video Technology System corporate identity.

2. Psychoneuroimmunology: UCLA research program exploring the mind's effect on the immune system.

3. Casablanca Fan Company: 80 page catalog detailing the materials and specification for full line of ceiling fans and lighting fixtures.

4. McDonnell Douglas Corporation: Last annual report prior to the acquisition by Boeing Corporation.

5. Petal Fresh: Packaging system for line of body and hand lotions.

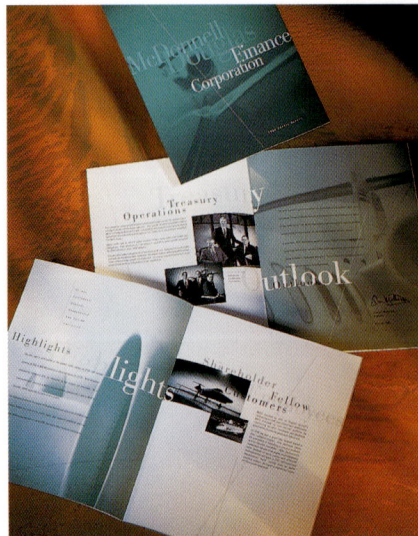

4.

5.

1.

3.

4.

2.

1. Kenwood USA: Automotive stereo and speaker brochure.

2. Boeing: Annual report for the finance division of the Boeing Corporation.

3. Grand Cru: Logo for a rare wine investment fund.

4. WTA: Western Typographers association logo.

CORE
SOFTWARE

1.

2.

3.

4.

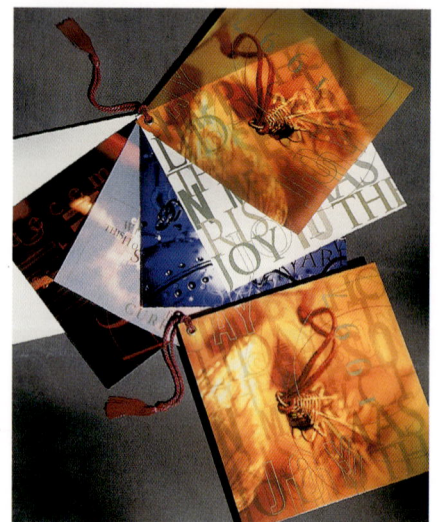

5.

1. Core Software: Corporate identity for a global imaging company.

2. Muse X Editions: Identity developed for publishing of archival fine art IRIS prints.

3. Art in Venice: Self published desktop calendar featuring various artists living and working in Venice Beach, California.

4. MGM: A line of 30 different titles packaged under a global "MGM Greats" system for the international market.

5. Holiday Card: Speciality greeting card designed in conjunction with a printer, highlighting both design and printing capabilities.

1.

2.

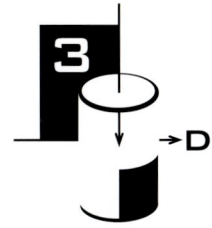

4.

5. Oasis

3.

1. Panagon: Software packaging system designed for the FileNet Corporation Panagon line.

2. Mitsubishi Motor Corp: Point of sale accessory rack brochure system.

3. Kenwood USA: Product brochure featuring Kenwood's full line of Personal Audio components.

4. 3-D: Identity for electronic imaging and data storage system.

5. Oasis: Software company retreat logo.

ValueNET®

1.

2.

3.

1. ValueNet: Identity developed for the Value Added Reseller Division of the FileNet corporation.

2. Tonga: Logo for a tropical themed sports and swimwear line.

3. Columbia TriStar: Screenings brochures featuring new and returning television programming and feature films.

4. Unilab Corporation: Annual report for California's largest independent lab corporation.

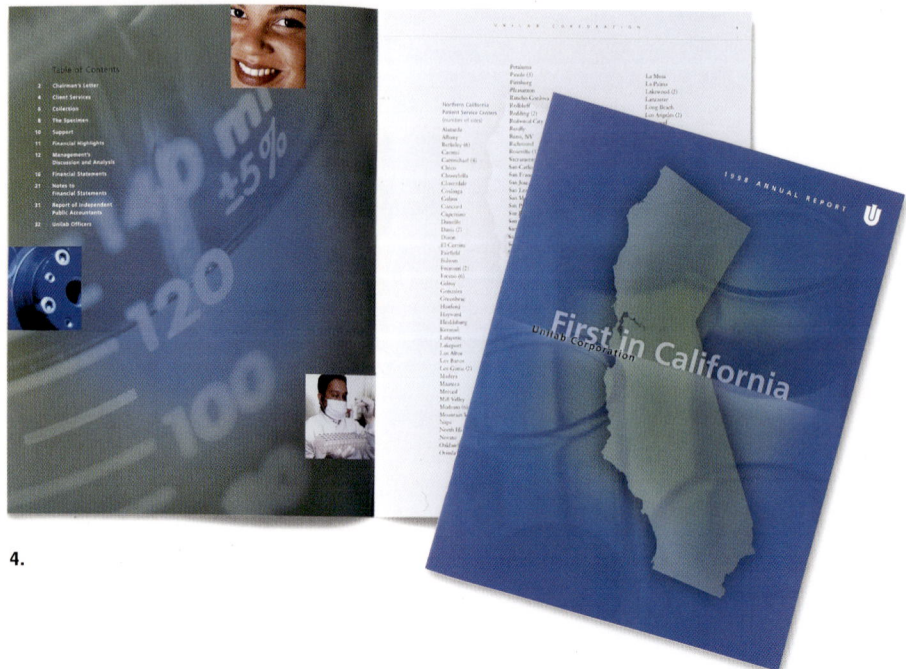

4.

Warren Group Graphic Design
622 Hampton Drive
Venice, CA 90291 USA
310.396.6316
www.studiodeluxe.com

1

WARREN GROUP

If it was ever true that the "medium is the message,"as sixties media guru Marshall McLuhan said, the Warren Group is here to prove otherwise. Despite these tech-heavy times, this exceedingly stylish Venice USA design firm strongly believes the message is the medium. Everything begins with the story the client is trying to tell.

The Warren Group puts this design philosophy into practice with every project they undertake. While their visual vocabulary is elegant, inventive, even beautiful, it's also infused with strategy and purpose.

This is a small firm that does big work, big where it counts: in originality and results. Since its founding in 1984, the Warren Group has defined itself as "boutique" in the largest sense of the word, providing exclusive services across all print media.

You can see their fresh sensibility and marketing sense in identity systems, collateral, advertising, packaging and product

2

naming, merchandising, annual reports, even film titles. One hallmark is an envelope-pushing use of illustration and photography. Another is smart, targeted writing. The Warren Group seeks out the most fertile collaborations with other creative professionals. In fact, their collaborative spirit sets this firm apart and extends to the way they view their clients.

As a consequence, the Warren Group enjoys many long-term client relationships. Their résumé includes such luminaries as the Walt Disney Company, ABC Capital Cities, Mattel, Dick Clark Productions, Magic Hour Pictures, Childrens Hospital Los Angeles, USC School of Cinema-Television, USC School of Engineering and The Annenberg Center for Communication, plus a growing list of entrepreneurial companies.

Another byproduct of telling effective stories: the work has won top honors from all the major design and communications organizations. Even the U.S. Library of Congress has taken notice. It selected the Warren Group for inclusion in its Permanent Design Collection.

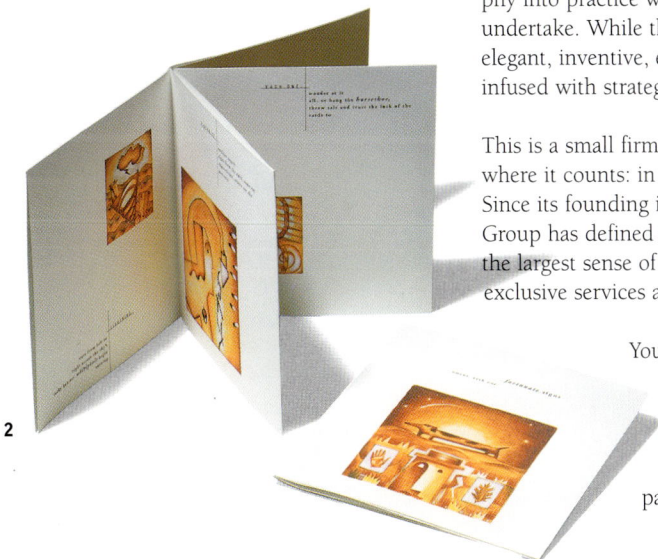

3

1. Previous spread: The studio and Phoebe.

2. Previous spread: Fortunate Signs, self-promotion, with illustrator Julie Scott and writer Candace Pearson.

3. USC Health Magazine, produced quarterly for the University of Southern California.

4. Overland Estates, Wines from the Northwest, naming, packaging, collateral

4

5

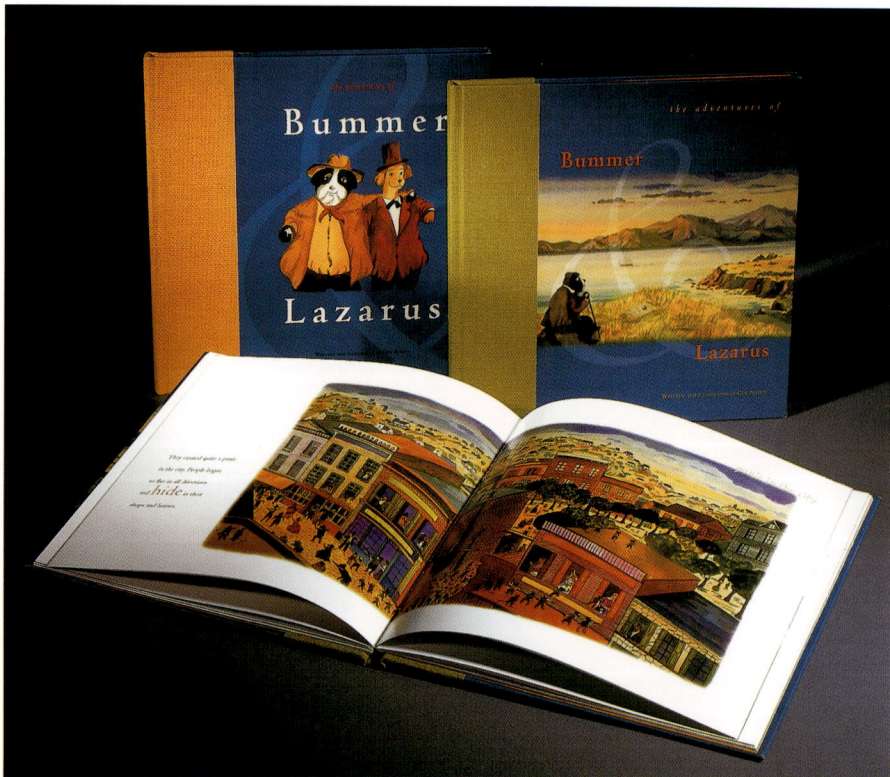

6

5. Simply Pooh merchandising development, Walt Disney Company.

6. Bummer & Lazarus, children's book by artist Guy Buffet, published by Diversified Publishing.

7. Imagine Magazine, annual report issue, Childrens Hospital Los Angeles.

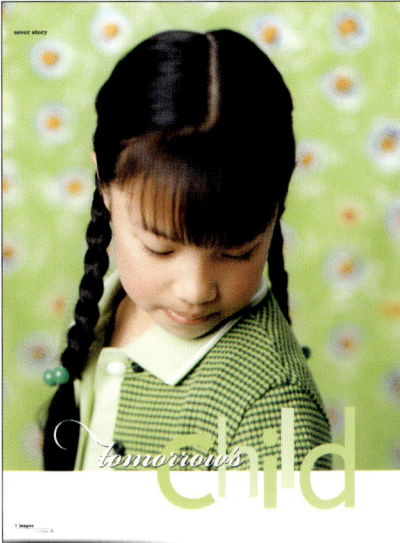

Tomorrow's
Child

By Candace Pearson

imagine

Caring for Tomorrow's Child

Annual Report Issue

7

explore

8

"By focusing people and resources in growth areas in which it was equipped to play an especially prominent role, the School of Engineering has risen tremendously in stature. As president of USC and as a faculty member of our school, I am proud of the momentum it has developed in recent years."

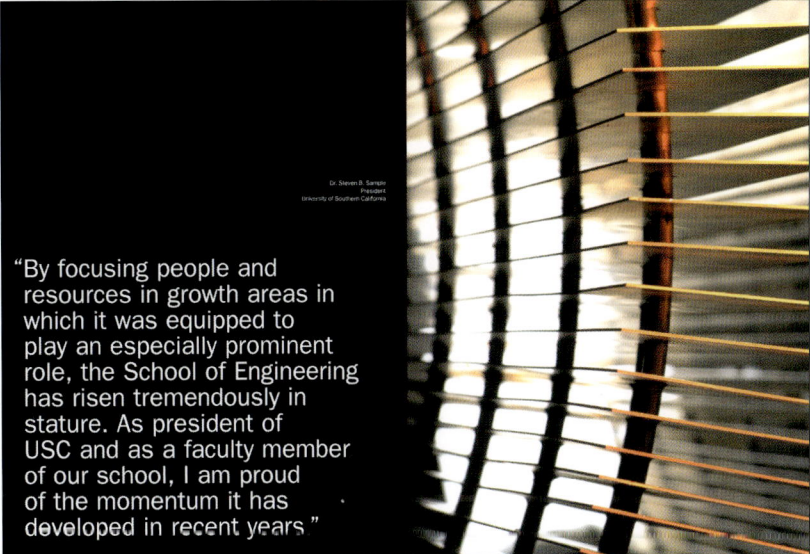

Dr. Steven B. Sample
President
University of Southern California

where the future is taking shape.

research and graduate education

university of southern california
school of engineering

00|01

8. The Volkswagen Bug Book, with author Dan Ouelette and publisher Angel City Press.

9. Research and Graduate Education brochure, USC School of Engineering.

9

10. Capabilities brochure, EC2, The Annenberg
Incubator Project, The Annenberg Center for
Communication.

10

Mires Design
2345 Kettner Boulevard
San Diego, CA 92101
619.234.6631
f: 619.234.1807
www.miresdesign.com

MIRES DESIGN

Founded nearly 15 years ago, Mires Design has steadily grown to become a respected national provider of inspired visual thinking and brand-building solutions to market-leading companies such as Qualcomm, Nike, Taylor Guitars and Harcourt Brace.

Collaborators and consensus-builders by nature, Mires Design's project teams take a rigorous yet intuitive approach to understanding their clients' needs and objectives. "My best work is always in concert with others — and that includes clients," says Scott Mires, the company's founder and one of its three principals. "I firmly believe that when you surround yourself with good people, good things are bound to happen."

From global leaders to visionary start-ups, Mires' clients share one thing in common: An intensely competitive desire to strengthen their market presence and realize their brand potential.

"We start by asking 'Why?' not just 'How?'" says Mires principal John Ball. "Our search for answers often takes us outside the confines of our studio and into the marketplace, into the culture, and into the minds of our clients and their audiences."

Clients value the level of communication and involvement that Mires' friendly yet intensely quality-driven culture helps to foster. And they look to Mires for solutions that combine insight, follow-through and impeccable execution. "The best solutions aren't just about strategies and ideas," says Mires principal Jose Serrano. "They're also about looking great."

Above all, whether they are seeking to differentiate themselves in the marketplace, establish a consistent point of view, or make a compelling emotional appeal to consumers, clients come to Mires for the strategies, systems and tools that make their brands work.

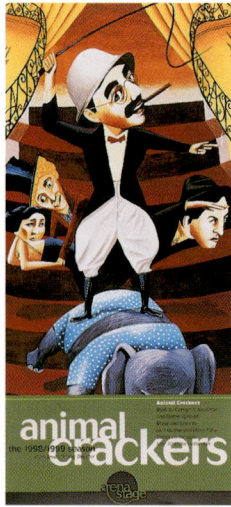

1

2

3

4

1. Arena Stage 1998/1999 Season Posters
2. Arena Stage 1998/1999 Season Catalog
3. Taylor Guitars 1999 Catalog
4. Taylor Guitars 1995 Limited Edition Catalog
5. Taylor Guitars Neon Sign

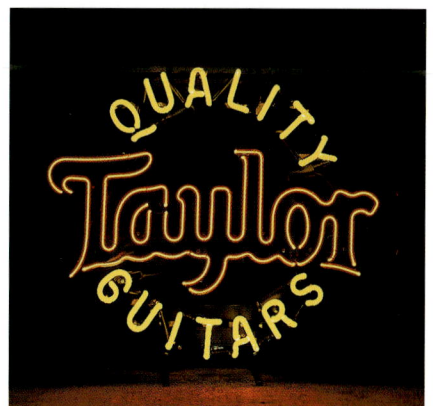
5

1

2

3

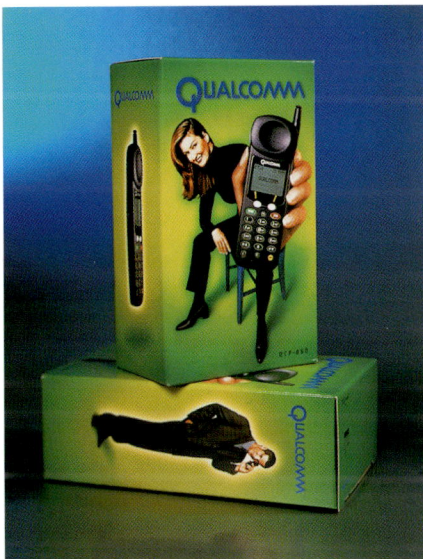

4

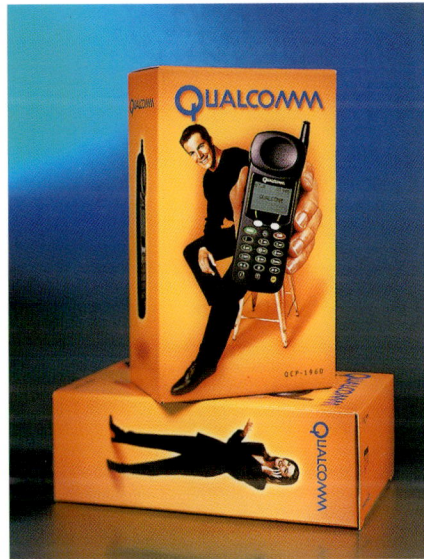

5

6

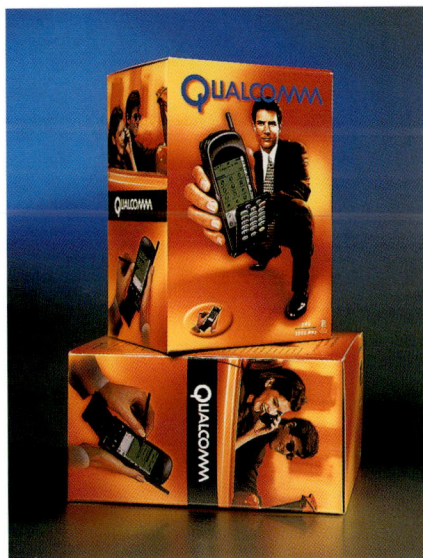

7

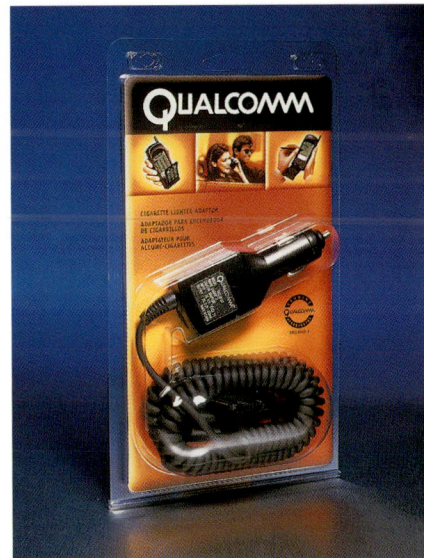

8

1. Qualcomm Q Lady Packaging
2. Qualcomm TGP Packaging
3. Qualcomm TGP Accessory Packaging
4. Qualcomm 5GP Packaging
5. Qualcomm 5GP Packaging
6. Qualcomm Accessory Packaging
7. Qualcomm PDQ Packaging
8. Qualcomm Accessory Packaging

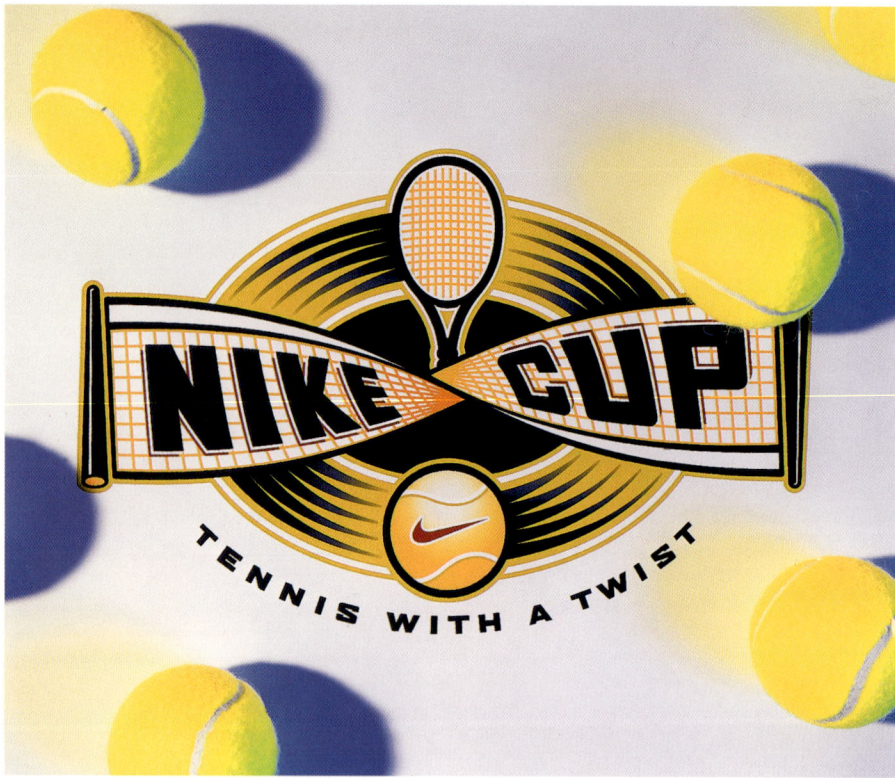

1

2

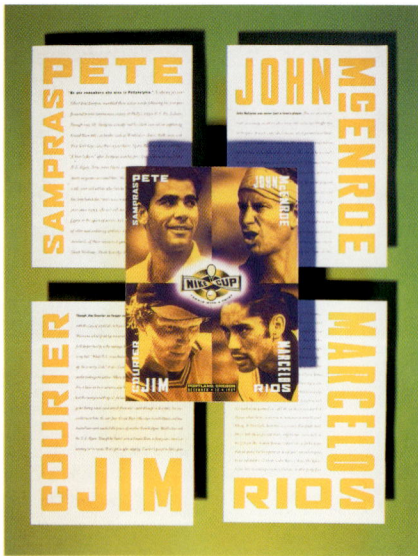

3

4

1. Nike Cup Logo
2. Nike Cup Banners
3. Nike Cup Brochure
4. Nike Cup Paddles
5. Frescante Countercard
6. Frescante Poster
7. Frescante Pin

5

6

7

95

Regional Theater
Restaurant
Nike Promotion

Automotive Traction Products
Clay Tile Manufacturer
Golf Website

Premium Skybox Program
Folding Keyboard
Green Field Paper Company

Internet Appliance Developer
Yellow Pages
Premium Acoustic Guitars

Rock and Roll Promotion
Internet Gaming Company
Nike Promotion

User Recognition Program
Information Management Company
Internet Service Provider

Point Zero
4223 Glencoe Avenue, Suite A223
Marina del Rey, California 90292
310.823.0975
info@pointzero.com
www.pointzero.com

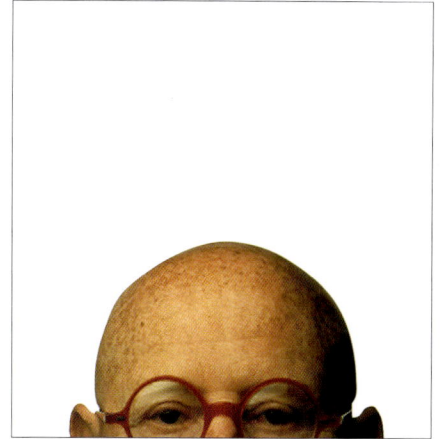

POINT ZERO

We could use this space to philosophize about the importance of branding or espouse our theories on strategic partnerships, but haven't you heard enough of that? Fact is, any creative firm worth their salt can go on and on with pie-in-the-sky marketing gobbledygook. We're more concerned about what's really important; developing effective, no-nonsense, exquisitely produced communications materials.

As a design firm Point Zero qualifies as one of the finest in the world. However, our talents extend far beyond that archaic term. As we've grown and evolved, we've redefined the very definition of our business. A design firm, communications firm, advertising agency, marketing consultancy and web developer, all in one – the Creative Enterprise.

We do things a little differently at Point Zero. Every project begins with a pencil, a blank piece of paper and a brain, not with a technician moving pictures around on a monitor. After forty years (before we became Point Zero we were called Runyan/Hinsche & Associates), we've learned one valuable lesson: Good ideas are a precious and elusive resource and no amount of technical proficiency can replace them.

Even our offices are engineered to nurture creativity and new ideas. People bring their dogs to work, music is always playing and lunch, prepared by our Creative Director, Jim Guerard, is a near-religious experience. Furthermore, a state-of-the-art 50" plasma TV (excellently constructed by our client, Pioneer Electronics) is the centerpiece of a Monday Night Football ritual attended by friends and clients alike. The point is, we're serious about producing great design, but we're also experts at having fun.

1

2

1. Promotional Kit for Hyundai Motors
2. Brochure for Saleen Performance
3. Brochure for Samsung Motors
4. Collateral for Pioneer Electronics
5. Annual Report for Iomega
6. Annual Report for K2
7. Mandalay Bay In-Room Service Directory

3

4

5

8

9

8. Identity for Beckman Coulter
9. Identity for Pacific Graphics

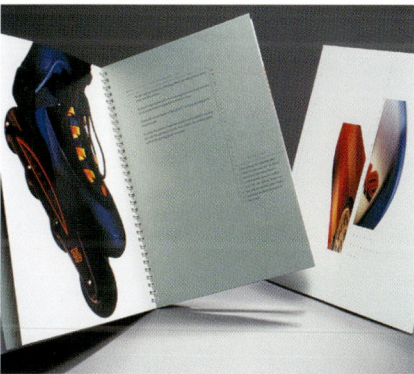

6

7

1

2

3

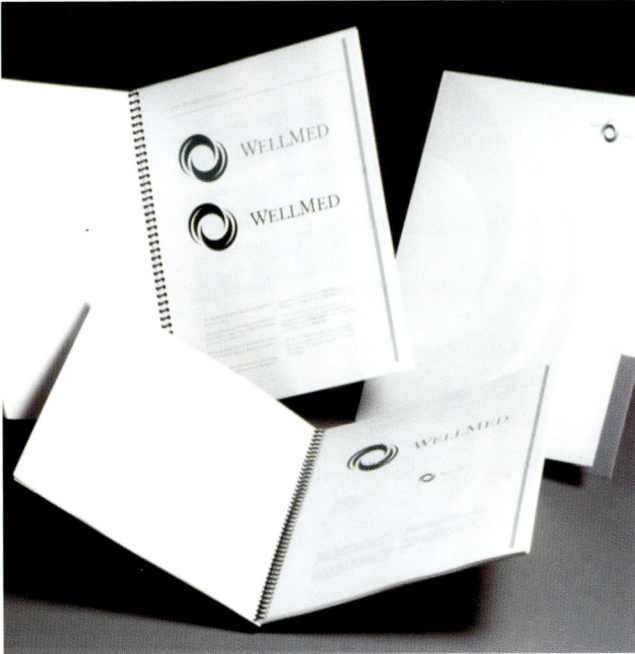

4

5

7

8

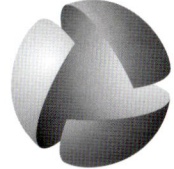

9

1. Exhibit for US Holocaust Memorial Museum

2. Exhibit for Bridge Medical

3. Exhibit for CorVel Corporation

4. Identity for WellMed

5. Annual Report for CorVel Corporation

6. Annual Report for QLogic

7. Identity for WellMed

8. Identity for Edje Boards

9. Identity for Bancentro (Mexico)

6

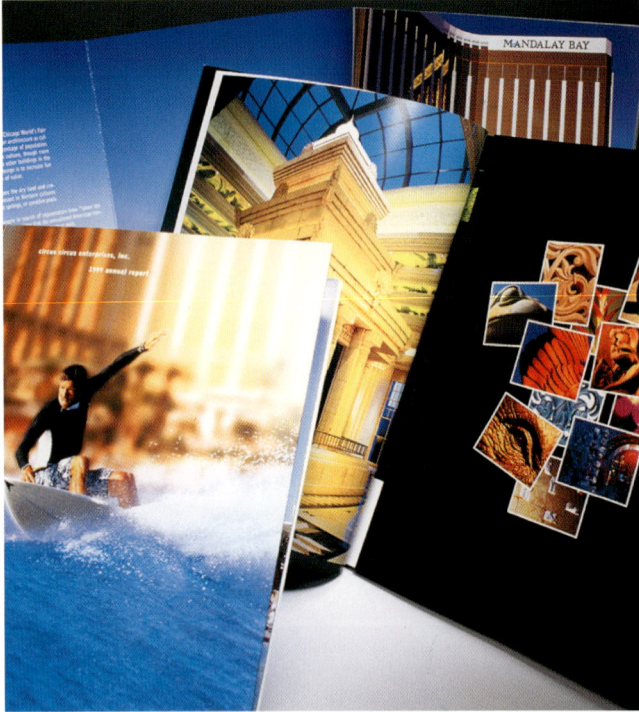

1

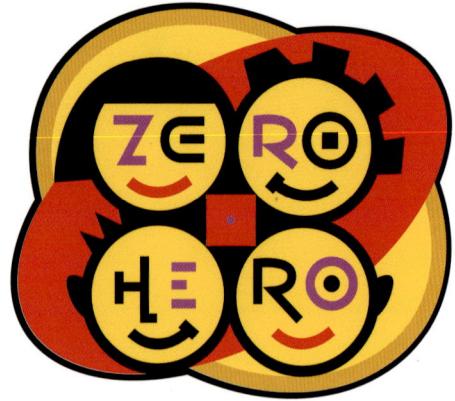

2

3

4

1. Annual Report for Circus Circus
2. Zero Hero Logo
3. Annual Report for CSC
4. Capabilities Brochure for Big Fish
5. Environmental System for 1999 Women's World Cup

5

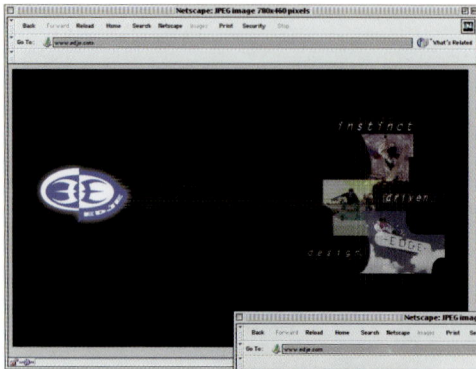

1

2

3

4

1. Web Site for Edje Boards
2. Identity for Big Fish
3. Identity for Caremark
4. Identity for Bridge Medical

James Robie Design Associates
152-$^{1}/_{2}$ N. La Brea Avenue
Los Angeles, California 90036-2912
323.939.7370
jrobie@robie.com
www.robie.com

JAMES ROBIE DESIGN ASSOCIATES

At James Robie Design Associates we strive for a balance between the strategic and the creative in our work, knowing that one tempers and informs the other. We approach each assignment with open, inquiring minds, recognizing how important it is to integrate the "spark" with a systematic, thoughtful process. The result is that we consistently produce durable, sophisticated design for our clients both large and small.

Our work is grounded in classic principles of design, emphasizing clarity, legibility and communication. What makes it soar is the imagination we bring to each project. Our office is highly structured for clear communications and streamlined project coordination, yet it fosters freeform creativity. We strive to produce design that is simple; at the same time it can support the most complex of information. Our work is unassuming, never calling attention to itself, yet it is exciting. It is quantifiable, inasmuch as it supports and strengthens clients' marketing strategy and ensures a good return on their investment. But we also infuse our design with quite a bit of the intangible – some heart and soul.

JRDA has built a reputation since 1978 for effective award-winning work, integrity and sound designer-client relationships. A partial list of clients includes Northrop Grumman, The J. Paul Getty Trust, TRW, Mercury General Corp., Lockheed Martin, PIMCO, Manning Selvage and Lee, Teledyne Technologies, Center Trust, Typhoon and Hump Restaurants.

1

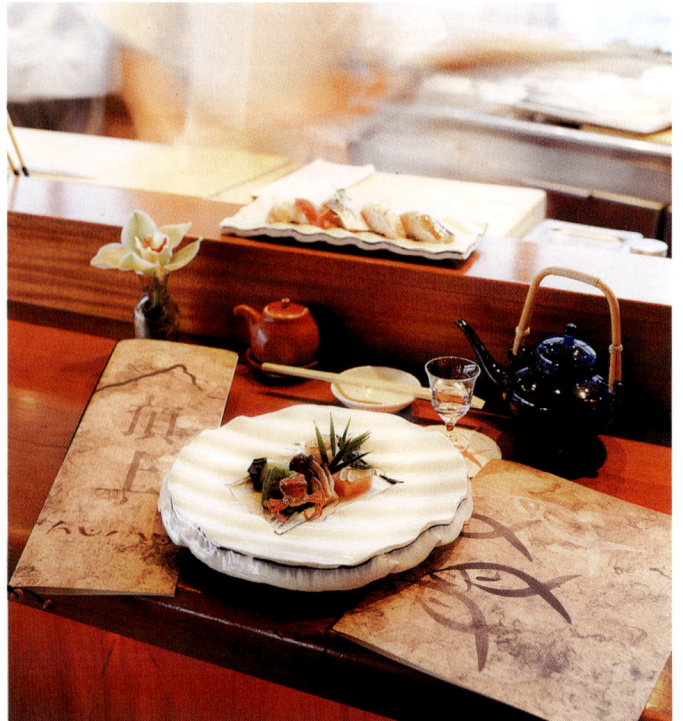

1. The Hump Sushi Bar & Restaurant
Program Identity

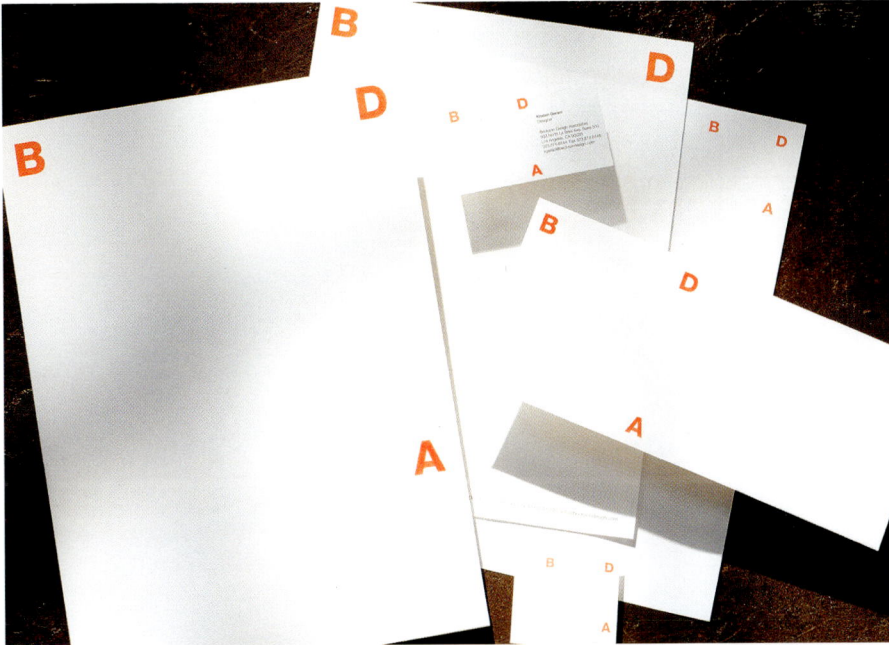

1

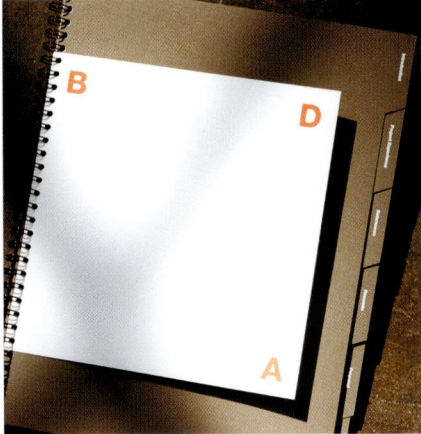

B

D

A

2

1. Beckson Design Associates Identity Program
2. Lescher Public Relations
   Capabilities Brochure
3. Kato Industries Identity
4. Luzero Identity
5. Getty Fitness Center Identity

3

LUZERO

4

GETTY *fitness*
CENTER

5

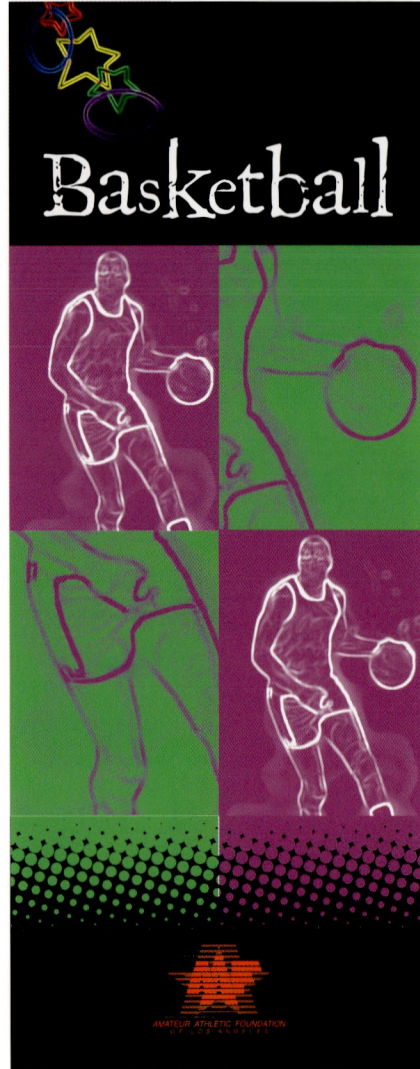

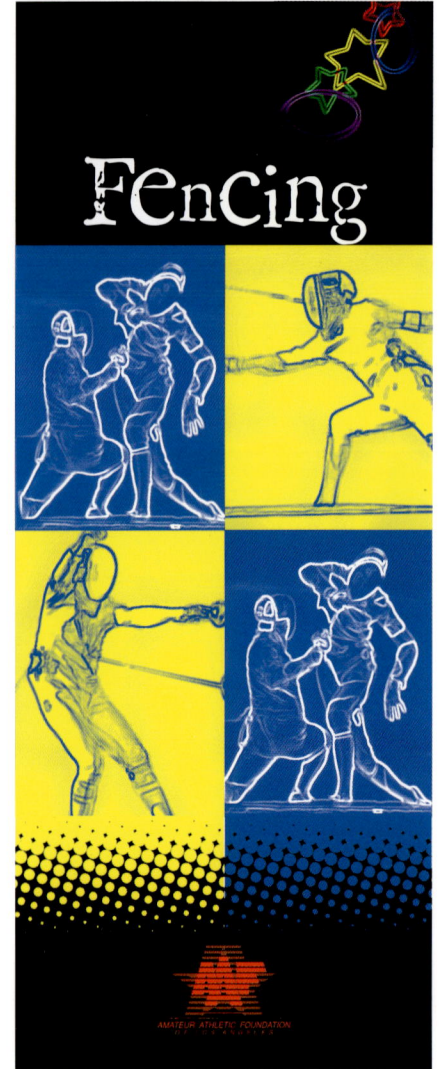

1

1. Amateur Athletic Foundation - Youth Olympic Sports Program Environmental Signage

2. Foundation for the Junior Blind "Share Our Vision" Identity

3. Allegheny Teledyne Identity

2

3

1. J. Paul Getty Trust Benefits Package
2. J. Paul Getty Trust Opening Staff Survival Kit
3. J. Paul Getty Trust Information Institute
   "Protecting Cultural Objects" Report
4. J. Paul Getty Trust Benefits Posters

1

2

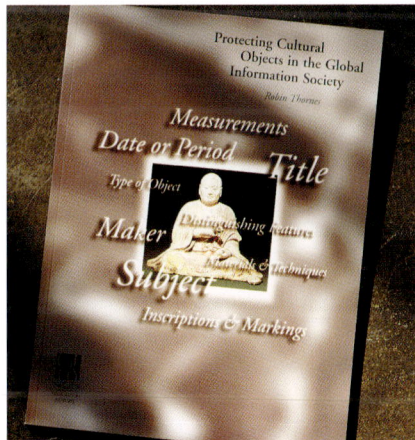

3

4

1. Jalate Ltd. Annual Report
2. Variflex Annual Report
3. Korn/Ferry International Annual Report

1

2

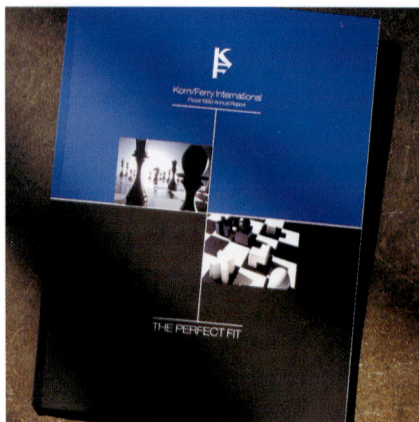

3

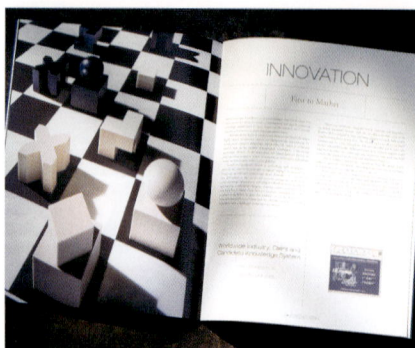

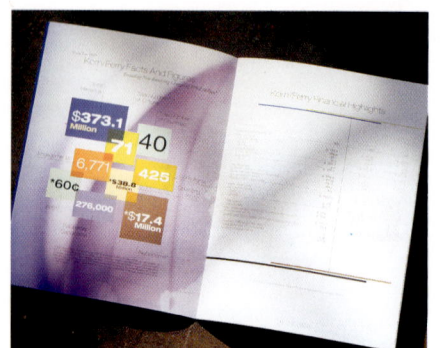

1

WorkWell

2

3

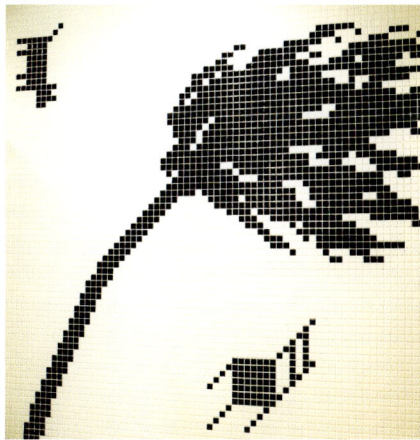

4

5

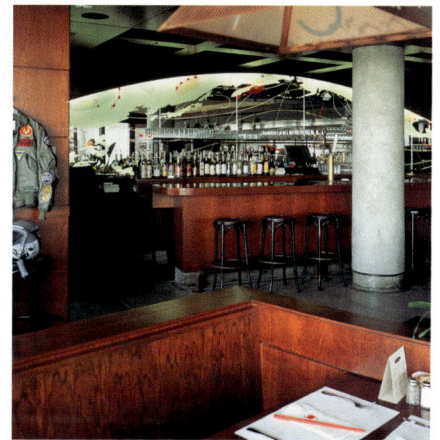

6

1. Lockheed Martin VentureStar Identity
2. Hughes WorkWell Health Program Identity
3. Los Angeles Convention Center Identity
4-5. Typhoon Restaurant Restroom Mosaic
6. Typhoon Restaurant Bar Mirror Design
7. Typhoon Restaurant Identity Program

7

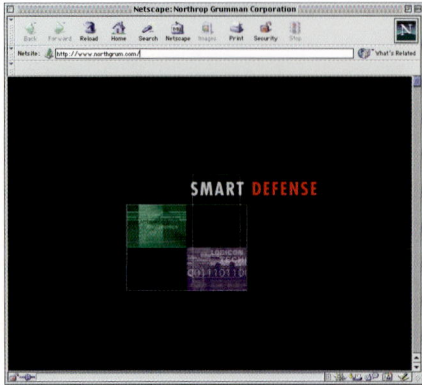

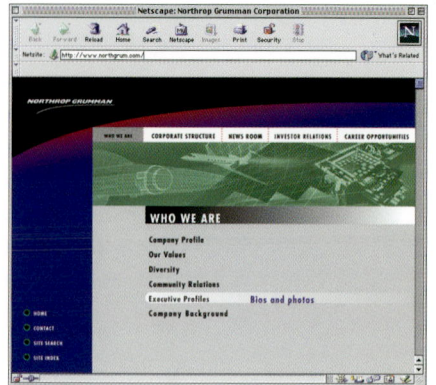

1

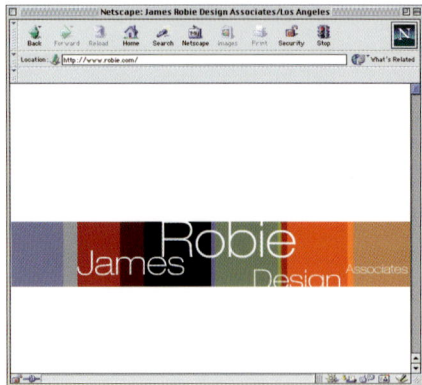

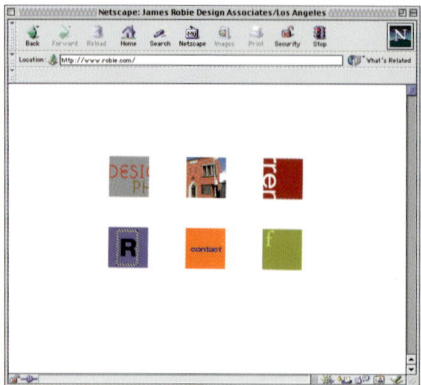

3

2

4

1. Northrop Grumman Web Site Proposal

2. James Robie Design Associates Web Site

3. James Robie Design Associates
   Identity Program

4. Self Promotional Brochure

Hershey Associates
1336 Fifth Street
Santa Monica, CA
90401-1415
310.656.1001 Phone
310.656.0613 Fax
888.669.1001 Toll free
www.hersheyassociates.com

HERSHEY ASSOCIATES

Our firm is a 22+ year partnership recognized nationally for creative excellence. Hershey Associates is consistently listed in the top 100 women owned businesses in Los Angeles.

We are a team of design and marketing professionals who partner with you, to solve communications problems, and develop strategic marketing solutions that meet your goals.

Our clients include leaders in healthcare, finance, consumer goods, technology, entertainment, utilities and non-profit.

We are communication consultants who listen, lead and get results!

Our services include:
Advertising Campaigns
Annual Reports
Branding Development
Capabilities Packages
Communication Audits
Communication Plans
Consulting
Corporate Collateral Material
Direct Mail
Environmental Graphics
Event Materials
New Product Packaging
Promotional Materials
Website Design

Hershey Associates: The collaboration of innovative design and strategic marketing.

1

1. Glendale Community College
2. Susan M Love MD
3. Keith Beer
4. Christopher Street
5. National Film Preservation
6. Circle City Association
7. Gas Company ERC
8. Hair Phd

2

3

4

National **Film Preservation** Foundation

5

6

7

8

1

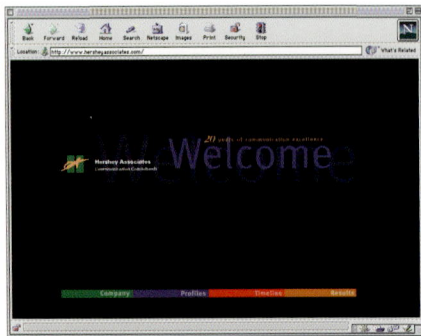

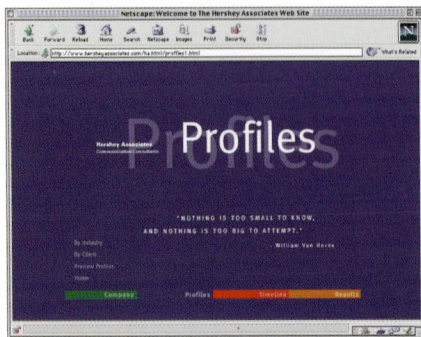

2

3

4

5

1. International Haircolor Exchange
2. Hershey Associates Website
3. Art Director's Los Angeles
4. Pacific Oaks
5. Liberty Hill Foundation
6. Schwab, Bennett & Associates
7. Medsite Urgent Care
8. Jelly Bellies

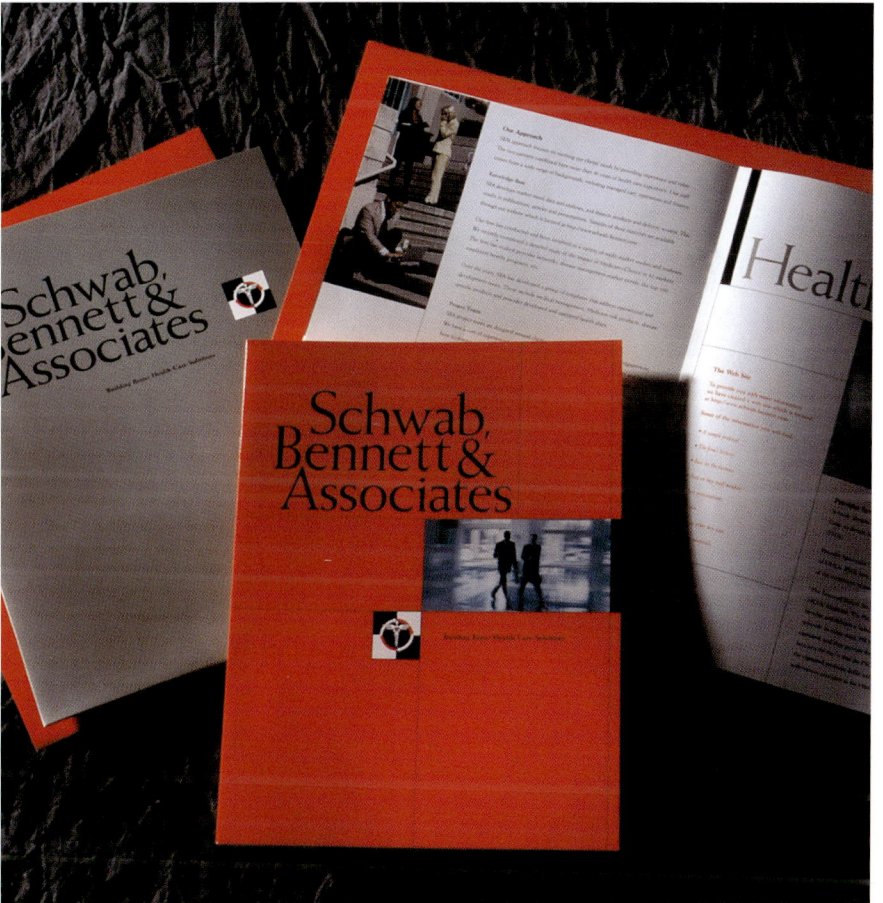

6

7

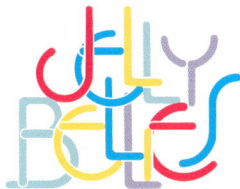

8

1

1. Para Los Niños
2. Los Angeles Urban League
3. Dr Pepper
4. Orange County's Credit Union
5. Hamilton House
6. YWCA
7. CEL & Associates, Inc.
8. Cellular One

2

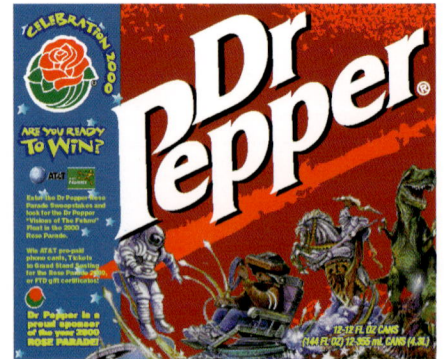

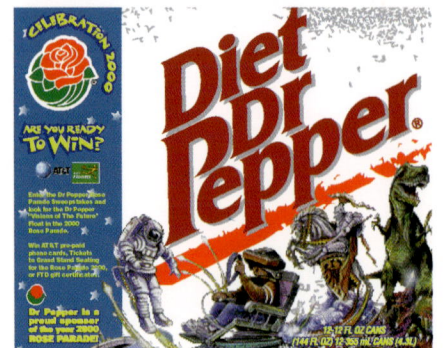

3

4

5

6

7

8

1

1. Tournament of Roses
2. Saint Francis Medical Center Neo-Natal Unit
3. GoBonzo!com Website

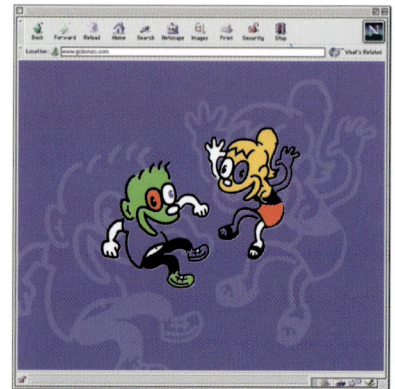

2

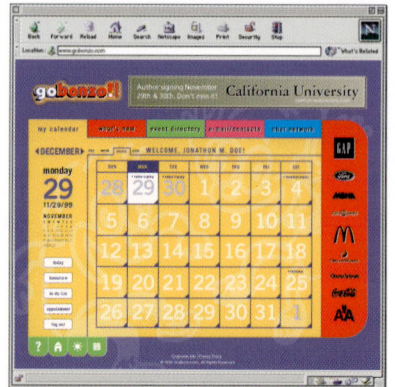

3

1337 Third Street Promenade
Second Floor
Santa Monica, CA 90401
Tel 310.576.1070
Fax 310.576.1074
www.sargentberman.com

SARGENT & BERMAN

Sargent & Berman has created and implemented a full spectrum of marketing and design-including corporate identities, brand packaging, collateral programs, advertising campaigns, and new media.

Clients include global leaders Sony, Bandai America, Sunkist, Princess Cruises, and Mattel as well as numerous leading regional companies. Some of these clients have been working with S&B for more than 10 years. In fact, over 70% of their business derives from long-term relationships. This kind of loyalty is cultivated by remaining faithful to the only design philosophy that seems to produce genuine marketing results. Which is this: Outstanding creative executions not based on focused marketing strategies are

ineffective, while sound strategic thinking will always break through the marketing clutter if it is given powerful creative expression. As the following examples demonstrate, every project is a unique event that must be understood within the context of a company's overall marketing plans and goals. Over the past decade, S&B has provided marketing solutions to companies in industries as diverse as technology & telecommunications, toys, travel & tourism, health care, fashion, food products, and entertainment.

1

2

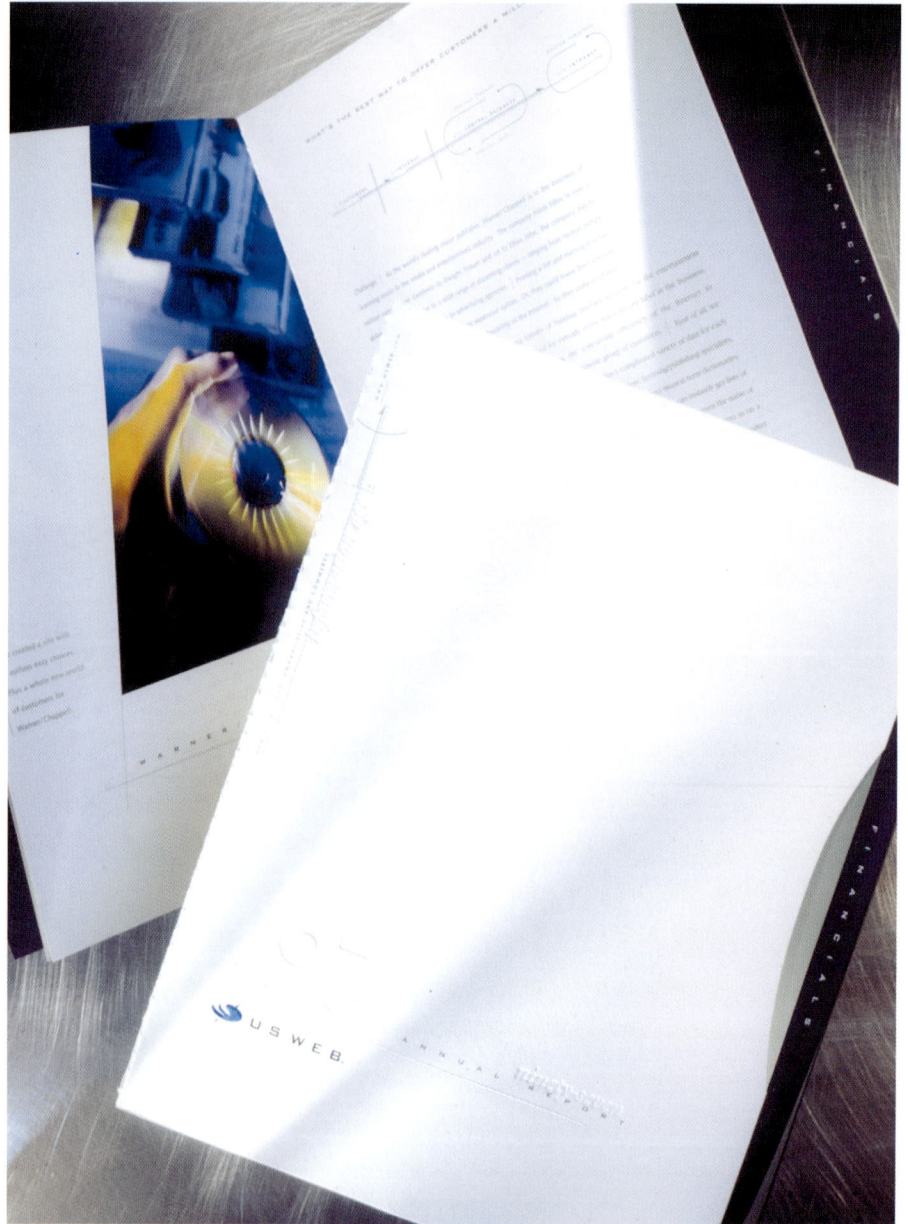

3

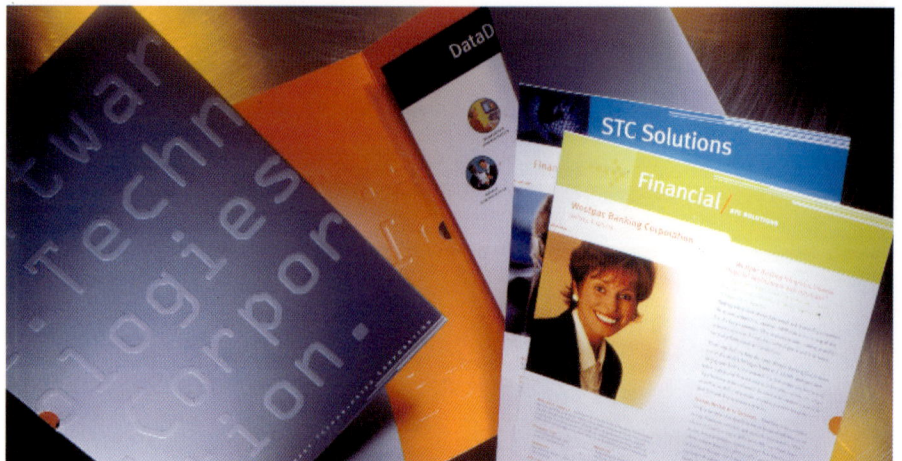

4

1. USWeb Corporate logo

2. Harvard Medical School logo

3. USWeb annual report

4. Software Technologies Corporation
sales kit and collateral

1

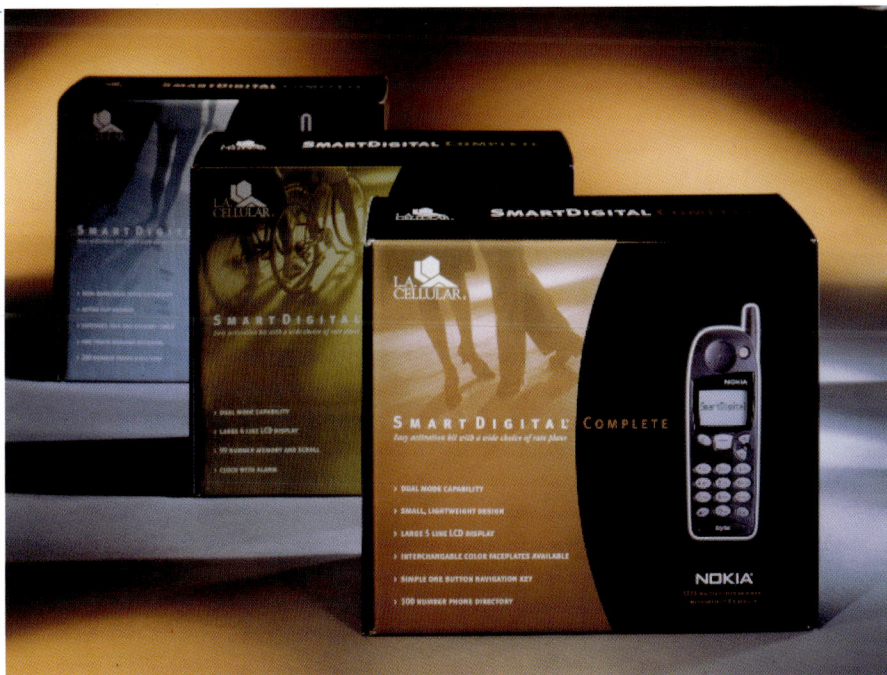

2

1. L.A. Cellular sales kit
2. L.A. Cellular packaging system
3. L.A. Cellular collateral system

3

1. "Umptee 3" style guide
2. "Godzilla-The Series" style guide
3. "Stuart Little" style guide
4. Sony Pictures Consumer Products
   sales support material

1

2

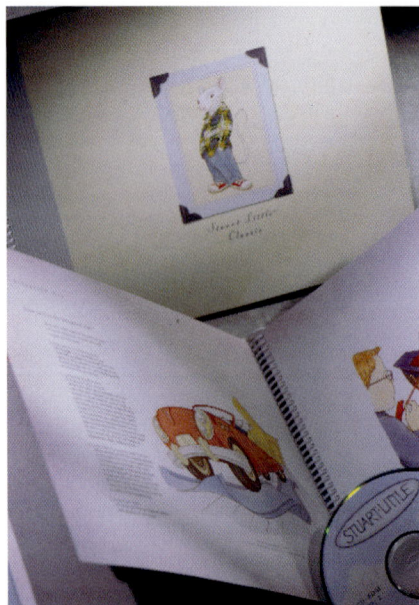

3

4

1

2

SEA PRINCESS

3

SUN PRINCESS

4

DAWN PRINCESS

5

6

1. SmartWorks identity and packaging
2. Voyage of Discovery menu and merchandising
3. Logo for Sea Princess
4. Logo for Sun Princess
5. Logo for Dawn Princess
6. Hansen's Natural packaging for children's juice product

MAPLE
D R I V E

1

1. Maple Drive restaurant logo
2. Sedlar Foods packaging system
3. 72 Market Street cookbook

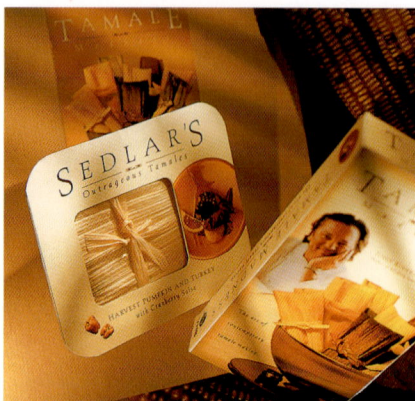

2

3

1

2

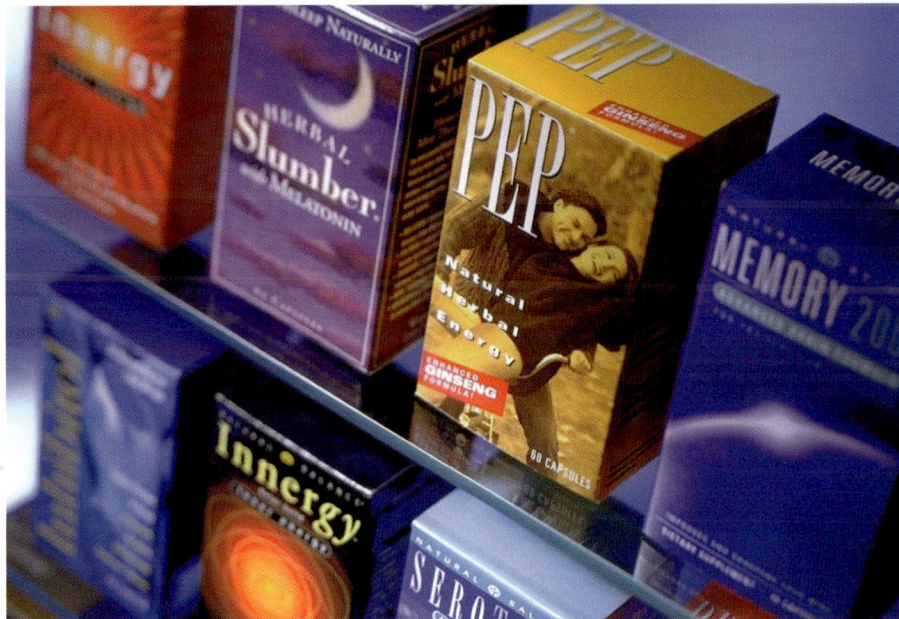

3

1. Power Rangers brand packaging
2. WWF brand packaging
3. Natural Balance, Inc. brand packaging

1

3

4

5

2

1. Crane America identity
2. Advanced Travel corporate brochure
3. Anderson Printing logo
4. Urban Slam Jam logo
5. Advanced Meeting Partners logo

Glendale California
Telephone 818 243 6800
Facsimile 818 243 7626

San Francisco California
Telephone 415 386 0875
Facsimile 415 386 0876

www.huertadesign.com

HUERTA DESIGN

Creativity is our passion. For more
than 37 years, Huerta Design has been
devoted to the success of our clients,
large and small.

A thorough understanding of each of
our clients' marketplaces is the secret to
our longevity, backed by the ability
to respond with effective, leading-edge
creative that provokes response while
maintaining corporate integrity.

Huerta Design. The experience to lead...
the strategy to succeed.

1

2

3

4

5

6

7

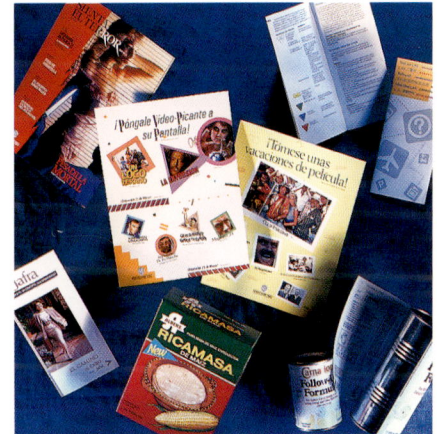

8

1. Foil wrap and packaging for an Easter chocolate promotion
2. Advertising, coupons and point-of-sale for children's toothbrushes
3. New logo and image campaign for a television postproduction and satellite delivery company
4. Annual reports for a national computer hardware leasing company
5. Face labels and packaging for promotional CDs
6. Label design for a line of salsa products
7. Brand identity and application to paper goods for a national pretzel franchise
8. Bilingual collateral, packaging and promotional materials

1

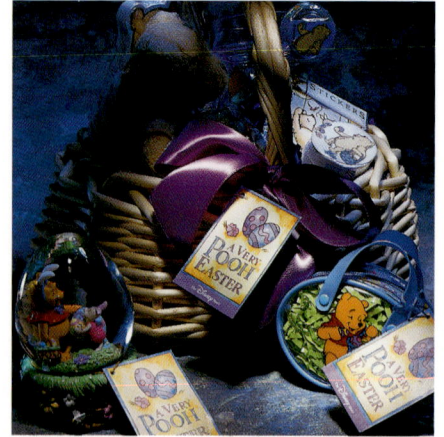

3

4

5

2

6

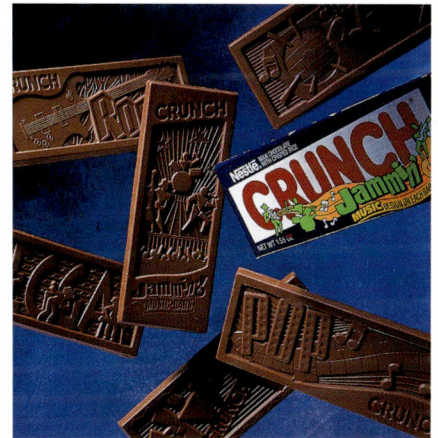

8

7

1. Packaging for a line of soy-based health products, including canisters, boxes and bars

2. Product brochures for a medical instruments company

3. Concept and identity implementation for a Pooh Easter product line

4. Package design for a Christmas candy promotion

5. Logo for a theme-designed pen collection

6. Product packaging for a line of computer printable cards

7. Product design, point-of-purchase and collateral materials for a theme-designed pen collection

8. Bar molds and wrapper graphics for a special chocolate promotion

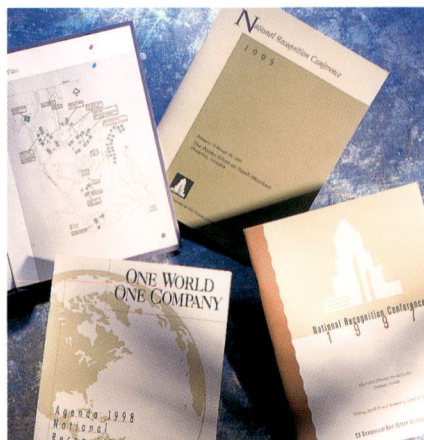

1

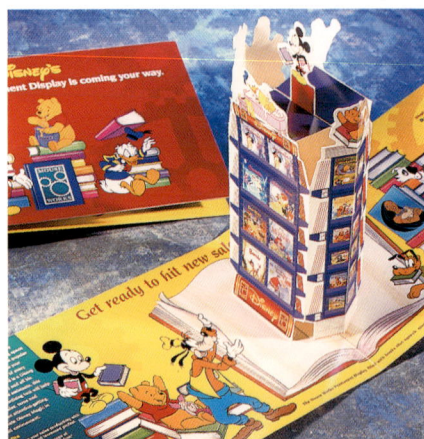

2

3

4

5

7

LATIN BUSINESS ASSOCIATION

8

6

1. Collateral materials for a national real
   estate company

2. Pop-up sales brochure for a major corporation's
   publishing division

3. Barrel, label and blister cards for a line of
   marker products

4. Sales program materials for a worldwide food
   corporation's chocolate division

5. Packaging and product catalogs for a national
   toy company

6. Packaging for domestic introduction of a line
   of international soups and sauces

7. Product packaging design for a line of computer
   printable cards and machineable labels

8. Corporate identity campaign for a national
   business association

1

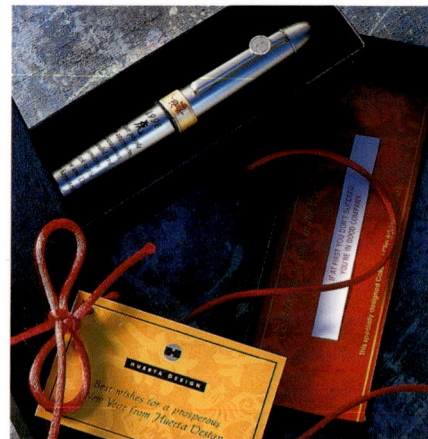

4

2

5

1. T-shirt graphics for annual 4th of July promotion
2. Packaging and labels for annual Cinco de Mayo promotion
3. Assortment of temporary tattoos for a special promotional mailing
4. Pen graphics and packaging for annual Chinese New Year promotion
5. Novelty 50s-themed birthday party invitation kit

3

Creative that sticks.

Morris Creative
660 9th Avenue, Studio 3
San Diego, CA 92101
619.234.1211
Toll Free 877.234.1211
headhoncho@morriscreativeinc.com
www.morriscreativeinc.com

MORRIS
CREATIVE

MORRIS CREATIVE (Stellar Solutions)

Think...Visual communication is about problem solving. An intelligent solution comes when a thorough process of thought is applied.

Feel...Intuition and feeling are the cornerstones of good visual communication. An emotional approach gives design a human touch.

Work...Brilliant design is nothing without hard work.

This philosophy is what drives Morris Creative. It's what makes their work award-winning, but more importantly, it's what makes their work effective and appropriate for the clients they work with.

Steven Morris, the principal of Morris Creative, first set up shop in San Diego in 1994 after relocating from Washington, D.C. After much success on the east coast, he hoped to combine his know-how with a lifestyle which suited him better. His hopes were realized. Morris Creative's work has won numerous awards and is regularly featured in many national and international design publications. The business and client base has also grown in keeping with the critical success.

Morris Creative provides a variety of creative and strategic services, including brand development, corporate identity, packaging, toy and game design, corporate collateral, interactive design and more.

A lot of thinking, feeling, and working is evident throughout Morris Creative's portfolio. The work is energetic, creative, thought-provoking, effective, strategic and solution-oriented.

Think. Feel. Work. For Morris Creative it's not just a philosophy, it's a lifestyle.

1

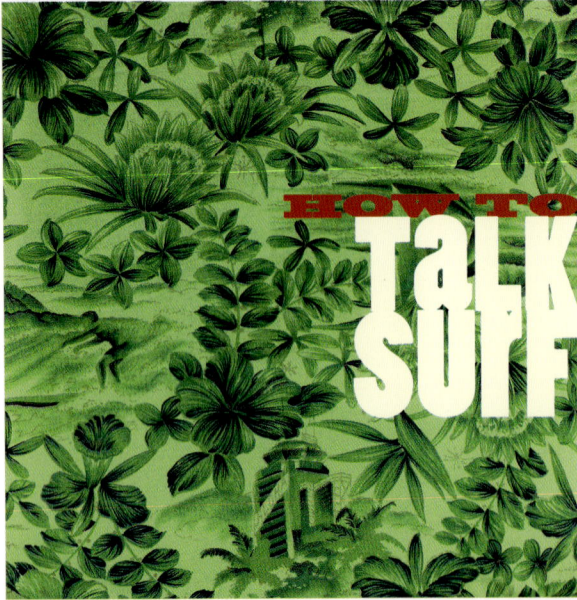

1. "How to Talk Surf" promotional book

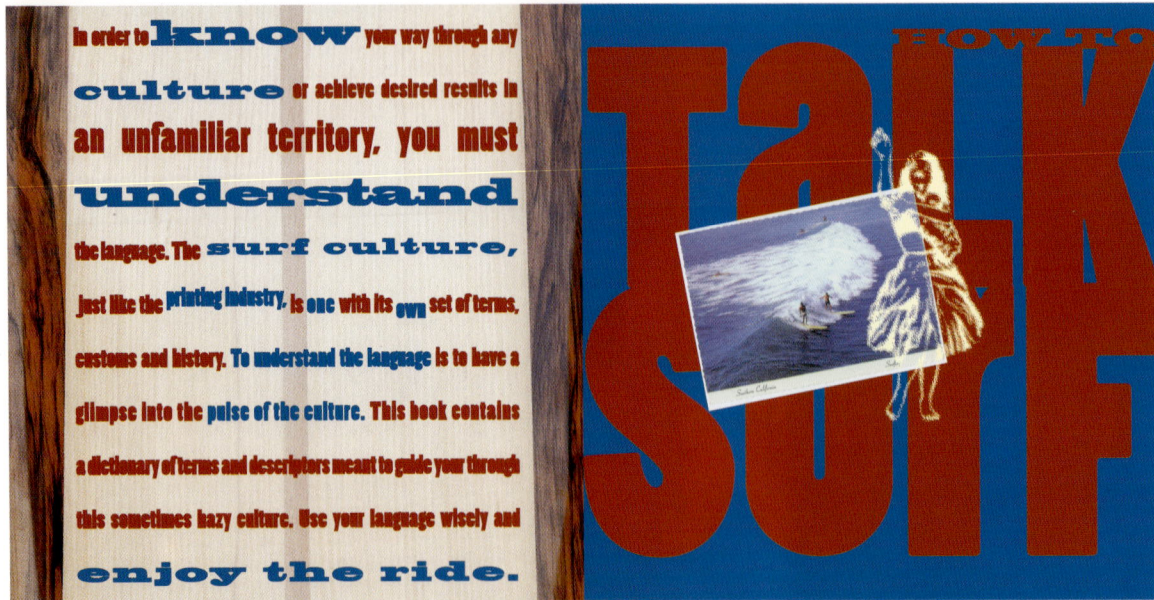

In order to **know** your way through any **culture** or achieve desired results in an unfamiliar territory, you must **understand** the language. The **surf** culture, just like the printing industry, is one with its own set of terms, customs and history. To understand the language is to have a glimpse into the pulse of the culture. This book contains a dictionary of terms and descriptors meant to guide your through this sometimes hazy culture. Use your language wisely and **enjoy the ride.**

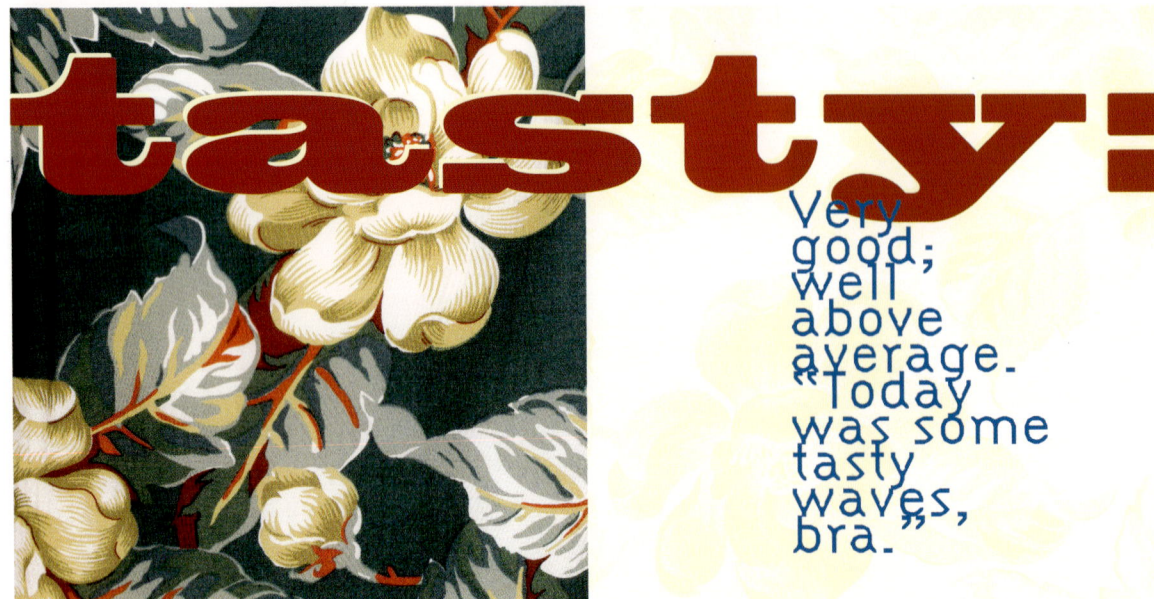

tasty: Very good; well above average. "Today was some tasty waves, bra."

3

1

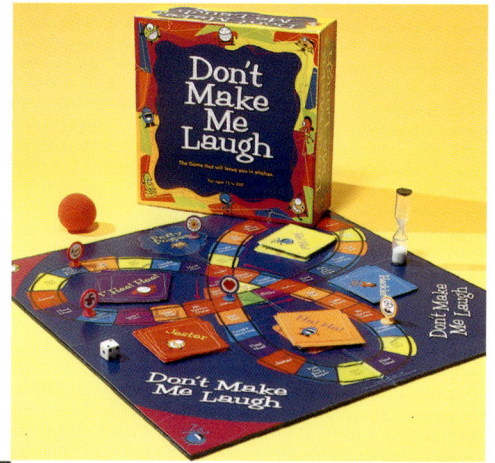

2

1. Mad Catz PC & Video Game catalogs
2. Mad Catz product packaging
3. Don't Make Me Laugh game product design
4. Project PACE product design

4

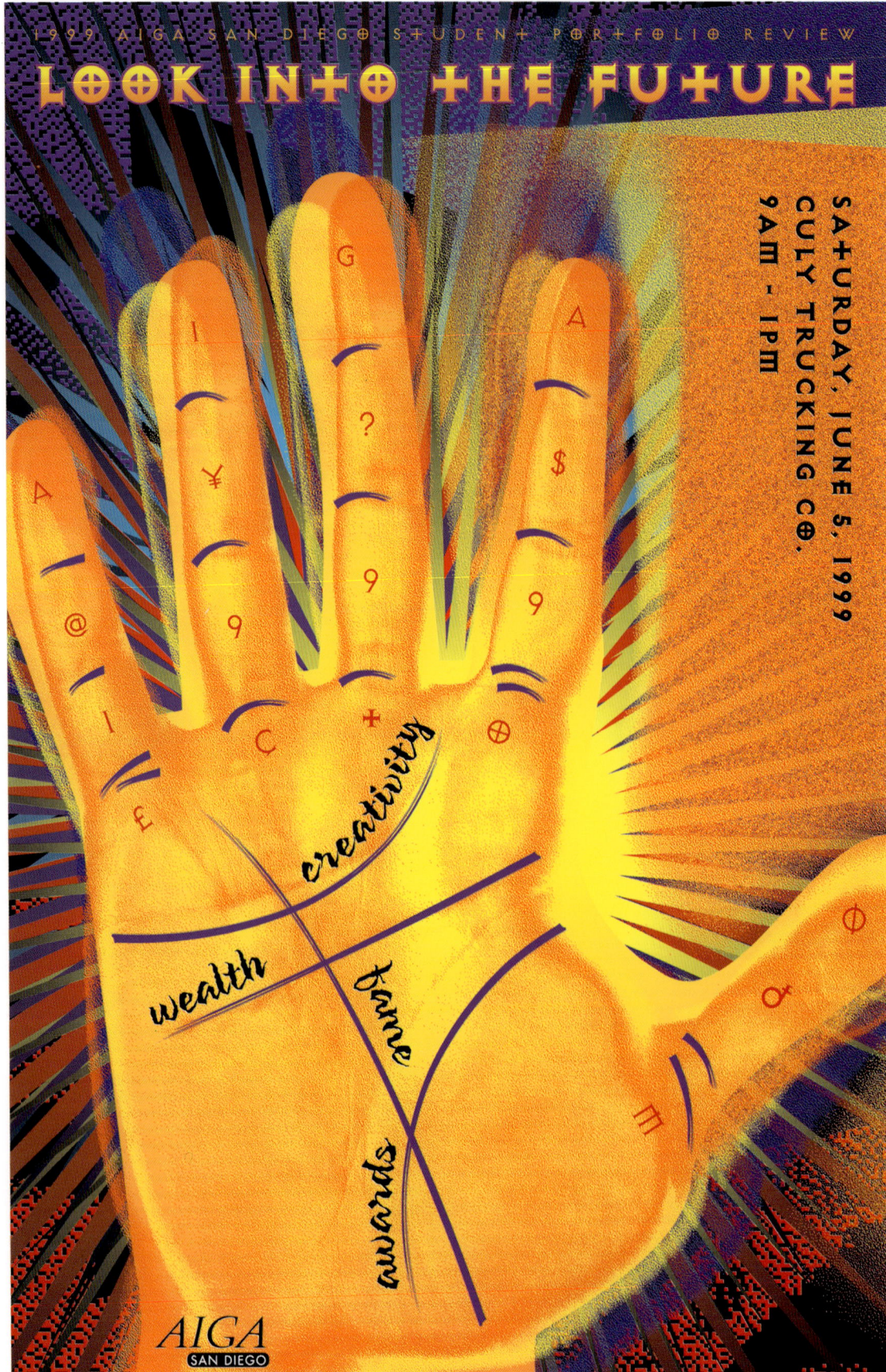

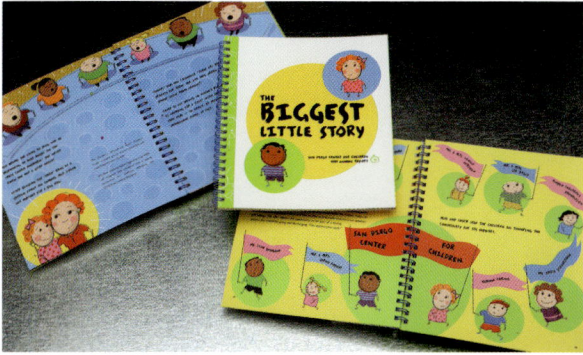

2

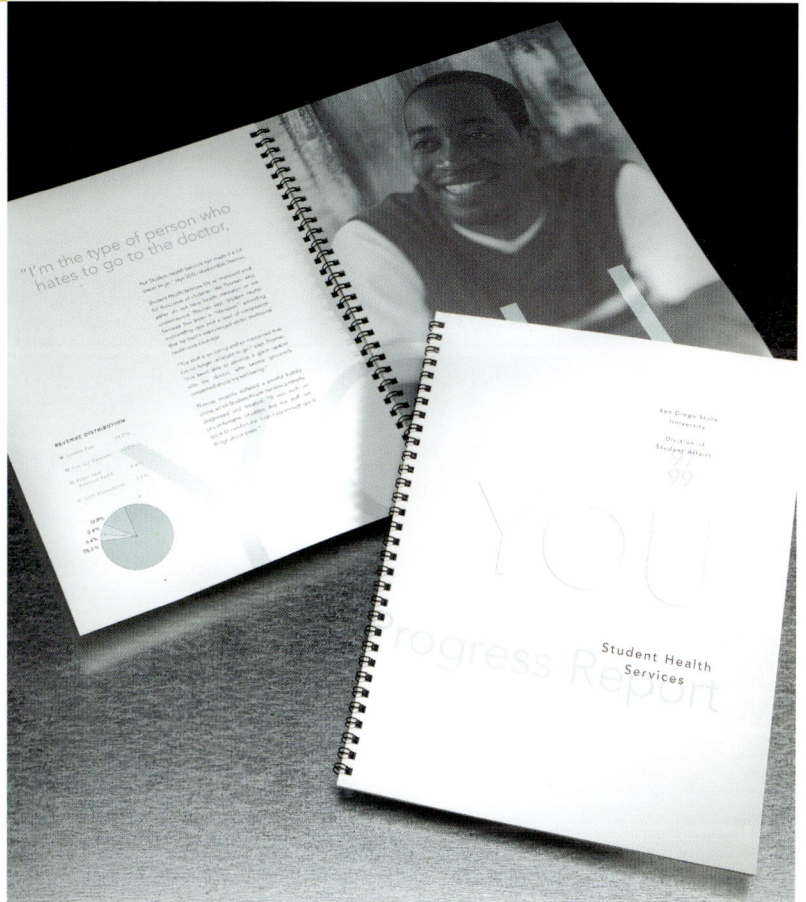

1. AIGA San Diego poster

2. Center for Children annual report

3. San Diego State University (Student Health Services) progress report

2. San Diego National Bank annual report

3

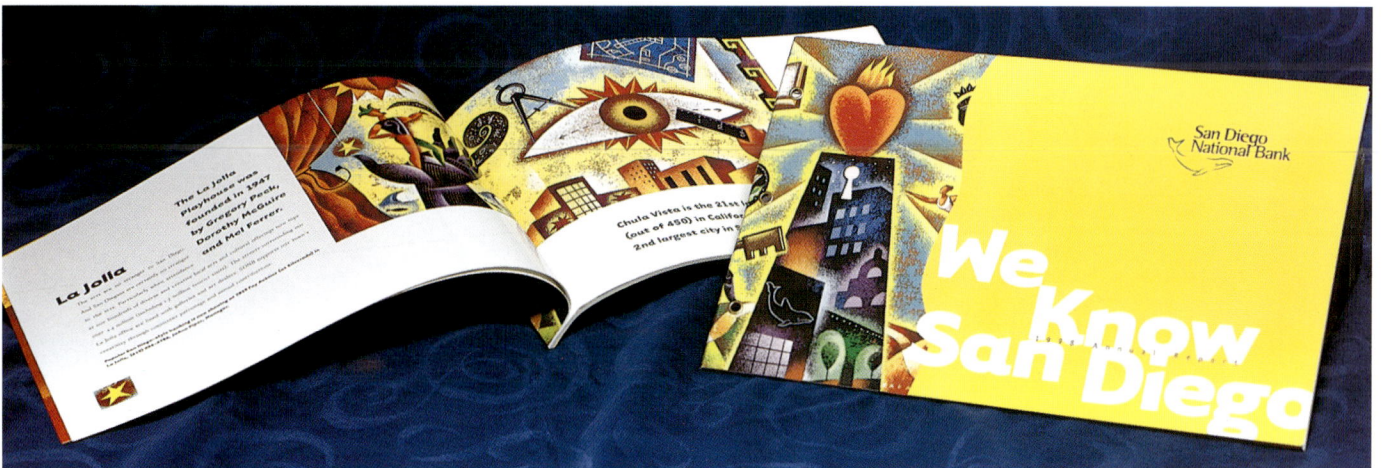

4

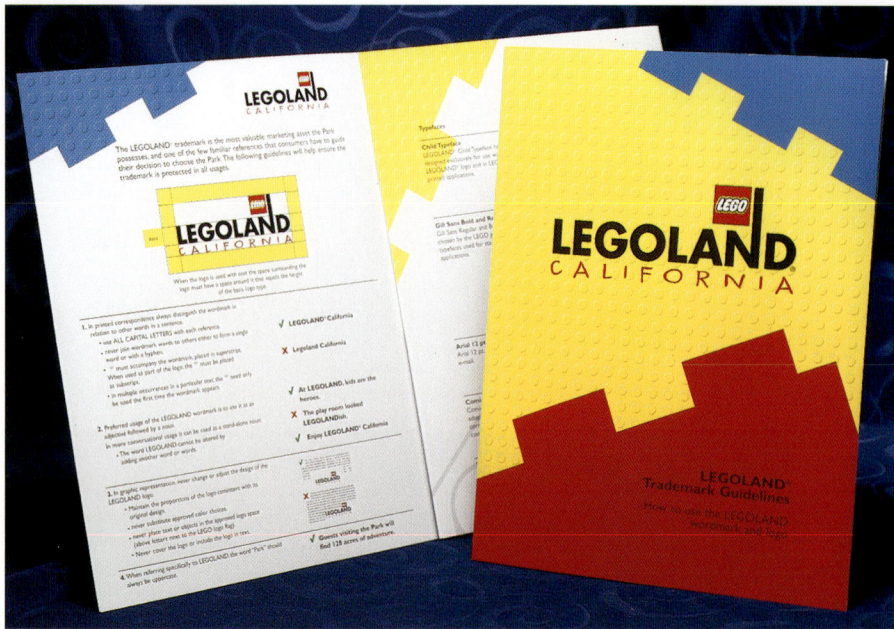

1

2

3

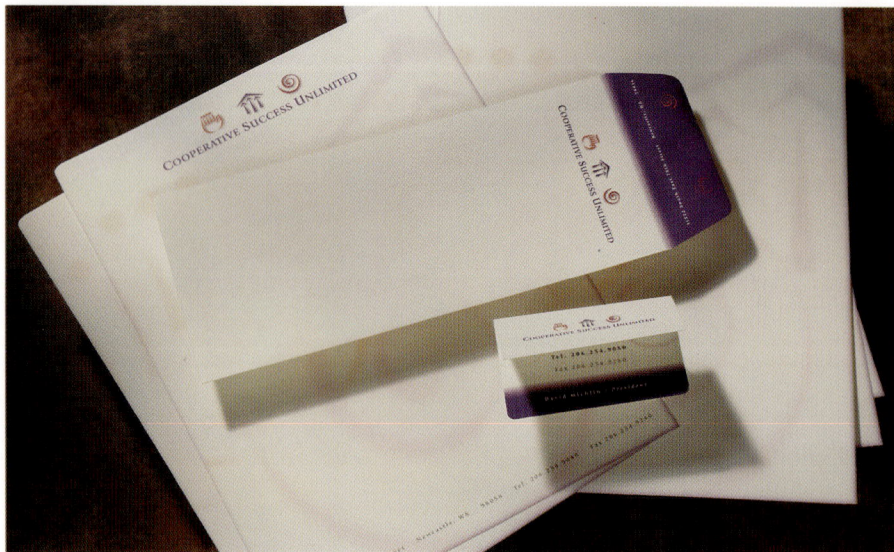

4

1. LEGOLAND California brand standards manual
2. Print Week '99 stationery design
3. Espresso Gourmet stationery design
4. Cooperative Success Unlimited
   stationery design

1

2

3

4

1. Tonka® brand product icons
2. Tonka® style guide interactive cd interface
3. Tonka® mass market product hang tag
4. Tonka® mid-tier product hang tag

1

2

3

4

5

6

7

8

9

1. Abby & Zoë's Playhouse brand logo
2. ebill.com brand logo
3. The Espresso Gourmet brand logo

4. Watters & Watters product line brand logo
5. venture-catalyst.com brand logo
6. Yoga Del Mar logo

7. Lolo Company brand logo
8. Kingsley Cards brand logo
9. Indigo Summers brand logo

THARP DID IT
50 University Ave. Suite 21
Los Gatos, California 95030
Tel: 408.354.6726
Fax: 408.354.1450
Web: www.TharpDidIt.com

San Francisco, California
Tel: 415.362.4494

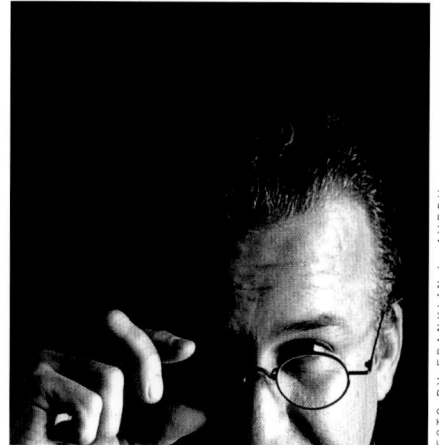

FOTO BY FRANKLIN L. AVERY

THARP DID IT   ⊤

THARP DID IT gets its noteworthy name from designer Rick Tharp. Established in 1975, the five-person studio is just as likely to *do it* for a Napa Valley restaurant as for a Silicon Valley start-up... for a family-owned Swedish toy company as for a jumbo-sized Japanese computer company. The studio's focus is on the disciplines of retail and corporate identity as well as packaging and environmental graphic design. In its twenty-something years the studio has been rewarded with everything from a free meal (for a restaurant logo) to the coveted Clio (for brand identity for its design for Mirassou Vineyards). The designers have even picked up a few Gold Medals along the way from organizations like the Society for Environmental Graphic Design in Washington D.C., the Vinitaly International Packaging Competition in Verona, Italy, and from The West Coast Show. The studio's work for BRIO Toys of Sweden is in the permanent collections of the U.S. Library of Congress and the Smithsonian Institution's Cooper-Hewitt National Design Museum.

Mr. Tharp's penchant for breaking rules has fascinated more than one corporate client. In the early '80s he designed the label for Sebastiani Vineyards' *Eye of the Swan wine*, whimsically turning the ordinarily lifeless UPC bar code into marsh reeds befitting its label theme. Tharp was arguably the first designer to enhance the UPC on retail packaging. When contracted to develop the complete identity program for one of California's largest county bus and light rail systems, Tharp began by recommending a brand new name to replace an acronym that nobody could remember. Full transit graphics, print guidelines, and standards manuals followed. The studio's innovative shoe packaging proposal for San Francisco based retail giant the GAP caught the attention of Hewlett-Packard's "old guard" leading the legendary computer company to contract Tharp Did It to break a few of its corporate standards for HP's retail environments and packaging.

According to Tharp, *"We don't break rules just to be breaking rules, but on the other hand, we don't let them get in the way either."* While the studio's client base has grown internationally, it's philosophy remains refreshingly provincial, *"Always do the right thing and always have fun doing it."*

T D C T J H T B I P C

1

1. poster for The Design Conference That Just Happens To Be In Park City
   (co-designers: Tharp, Berner, and Weller)

2. icons for TrukkE Winter Sports Boot Company
   The Walking, Working, Camping, Hunting, Fishing, Snowshoeing, Climbing, and Generally Goofing-off-in-the-Snow Boot

2

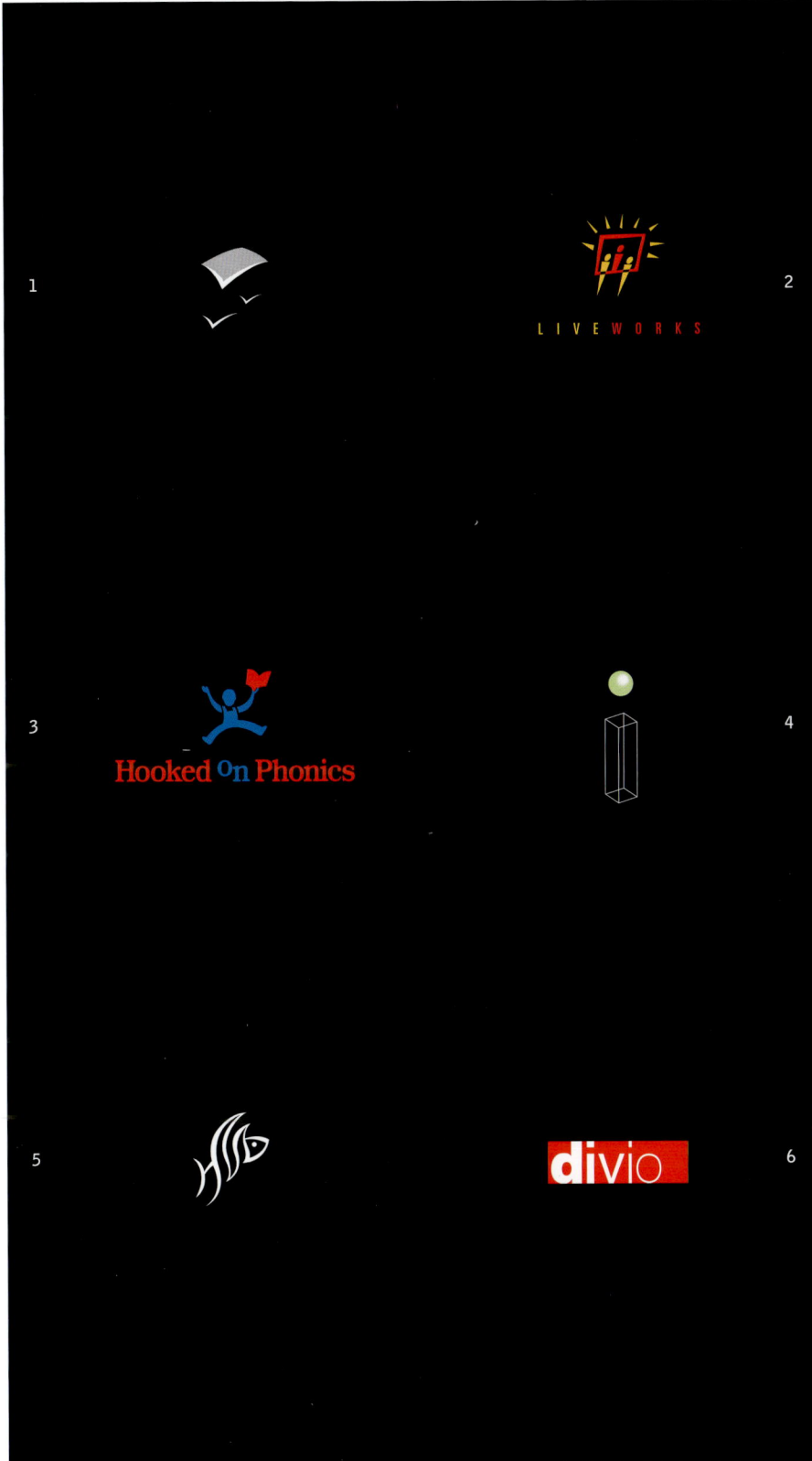

LIVE**WORKS**

Hooked On Phonics

divio

THE ORIGINAL dashBoard SINCE 1995 ™

7

1. logo for Bayshore Press (printer)

2. logo for Xerox's videoconferencing system
   (agency: The Stephenz Group)

3. logo for America's #1 home reading program

4. logo for Identity Packaging Corp.

5. logo for Steamer's, The Grillhouse

6. logo for video compression technology

7. identity for a bicycle without pedals

8. logo for NuTryx
   (internet training for senior citizens)

8

1

2

3

4

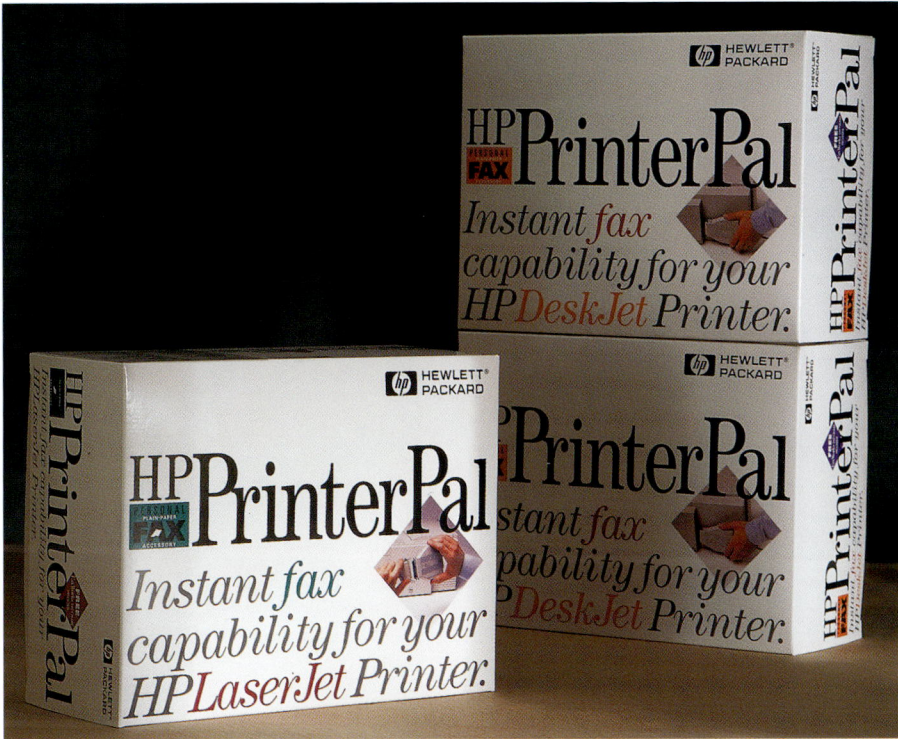

5

1. logo and label for a winery
2. wine label
3. brand identity and packaging
4. computer hardware packaging
5. bar code for Eye of the Swan wine
6. original painting and wine label
7. healthy snacks packaging

6

7

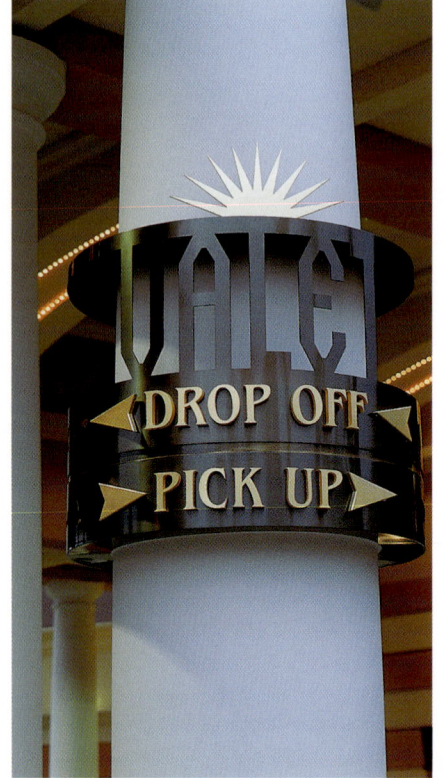

1

1. identity, signage, and environmental graphics for a casino
2. identity and fleet graphics for a mobile oil change service

2

1. restaurant identity, entryway, signage, and uniforms
2. placemats and signage for Steamer's, The Grillhouse
3. identity and packaging for LeBoulanger Bakery Cafes

1

2

3

graphic identity system and poster series for a film festival
featuring Gabriel Byrne, John Waters, and Rod Steiger

SAN JOSE FILM FESTIVAL 10
THURS. FEB. 24–SUN. MAR. 5, 2000
MAVERICK
FILMS/FILMMAKERS/TECHNOLOGY

CINEQUEST

WWW.CINEQUEST.ORG

10

TEN YEARS
RUNNING

TICKETS

DESIGN: THARP DID IT

Vigon/Ellis
10920 Ventura Blvd. Studio City, CA 91604
818.980.3777 www.vigonellis.com

photograph by Karen Beard

VIGON/ELLIS

Vigon/Ellis develops brand strategies and imagery that help its clients build their businesses and capture leadership. No matter how volatile and complicated the industry, or how broad the applications might be. Product Design, Packaging, Interactive, Electronic, Identity, Print, Web. More than executions, each element is the expression of our clients' core values, competitive differentiation and brand essence. Crafted in a way that cuts through in a nanosecond, but has relevance and impact for years.

Skin Essentials/Expressions

Gaining shelf space is the biggest challenge facing any company. Thanks to its breakthrough branding and packaging design, XpressionS gained distribution in virtually every major drug chain and mass merchandiser in the nation.

ELECTRONICA

Encyclopedia Electronica

The first all-original DVD consumer software product, Electronica represents a radical departure from traditional computer interface design. Electronica is both a television and computer product, which means that the interface had to work equally well on-screen 18 inches from the viewer, as well as across a room on a TV.

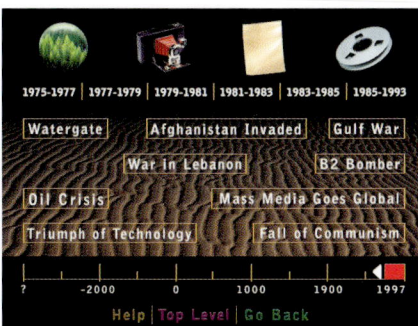

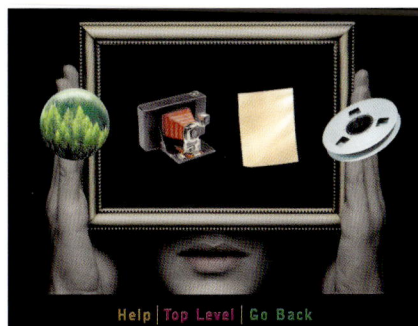

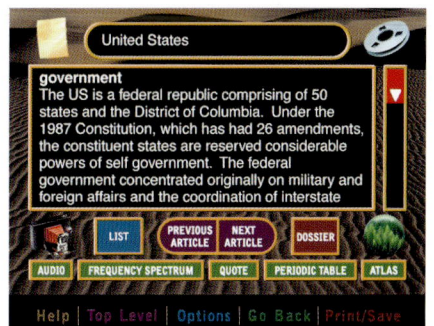

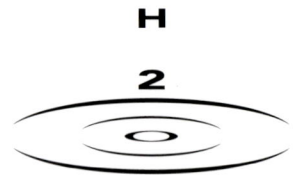

matinee
ENTERTAINMENT

DreamWorks

HEADSPACE

NOTEWORTHY

TOTAL
MULTIMEDIA

employers
group

PIX

BRAIN©

pronounced
TECHNOLOGIES INC

FRIEDLAND JACOBS
COMMUNICATIONS

WELK RESORT CENTER

Valley Crest

A mix of art and science, the imagery developed
for Valley Crest reflects its position as the
industry leader.

Adlink

A Top 5 cable TV branding campaign, this new
identity enabled Adlink to create and own the
category of "Targeted TV" advertising.

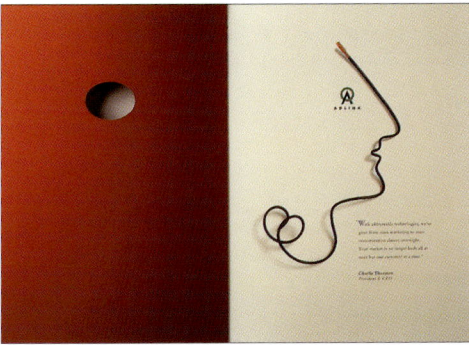

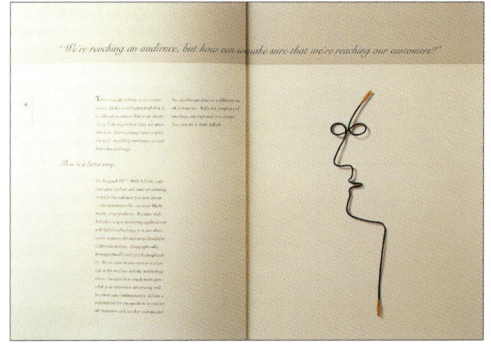

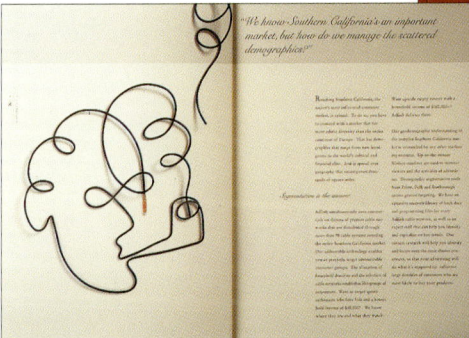

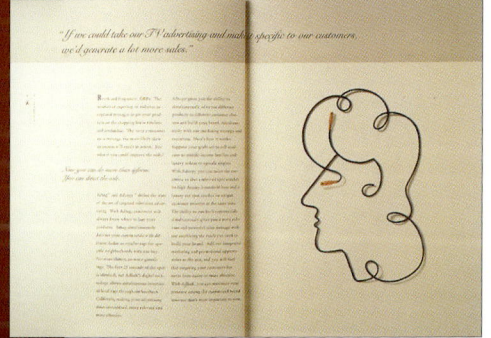

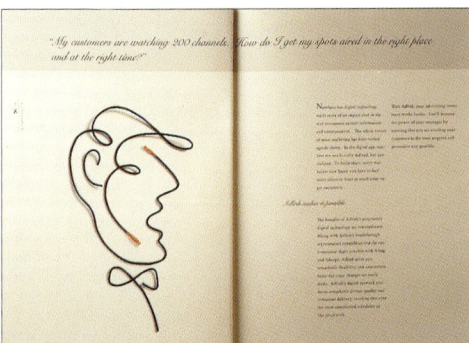

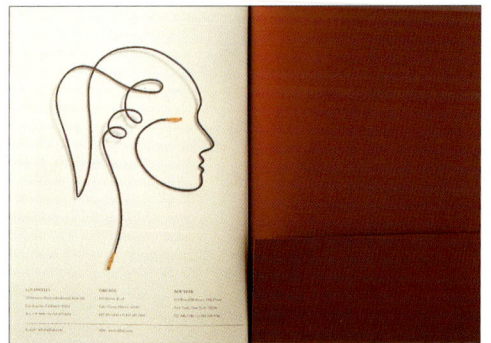

LOS ANGELES

it's all right here

Los Angeles Convention & Visitors Bureau

It isn't often that a firm that specializes in developing consumer and business-to-business brands has the opportunity to create a brand identity for a state of mind. Our approach was to show the sophisticated side of Los Angeles, the part that makes L.A. the world-class destination it truly is.

Mike Salisbury, LLC
Effective Brandesign
P.O. box 2309
Venice, California 90294
310.392.8779
mikesalcom@aol.com

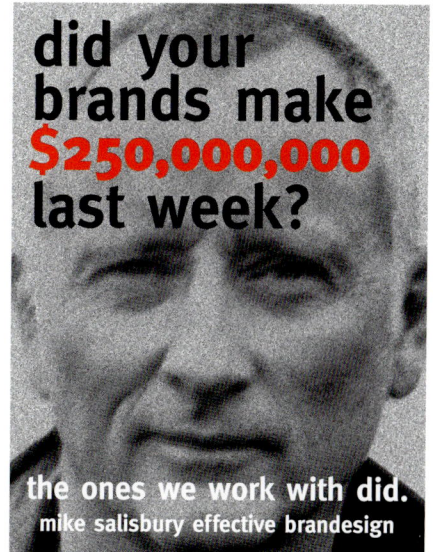

MIKE SALISBURY

"From Rolling Stone to Michael Jackson. From 501 Jeans, to Joe Camel, Mike Salisbury has been responsible for creating some of the most successful pop icons of our time.

He is the father of the 501 brand name and Michael Jackson's white glove.

Mike created corporate icons - the rainbow for Disney, the magician for George Lucas' Industrial Light and Magic and logos for PolyGram, *Raiders of the Lost Ark* and the California Angels baseball team, print and TV advertising campaigns for Levis, *Jurassic Park*, *Aliens*, VW, Mazda and MTV, packages for Bubble Yum, Mattel Toys, Kirin Beer and products for Suzuki and Honda.

He has designed branding programs including corporate identity, e-communication, advertising, packaging and public image for companies like Hasbro - the world's largest toy company - makers of Monopoly, Mr. Potato Head, Playskool, Lincoln Logs and more.

Mike took Gotcha Sportswear from a garage in Laguna Beach to over $200,000,000 in yearly retail sales with total branding - advertising, clothing design and merchandising concepts.

Salisbury has either designed from scratch or redesigned such publications as Rolling Stone, Playboy, West, Surfer, Surfing, Hot Rod, Motor Trend and The San Francisco Examiner. Mike's photography has been published in Vogue, Life, Newsweek, Esquire and Men's Journal magazine

He is also a writer for Men's Journal, Architectural Digest's new automotive magazine and Forbes magazines.

His work is in the permanent collections of The Smithsonian, The Library of Congress and The Museum of Modern Art. Mike has taught at UCLA, Art Center College of Design, and Otis.

He has been invited to speak in Brazil, Finland, Mexico City, New York, Chicago, Boston, Miami, Park City, Dallas, Seattle, San Francisco, San Diego and New Orleans.

Advertising creative director, editorial art director, graphic designer, TV commercial director, brand strategist - this fall, two books are being published on the work created by this image maker of the world we live in and buy in.

Mike Salisbury's creative work is the value added to the Gross National Product."

-Adweek

creating the biggest little number in clothing - 501 which equals $970,000,000.00. annually.

we helped scare up domestic ticket sales of $300,000,000.

1.

We proudly introduce the most imitated logo on earth.

See? You're imitating it right now. And you're not even playing Monopoly or Star Wars or Mr. Potato Head or G.I. Joe, or with Nerf balls or Tonka Trucks.

But you have, and you will.

And every time they make you smile, if you look closely, you'll see our smile grow just a little brighter.

2.

3.

1. Our new Hasbro corporate logo on the most famous boardgame in the world.

2. Wall Street Journal ad created by Mike Salisbury, LLC to introduce the newly created brand image that represents the family of the world's best known toys to the global financial markets as one entity.

3. Cross marketing the corporate brand and the world's favorite game brands with our designs for the Hasbro communication systems.

4. Hasbro corporate internet site featuring their new smile-the world's most well known symbol for fun and Hasbro's most important product.

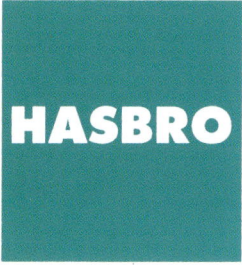

[before]

[after]

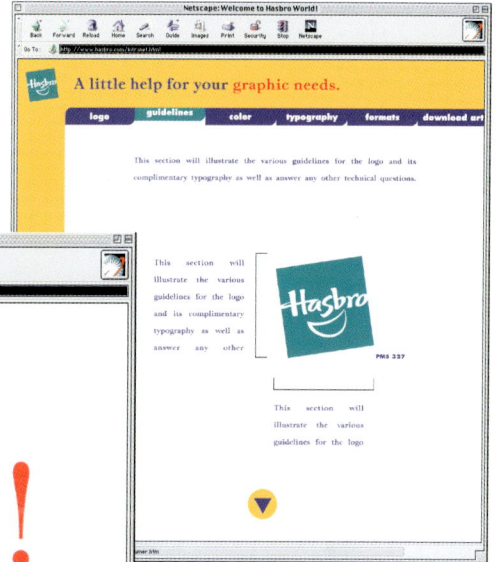

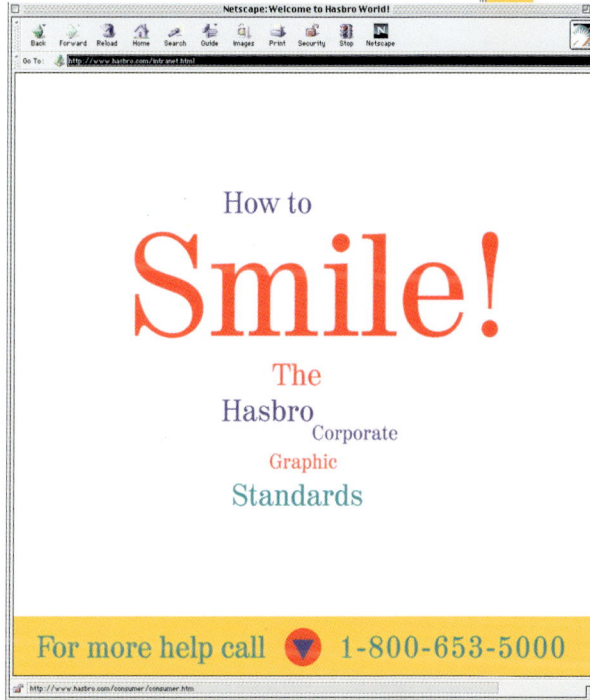

4.

our packaging design helps produce 640,761,832,409.701 total bubbles yearly.

the most anticipated computer game of the decade chose Mike for their entire brandesign program.

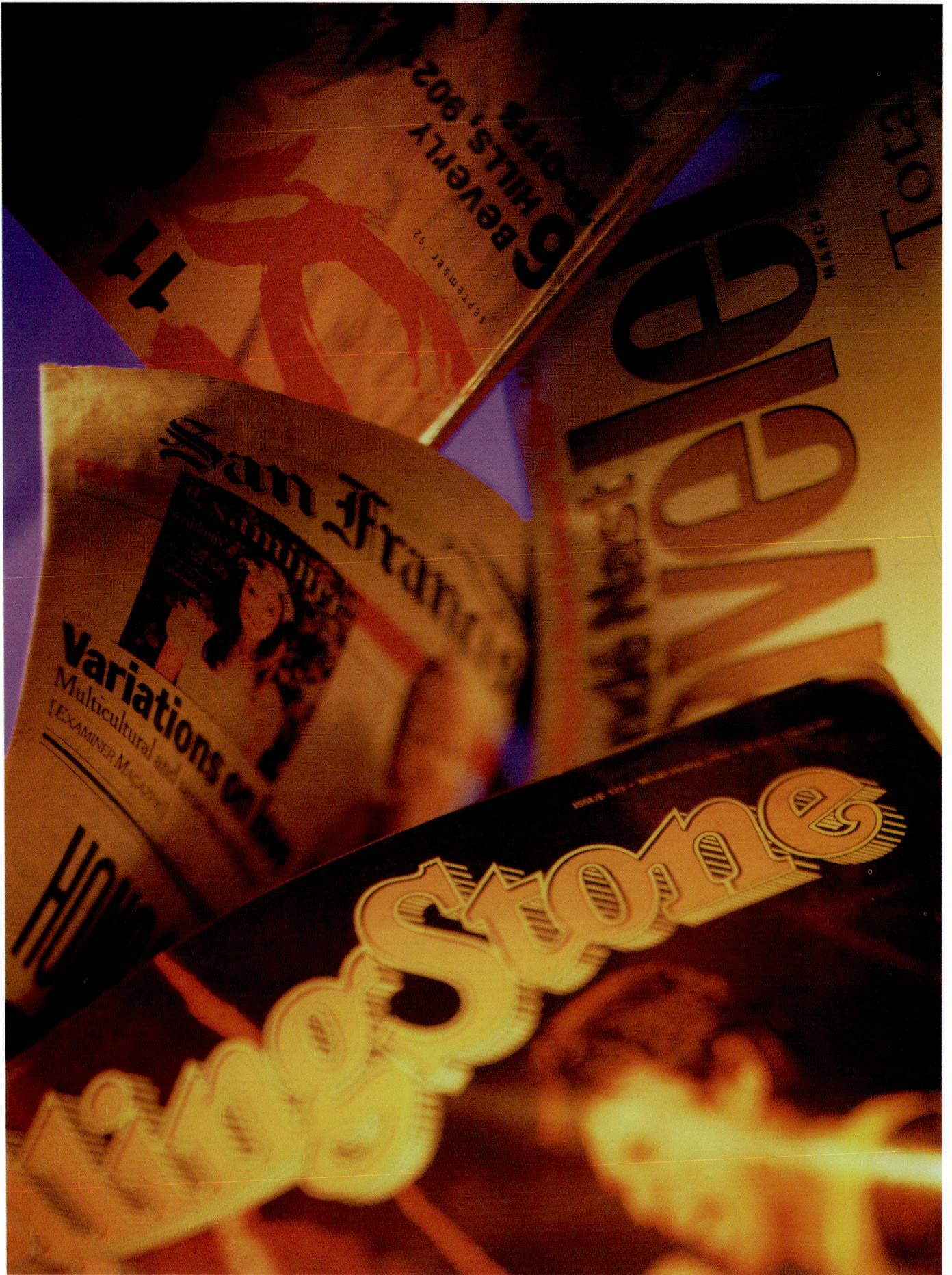

billions of pages turned with Mike Salisbury's publication design.

LAURA COE DESIGN ASSOCIATES

Laura Coe Design Associates
4918 North Harbor Drive, Ste. 206
San Diego, California 92106
619.223.0909
Fax 619.223.0939
www.coedesign.com

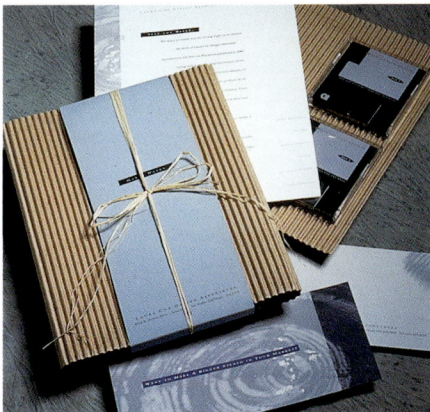

STRATEGIC BRANDING AND DESIGN
Walk into an inviting work environment
with purple carpets and multi-colored walls
and hear the seagulls and water splashing
in the background. This is Laura Coe Design
Associates. The LCDA creative staff, lead
by Laura Coe Wright, have been producing
the marketing integration of two and three-
dimensional images at this waterfront marina
in San Diego since 1985. LCDA offers strategic branding solutions incorporating dynamic
design solutions, unique identities, elegant
catalogs, inventive environmental graphics,
effective packaging, creative illustrations and
practical point of sale materials. Their extensive work in consumer products has enabled
them to produce strong brand identities from
product development and coloration, identity
and packaging through environmental design
and retail merchandising.

LCDA's work philosophy is simple. Listen,
think, then design. The key is to develop
an understanding of each client's marketing
goals and objectives by listening first. The
combination of experience, knowledge and
talent, along with the LCDA personal touch,
translates into effective visual solutions that
work for each client. "The thought process is
critical," Laura explains, "we are exceptional
problem solvers which allows us to be even
greater designers."

Over the years, clients have ranged from
local to international. San Diego is a great
place for clients to visit. With the internet,
travel is not always necessary, but LCDA likes
the personal interaction they are so well
known for. Clients have included SeaWorld
of California, Hewlett-Packard, Hang Ten,
Dennis Conner Sports, Titleist and Foot-Joy,
Sony and Taylor Made/adidas Golf.

"We love working together with our clients
to create the best overall solution," remarks
Laura. To better serve their clients' needs,
LCDA is expanding their design capabilities
to include industrial design by creating
a strategic alliance with an established
Midwestern firm. "We are excited about
the possibilities this brings… and we do
our best work when we are excited!"

1

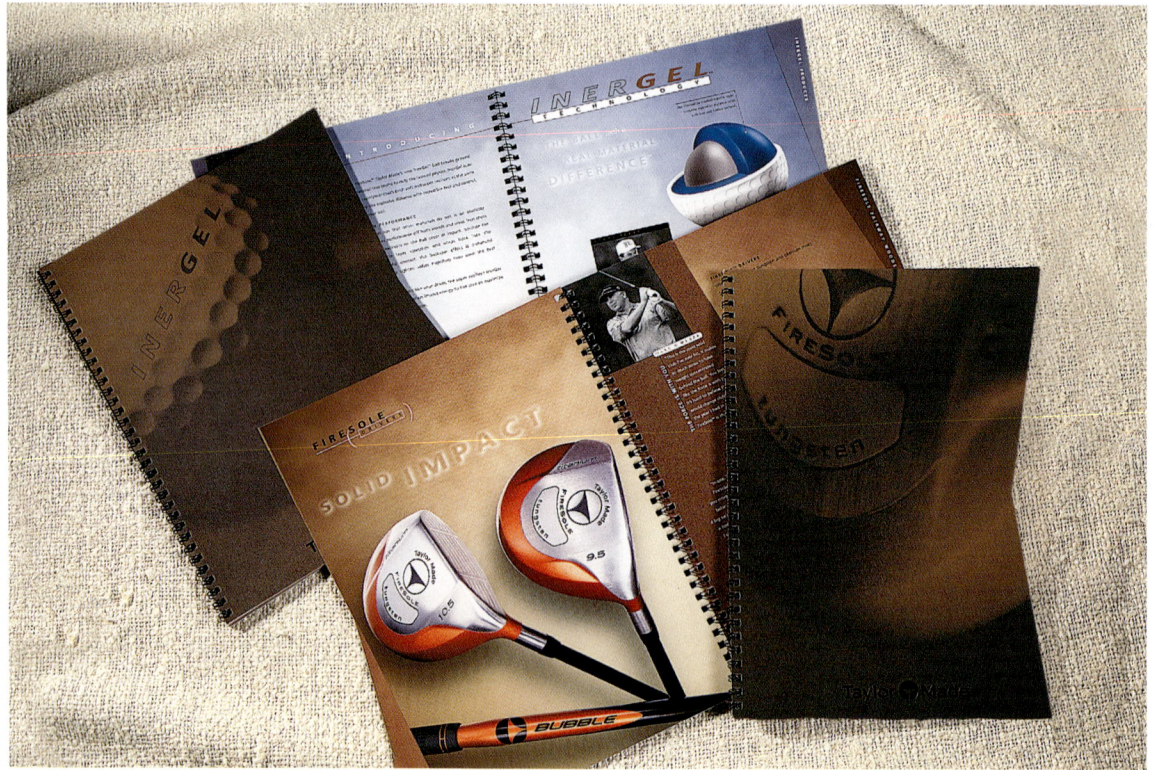

3

4

2

Branding Series for Taylor Made Golf:

1. Product packaging insert for React golf glove

2. Communication icons for print materials

3. Trade catalog of new products

4. InerGel golf ball counter display graphics and brochure

5. Environmental design for in-store and booth graphics, signage and product displays

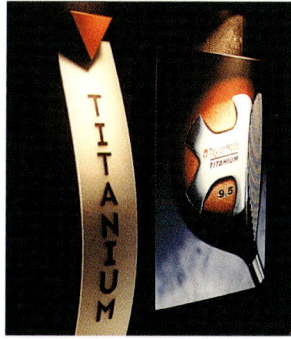

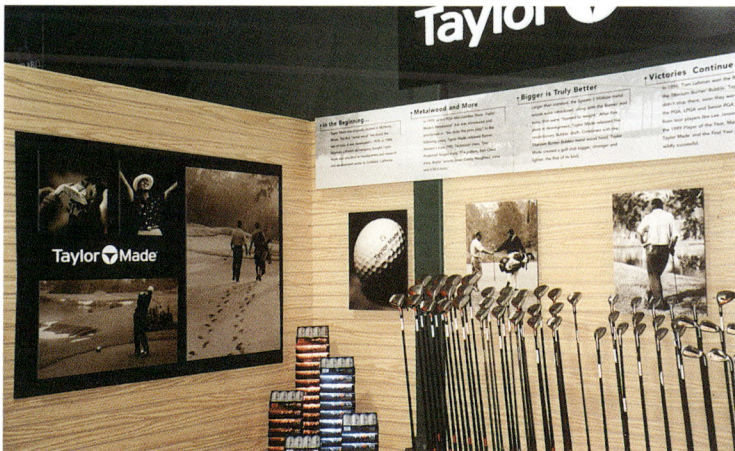

5

1. Promotion for Fox River Paper

2. Retail packaging for Hewlett-Packard

3. Communication icons for
   DataQuick Online Real Estate

4. Product development and coloration
   for 4 Sport & Play coolers

5. Point of purchase sample book and
   information pad for Hewlett-Packard

6. Capabilities brochure for Exponents,
   modular exhibit company

7. Web page illustrations and buttons
   for DataQuick Information Center

1

2

3

4

5

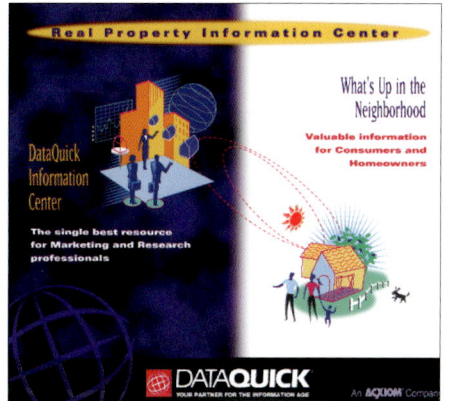

7

6

1

1. Packaging program for ProAction bicycle seats

2. Packaging for ProAction insulated water bottles

3. Software packaging and presentation kit for CostCore, legal management software

4. Brochure, video and poster presented in a custom teak box, used for fund raising for Dennis Conner Sports, Inc.

5. Cover and book design for Polly, a collection of photographs

2

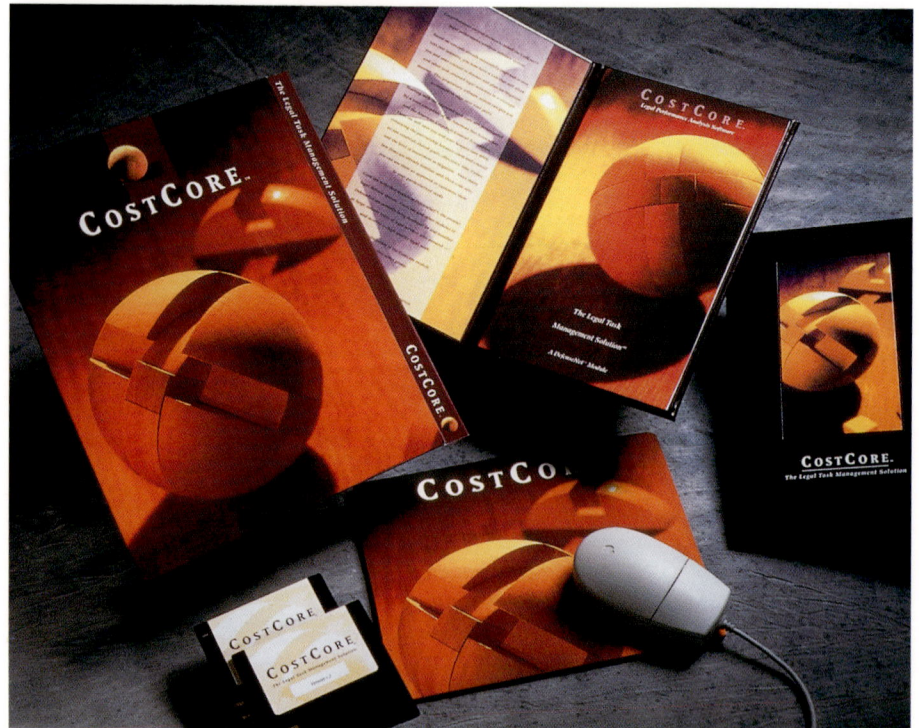

3

4

5

3

4

5

1. Educational brochure for SeaWorld
of California

2. Corporate identity for Active Motif,
a gene analysis company

3. Signage logo for SeaWorld of California

4. Packaging icon for Globalink Software

5. Internal logo for Salzman International,
Artist Representative

Michael Osborne Design
444 De Haro, Suite 207
San Francisco, California 94107
415.255.0125
fx 415.255.1312
mod@modsf.com
www.modsf.com

MICHAEL OSBORNE DESIGN

San Francisco-based Michael Osborne Design, Inc. (MOD) was founded by President and Creative Director Michael Osborne in 1981 with the goal of creating outstanding design for every client. He has achieved this within a creative climate where young designers, schooled in the latest techniques and technologies, are nurtured and developed into effective communication problem solvers. Today, with a staff of twelve, Michael Osborne continues to meet his aim with successful work in package design, corporate/brand identity, print collateral, and electronic media.

"We believe design is a process involving the collaboration of client, marketer, researcher, and designer," says Michael. "This process of working together to meet a set of given objectives leads to several solutions to any problem. The perfect solution is the one in which information is communicated in an innovative, strategic, and provocative manner. Arriving at the perfect solution is our profession – and our passion."

MOD has received awards from many competitions for outstanding design, including AIGA, the San Francisco Show, and several Clios. More importantly, these designs have proven their effectiveness in the marketplace with increased sales. MOD's work has been featured in Graphis, Communication Arts, The Society of Typographic Arts, American Institute of Graphic Arts, How Magazine, Step-By-Step Graphics, and numerous Print Annuals.

MOD has worked in many industries with such companies as The Learning Company, Intel Corporation, Trinchero Family Estates (formerly Sutter Home Winery), Nordstrom, Brown-Forman Beverages Worldwide, Wente Vineyards, Wells Fargo Bank, SFMOMA, Eastman Kodak, Gymboree Corporation, 3Com Corporation, Ansel Adams Gallery, Chronicle Books, and Yosemite Association.

Michael Osborne graduated with honors from Art Center College of Design in 1978. In addition to his work at MOD, he has been a faculty member at the University of California at Berkeley and currently teaches at The Academy of Art College. He frequently lectures at universities and colleges and has been a featured speaker at several Western Art Directors Club and AIGA events as well as at the A.D.A.C. Envision Design Conference.

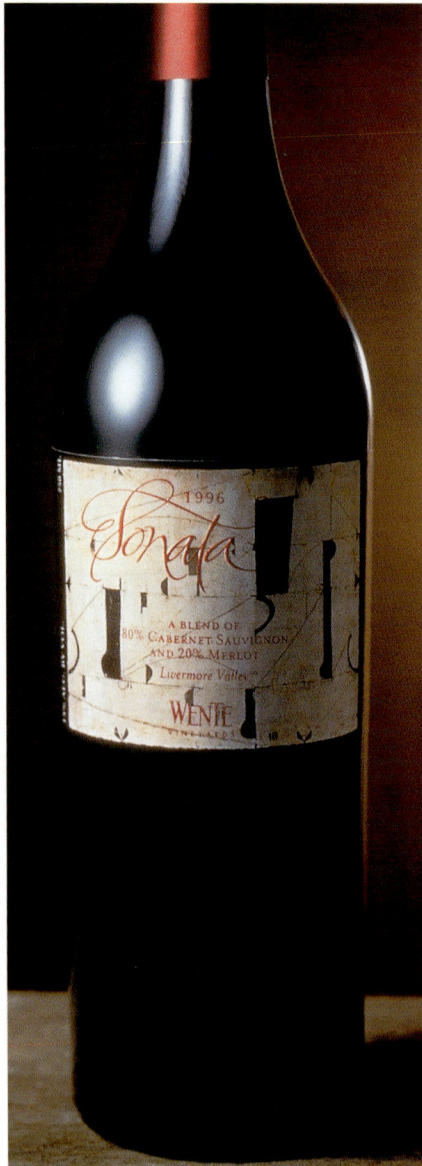

1

2

vitessa

3

AserA

4

1. Naming, packaging, and bottle structure design for Jack Daniel's Monogram Tennessee Whiskey, Brown-Forman Beverages Worldwide

2. Naming and packaging for Sonata, Wente Vineyards

3. Naming and identity for e-commerce business

4. Logo for e-commerce business

5. Print promotion for Atlanta-based specialty printer, Dickson's, Inc.

6. Identity for venture capital company

7. Wine packaging for Savona, Trinchero Family Estates

5

6

7

1

2

3

1. Logo for University of the Pacific Department of Athletics
2. Wine packaging for Soléo, Trinchero Family Estates
3. Packaging program for hardware peripherals
4. Identity program for USS Hornet historical museum
5. Logo for women's sportswear
6. Packaging for ESPN Digital Games
7. Packaging and brandmark for high-speed internet access products

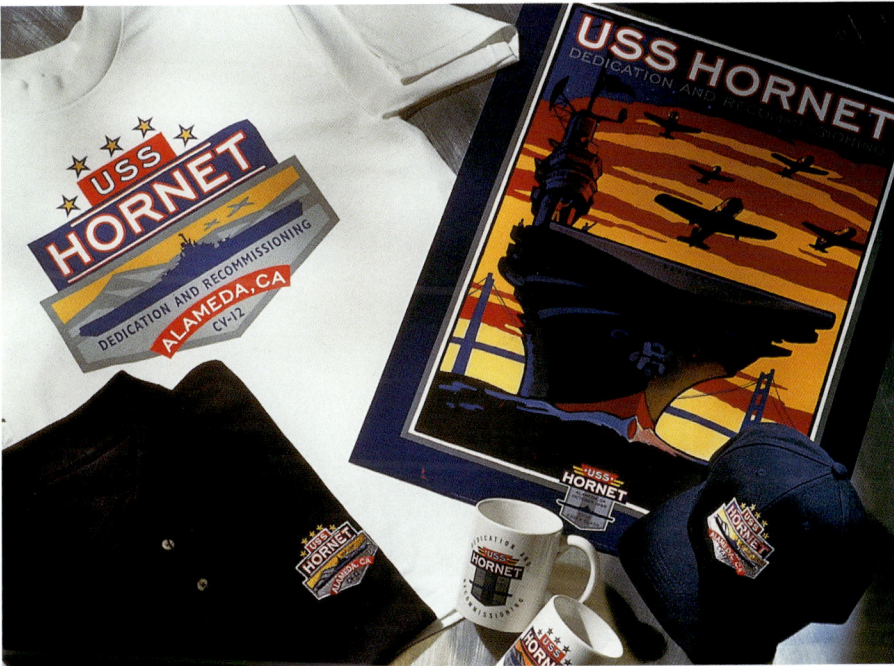

4

enginewear

5

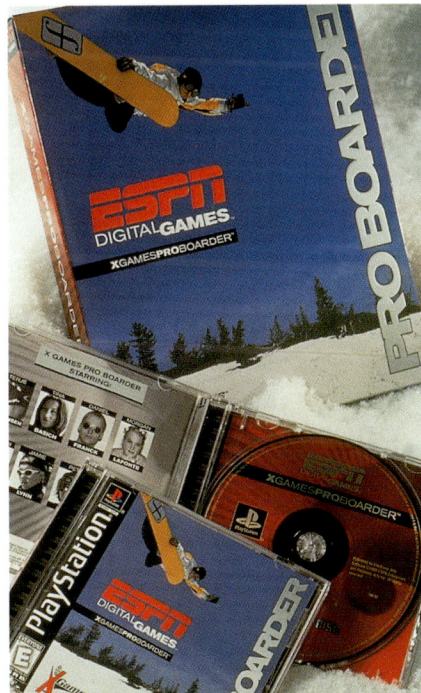

6

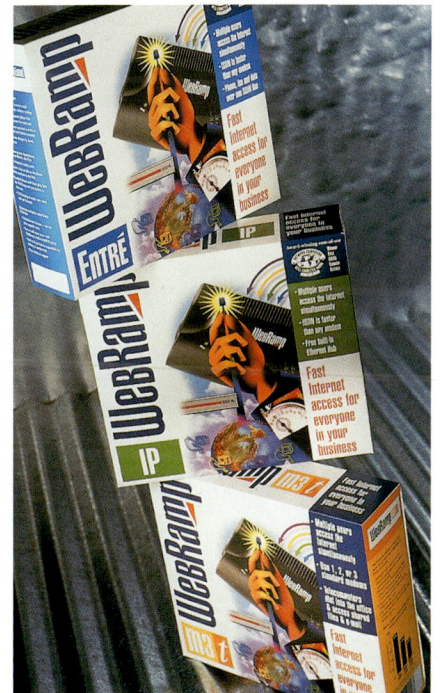

7

1

2

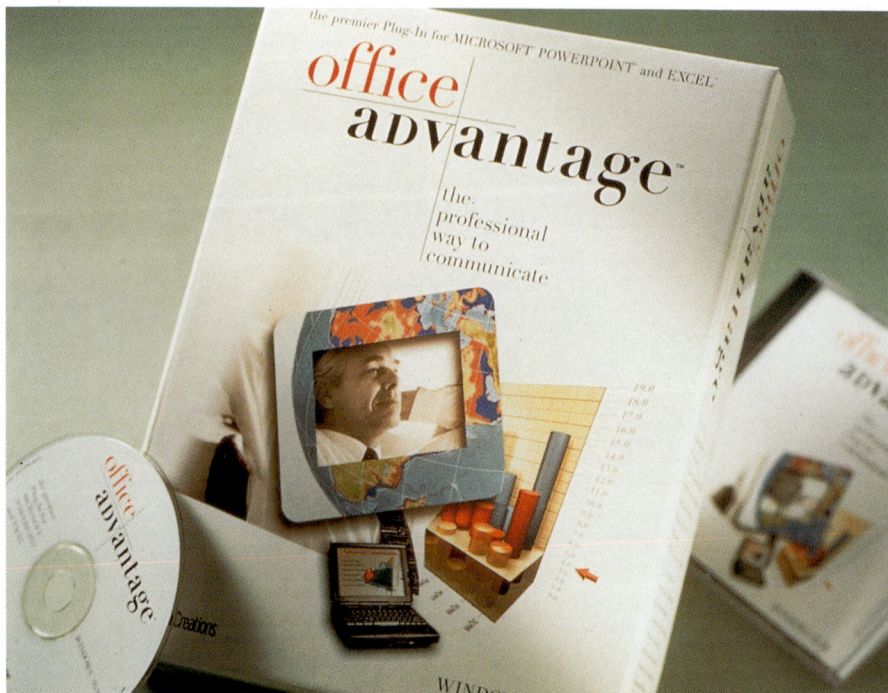

3

1. Logo for collegiate football bowl game
2. Packaging for a line of Italian varietals produced in California, Trinchero Family Estates
3. Software packaging for MetaCreations
4. Promotional merchandise for the SFMOMA MuseumStore
5. Promotional logo for the SFMOMA MuseumStore
6. Shopping bags for the SFMOMA MuseumStore
7. Language software packaging for The Learning Company

4

SAN FRANCISCO MUSEUM OF MODERN ART

5

6

7

1. Identity for design conference
2. Packaging for L'Ecosse Vineyards
3. Identity program for Opera House Theatre, Napa Valley

Morla Design
463 Bryant Street
San Francisco, California 94107
415.543.6548
www.morladesign.com
Creative Director: Jennifer Morla

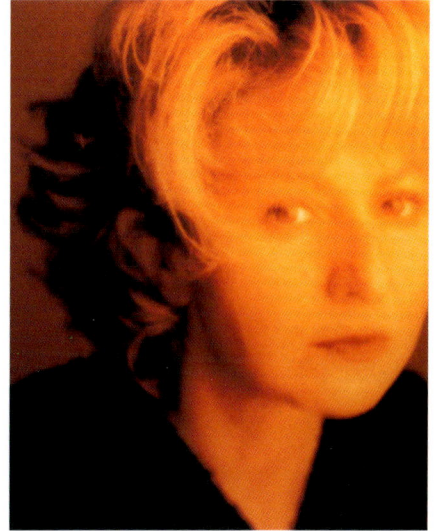

MORLA DESIGN

Morla Design has been instrumental in the image building of some of the country's largest and most visible corporations. Projects include packaging for Apple Computer and the Discovery Channel Store, the total corporate identity program for Wells Fargo Bank, an eighteen year collaboration with Levi Strauss & Co. on all aspects of their identity, including branding, print collateral, store design and interactive displays, numerous books for Harper Collins and Chronicle, broadcast and animation design work for MTV, a collection of Swatch watches, annual reports, as well as identity campaigns for experimental art organizations and museums. In addition, Ms. Morla has had solo exhibitions at the San Francisco Museum of Modern Art and DDD Gallery in Japan.

Details of our work follow.

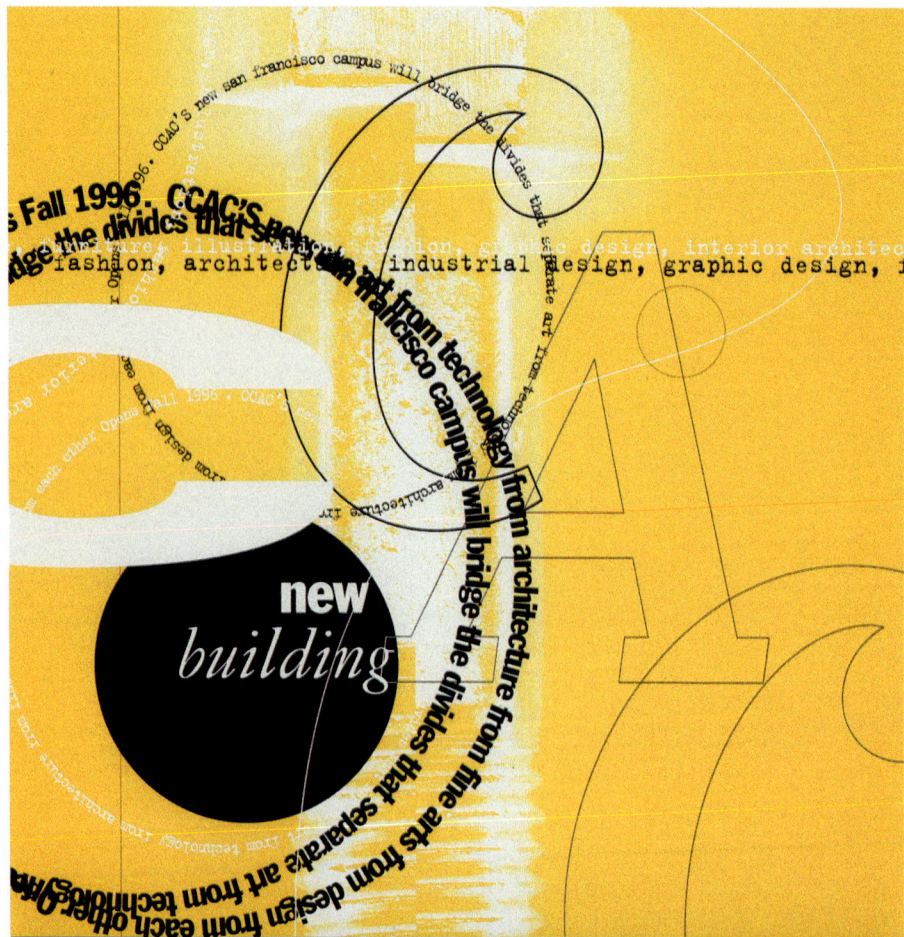

1. CCAC New Building Poster | 1999
   Client: California College of Arts & Crafts

2. www.morladesign.com | 1999
   Produced in collaboration with
   Razorfish, San Francisco

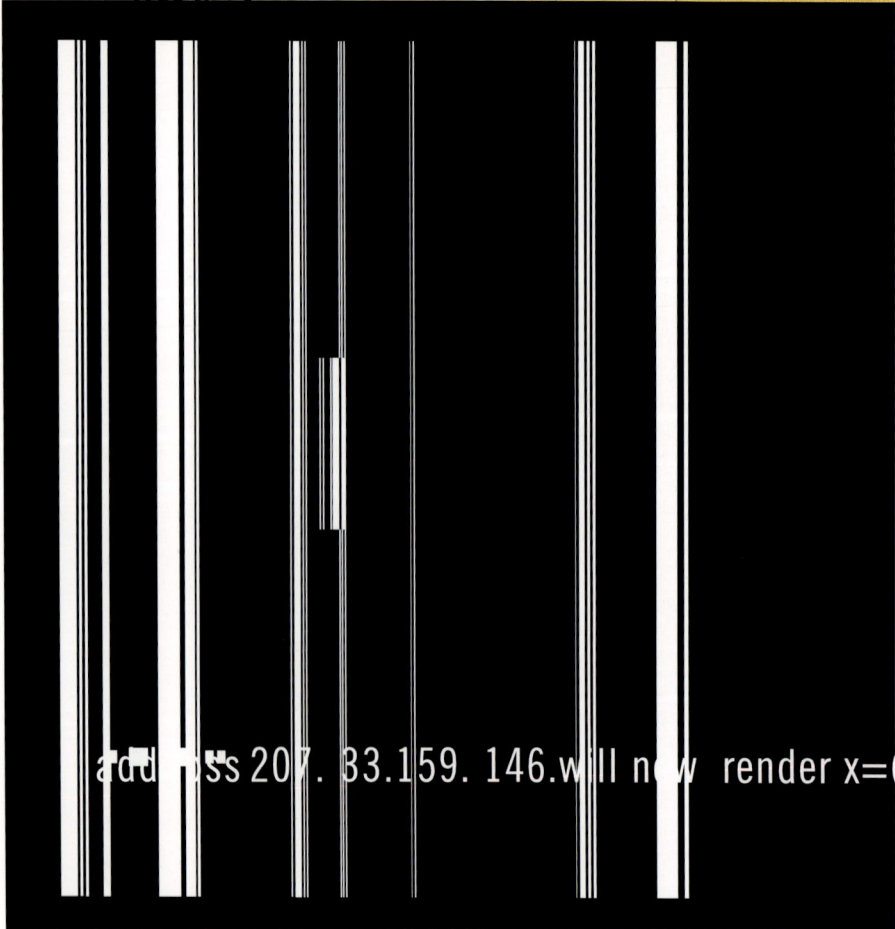

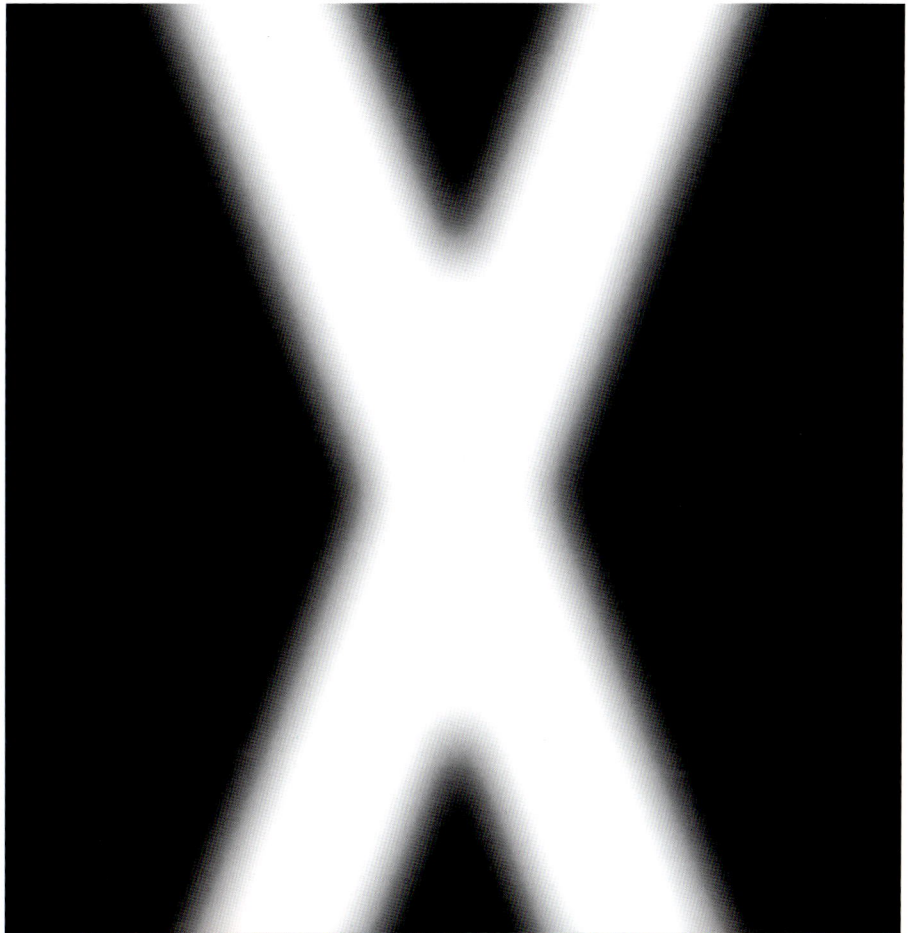

3. Capp Street Project Poster: A Study in Genetics
1995 | Client: Capp Street Project

4. Levi's Poster | 1998
Client: Levi Strauss & Co.
Illustration: Amy Guip

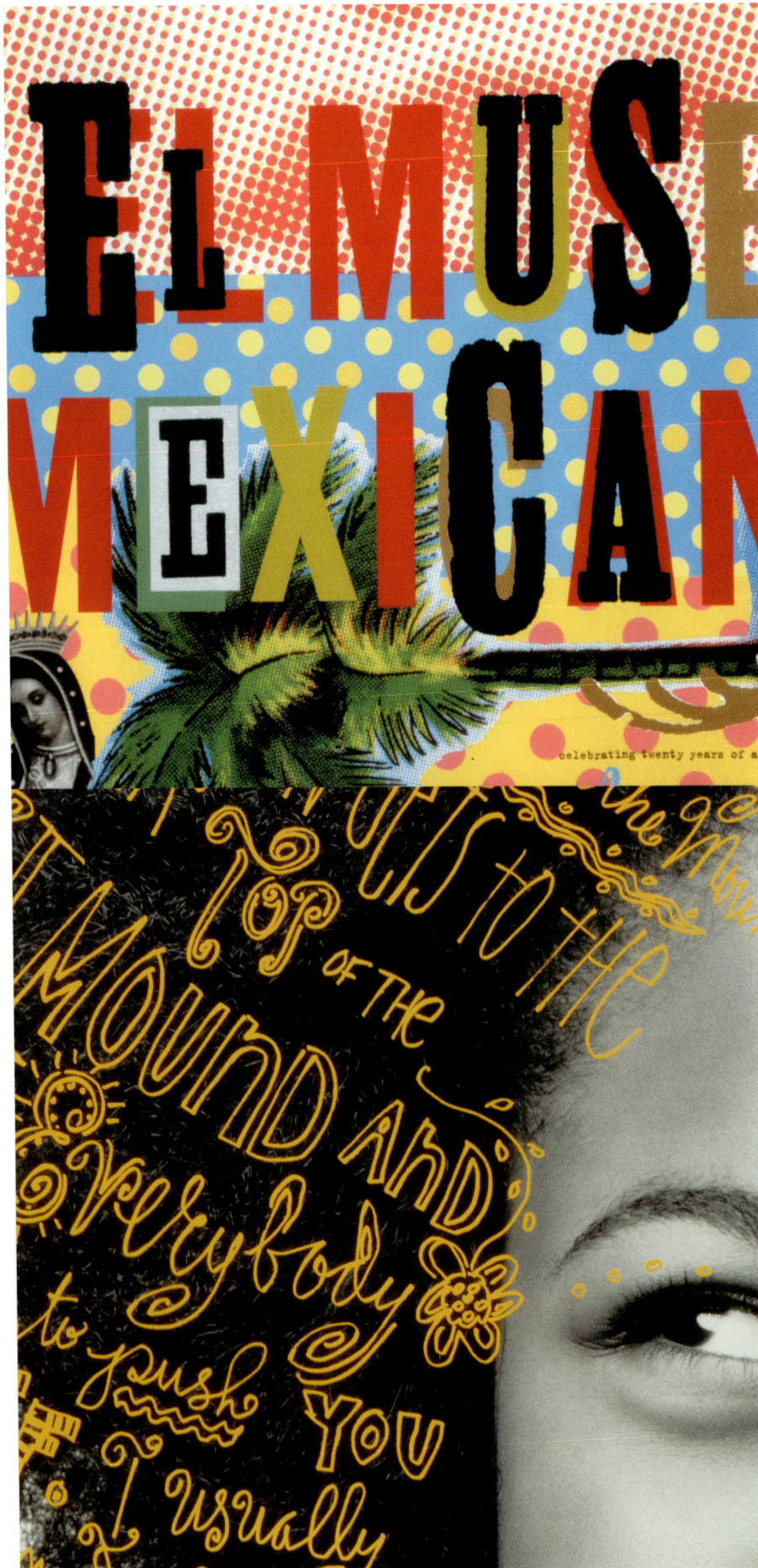

1. Mexican Museum Poster | 1996
   Client: The Mexican Museum

2. Levi's Poster | 1998
   Client: Levi Strauss & Co.
   Photography: Jock McDonald
   Lettering: Morla Design

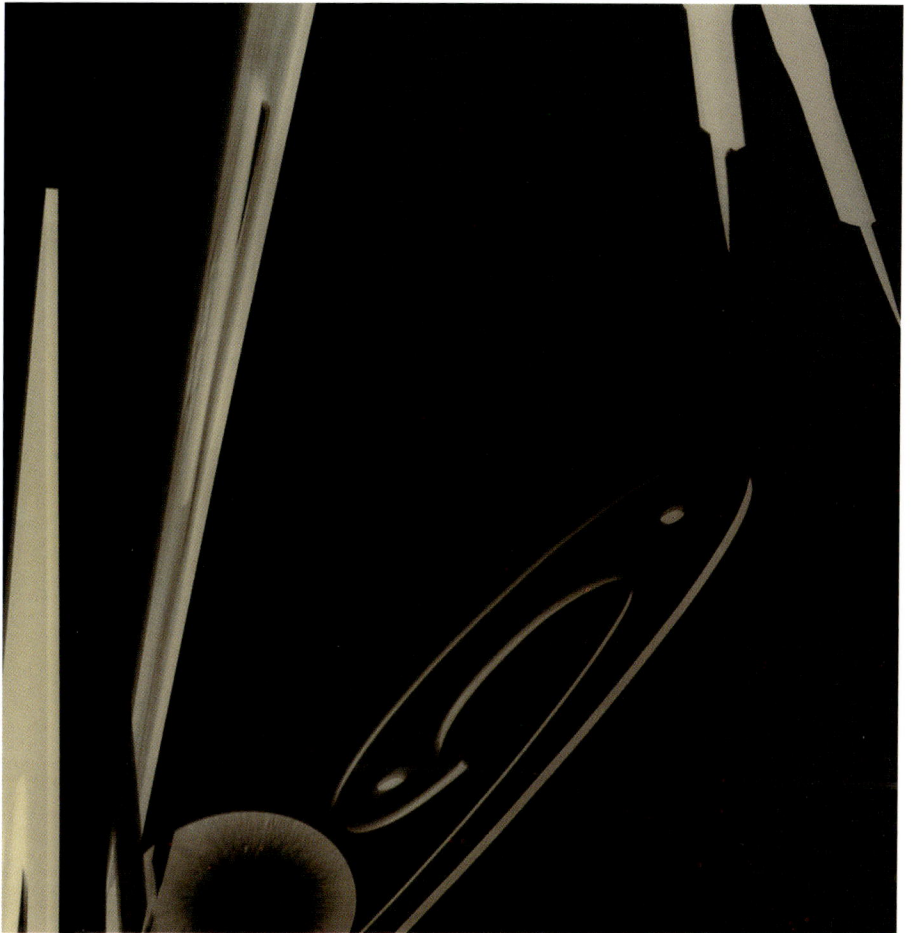

3. San Francisco International Airport
Annual Report | 1993
Client: San Francisco International Airport

4. The Logan Collection | 1999
Client: California College of Arts & Crafts

the shock of the

familia

The objects of ordinary life
as never before, designed t
manipulate taste and desire
is a design explosion under
and it is forcing us to see e
things in entirely new ways

From toothbrushes to Web
a guided tour.

DECEMBER 13, 1998 / SECTION 6

The New York Times Magazine

1. The New York Times Magazine Cover | 1999
Client: The New York Times

2. Apple Computer: QuickTime 2.0 | 1994
Client: Apple Computer

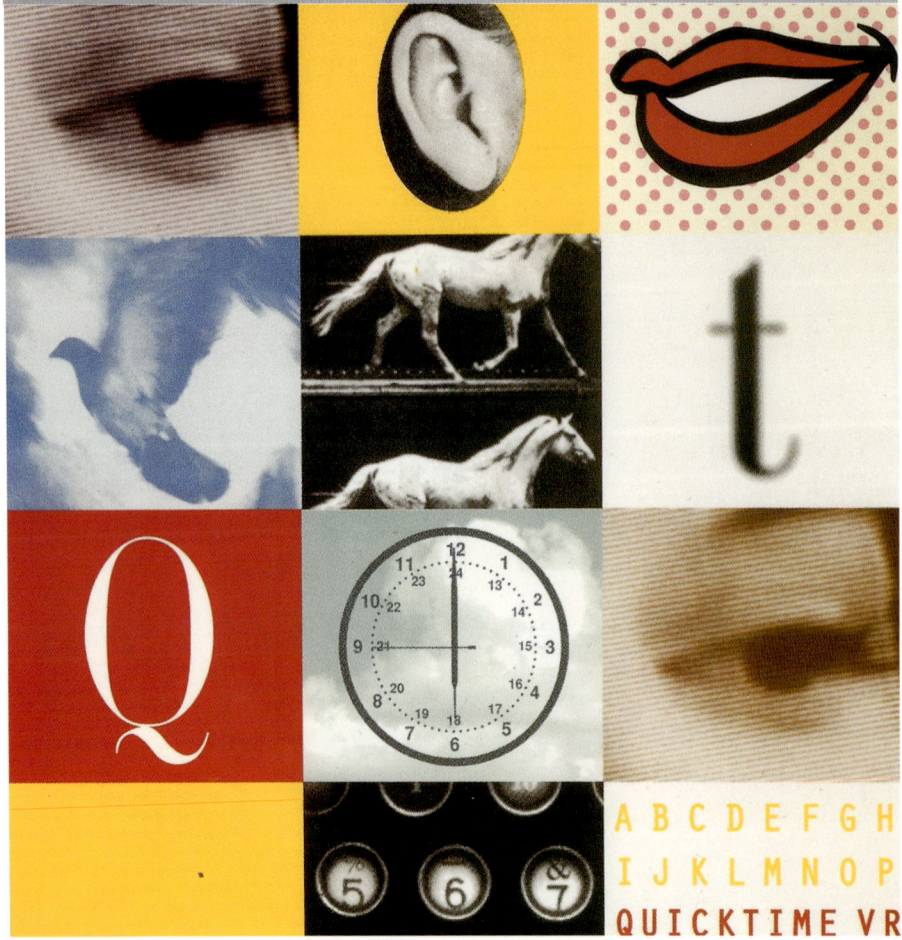

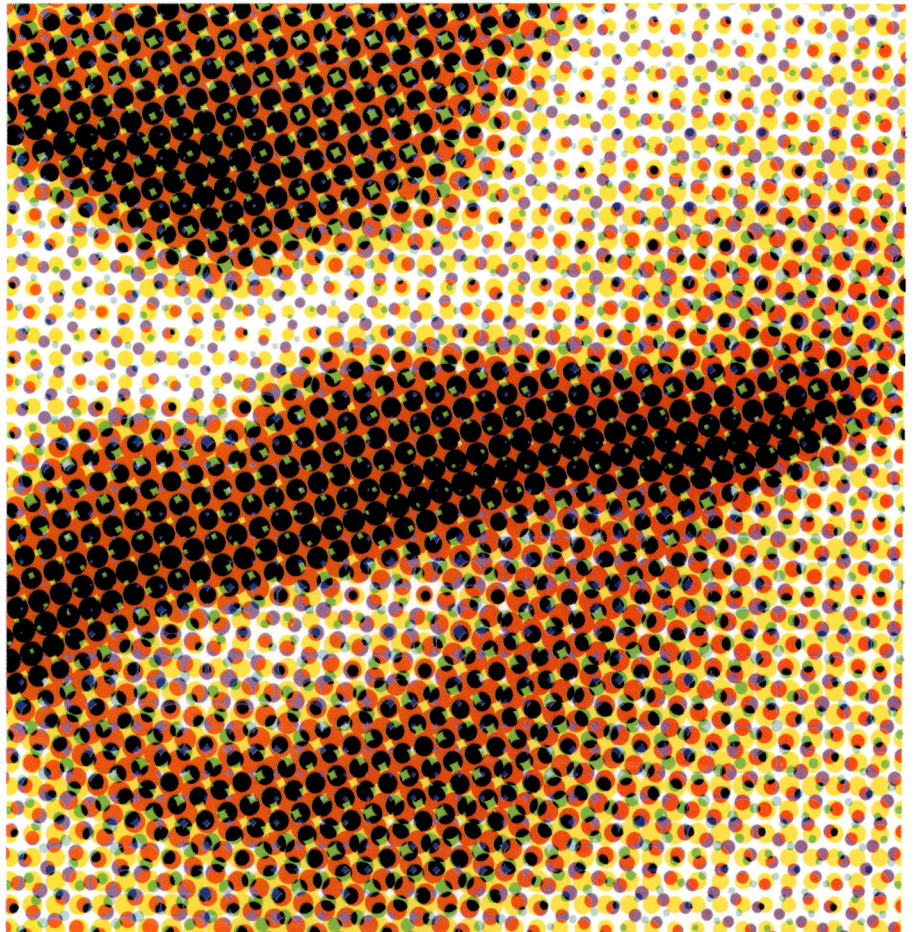

3. Appleton Paper Company Bus Ads | 1996
Client: Appleton Paper Company

4. Hewlett Packard Color Printer Ads | 1999
Client: Goodby, Silverstein & Partners

gloss.com

new langton a

new langton arts

nineteen nineteen ninety one
nineteen ninety one
to nineteen nineteen seventy s
to nineteen ninety seven

1. Gloss.com: Identity | 1999
Client: Gloss.com

2. New Langton Arts Catalog | 1998
Client: New Langton Arts

Miriello Grafico, Inc.
419 West G Street
San Diego, California 92101
619.234.1124
pronto@miriellografico.com
www.miriellografico.com

MIRIELLO GRAFICO, INC.

"I spoke to my son's second grade class recently about what I do for a living. I told them something that says a lot about our office: When you're a child, you are naturally curious. But as people grow older, most get less and less so. Now, if you can keep that gift, other people will hire you to be curious for them. Clients like to work with us because we are curious. We provide them a perspective that they are searching for.

We focus on building left-brain as well as right-brain skills. It's just not enough to design well. You also have to put yourself in the position of the client. There's nothing more important than that—it's where empathy and experience come from. We push ourselves aside so we can be there for the client and push them further than they thought they could go.

I feel we have a very unique environment here. We do our best work with a bit of resistance from each other; we provide an ongoing critique, challenge each other. That lets the best idea win. Sometimes when we're filling out a credits form for an award, it's hard to say who exactly did the work. There can be very key nuggets from many people.

We use good organization to preserve the time we need to think and create, time apart from the paperwork and meetings that can consume a project. The left brain provides the plan so that the right brain has room to be successful. We are also very thorough, a scarce commodity these days. Managing a project all the way to its completion is as important as the initial big idea.

Building a one-to-one relationship through our design is something we're very good at. I look at our business as part craft, maybe because of my training in Italy. There are very few businesses that offer customization anymore—the handcrafted shoes or the personally tailored suit. But we build every project from the ground up. Every design is crafted especially for that specific client. I'm proud of that. Because it's not only about creating a product or design: It's all about creating an experience. It's what the Italians do very well: use theater, fashion, song, architecture, food, and romance to create a unique experience. That's what makes a design magical." —Ron Miriello

1. Eastpak/Coleman brand identity and product graphics
2. Promotional notecard series
3. Qualcomm brochure system
4. Gallery One store identity

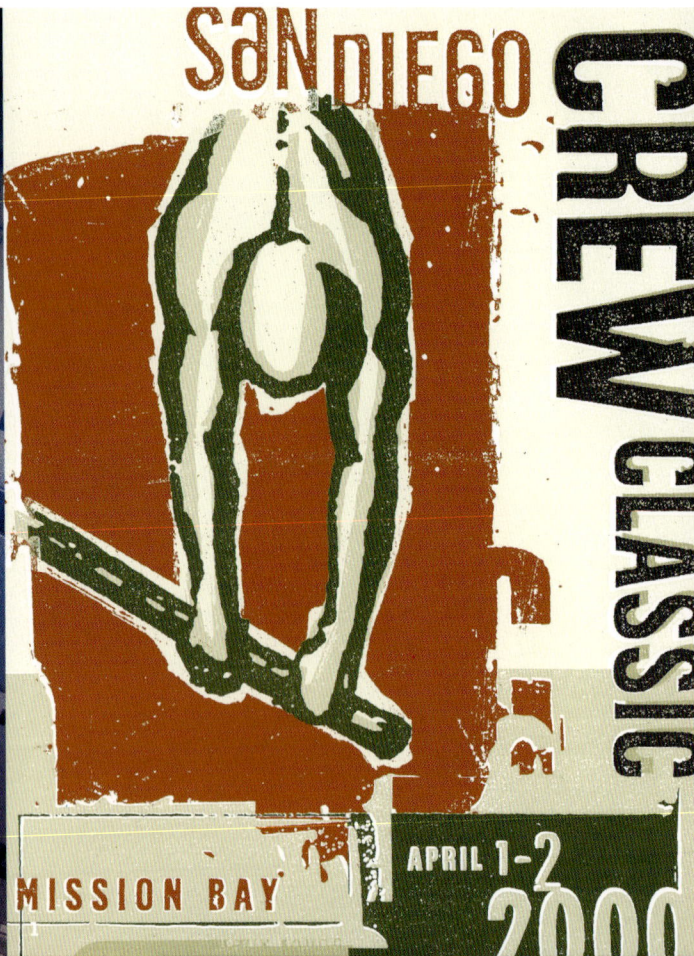

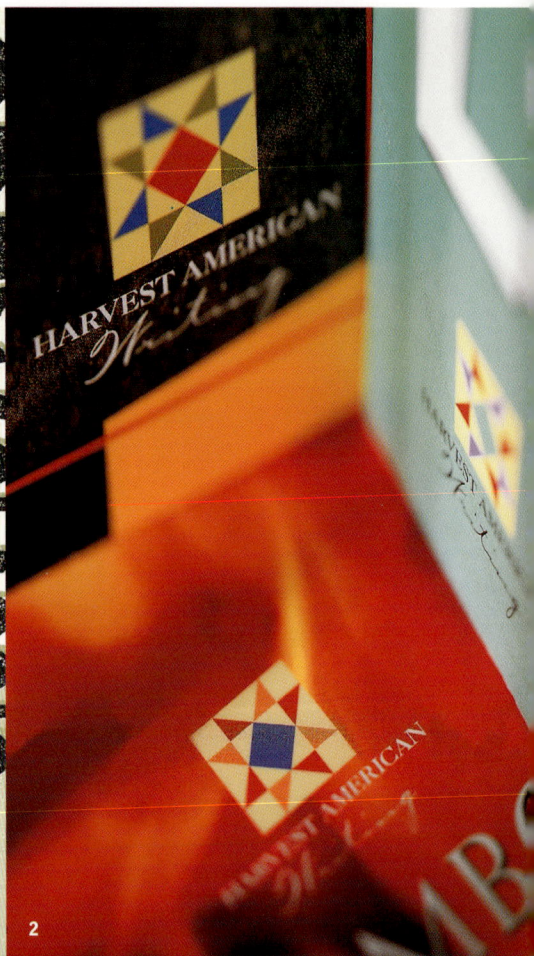

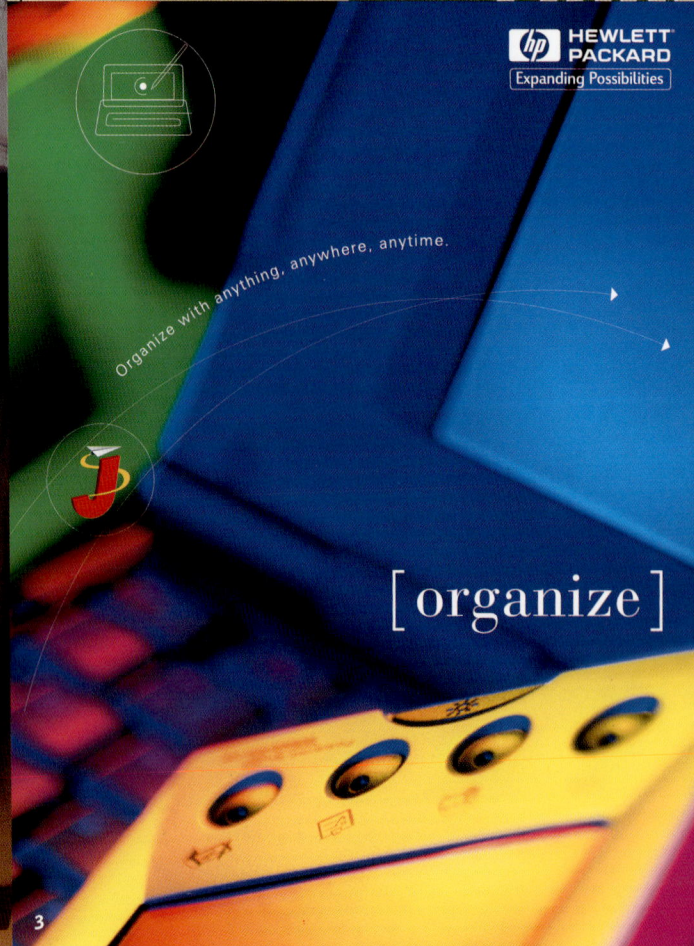

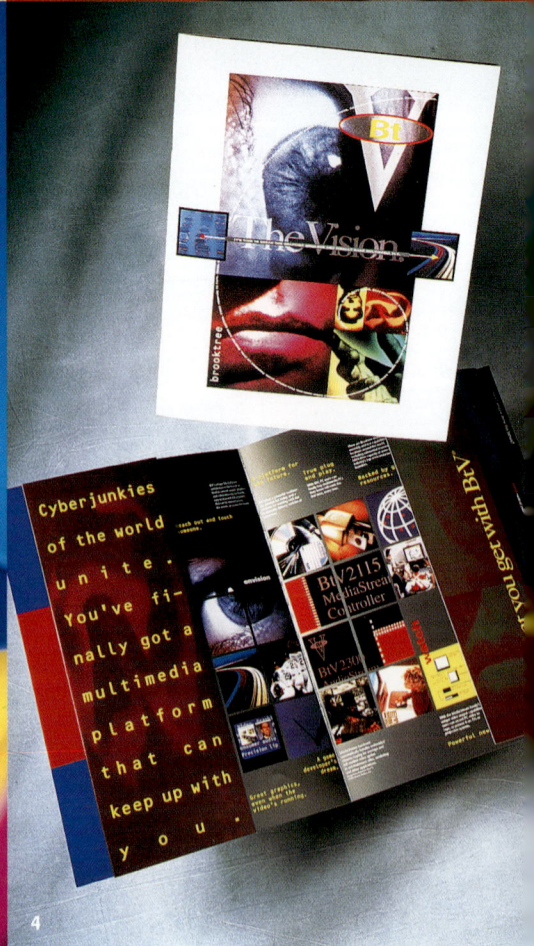

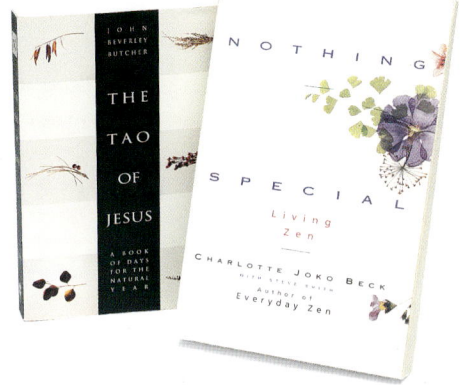

1. Crew Classic event graphic
2. Harvest American Writing imprint identity
3. HP JetSend exhibit graphics
4. Brooktree Semiconductor brochure
5. Harper San Francisco book covers
6. Carrier Johnson Wu Architects brochure
7. Harper San Francisco book series

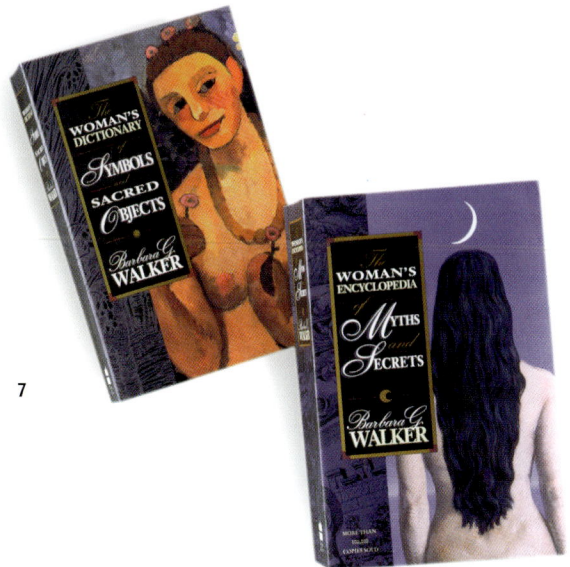

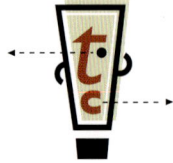

1

2

3

4

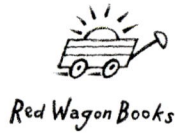

5

6

7

8

9

1. Technically Correct copywriting

2. The Old Globe Theater

3. Arnold Palmer Golf

4. Newport Communications

5. Red Wagon Books

6. Mootown Creamery ice cream shop

7. Newport Coast Oral Facial Institute

8. Ecnorrot Menswear

9. Divan furniture showroom

1. Nancy Lopez Golf brand identity

2. Ashworth Golf product brochure

3. Palmer Golf brand identity

4. Eastpak backpack identity

5. HP PhotoSmart packaging

6. Comdex tradeshow exhibit

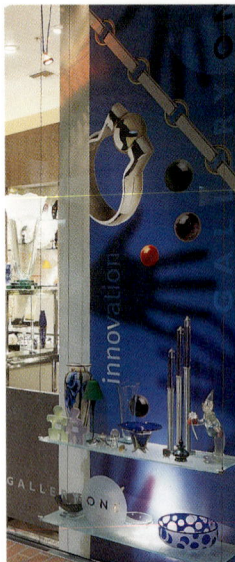

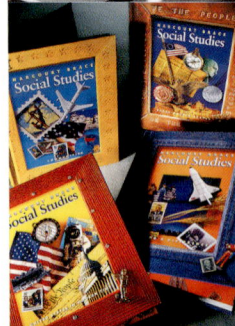

1. Omega Marine/Andromeda yacht brochure

Miriello Grafico, Inc.
419 West G Street
San Diego, California 92101
619.234.1124
pronto@miriellografico.com
www.miriellografico.com

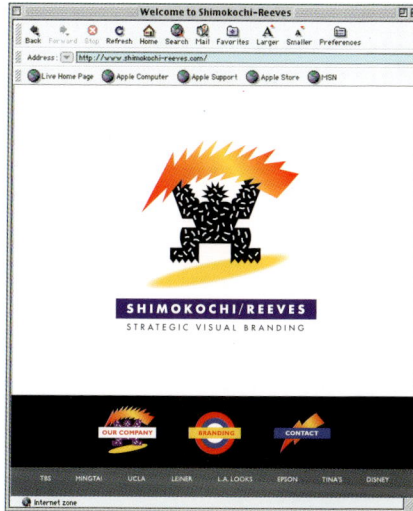

SHIMOKOCHI/REEVES

SHIMOKOCHI/REEVES
P: 323.937.3414
F: 323.937.3417
www.shimokochi-reeves.com

Shimokochi/Reeves has earned a reputation for providing highly marketable solutions with extraordinary results. Their track record includes some of the most recognizable identities of the past three decades.

The firm's strategic capabilities include identity, branding, packaging, print, environmental graphics, new media branding and name development. From years of working side by side with clients across a broad range of industries, Shimokochi/Reeves knows what it takes to create compelling brands that stand out in the global marketplace. Simply stated, the firm calls it - Strategic Visual Branding.

According to Shimokochi, branding has the power to convey any image you wish - it's the visual expression of your brand, the link between you and your target audience. In an ever-competitive environment, brands have only a few seconds to communicate their message. The challenge is to stand out - to create images that are fresh, engaging, and memorable. The company strategically analyzes what works, what doesn't and why. As the brand design experts on your team, Shimokochi/Reeves creates strategic branding solutions that speak to the hearts and minds of consumers - solutions that achieve results!

Mamoru Shimokochi, as Creative Director and Anne Reeves as Director of Marketing, bring thirty and twenty-five years design experience, respectively.

1

2

3

1-2. Zig Ziglar Network - Zinera: Brand identity
& packaging

3. Epson America, Inc.: Packaging system

AFTER THE FALL

1

2

3

1-3. Smucker Quality Beverages, Inc. -
After The Fall: Brand identity & packaging
system, 42 SKU juice line

1-2. Dep Corporation - L.A. Looks: Brand identity
& packaging system - proposed

3-4. Camino Real Foods - Tina's: Brand identity
revitalization & packaging system

1

2

3

4

1. Leiner Health Products: Brand identity & packaging - proposed
2-3. ROR Production Studios: Identity & communication materials

1

2

3

1

5

2

6

3

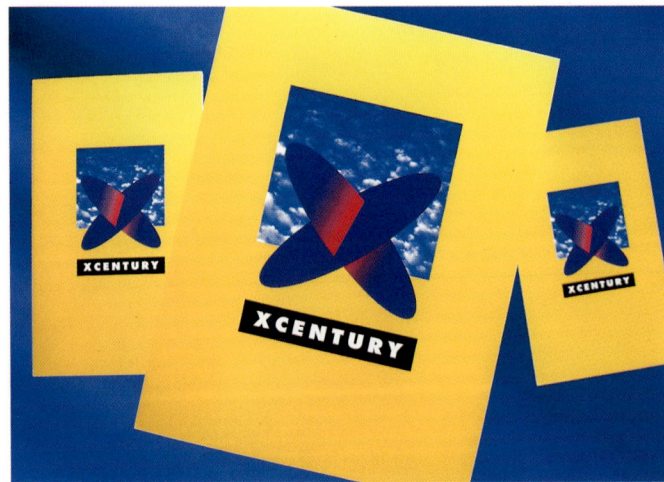

7

4

8

1-2. UCLA - Multimedia Center: Corporate identity program

3-4. Mingtai Insurance Co., Taiwan: Corporate identity program

5-6. Clothes The Deal: Corporate identity

7-8. X-Century Studios, Japan: Identity program

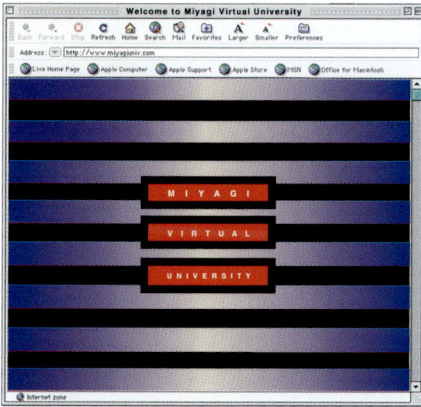

1

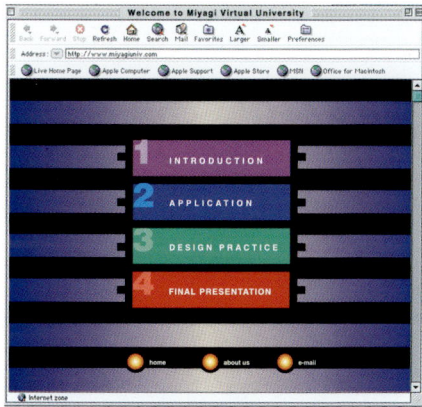

2

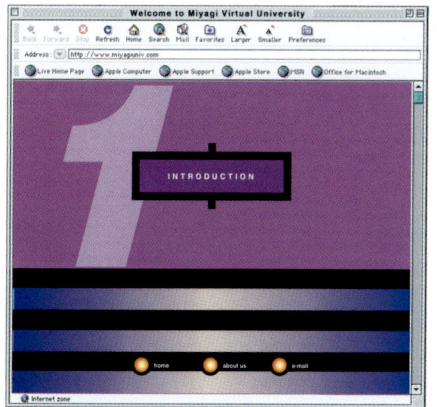

3

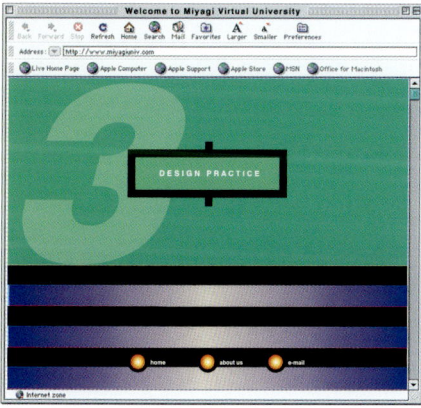

4

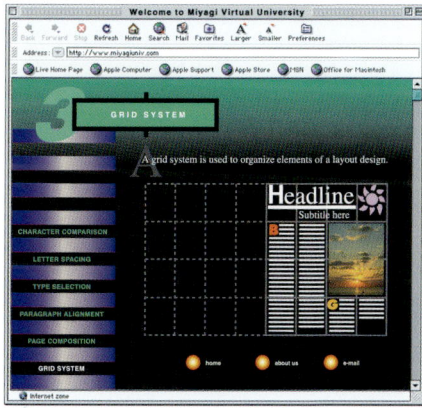

5

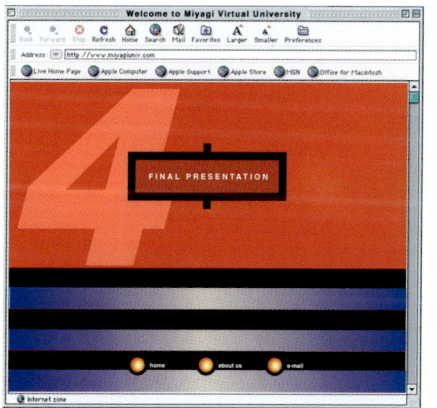

6

1-6. Miyagi Virtual University: Website design

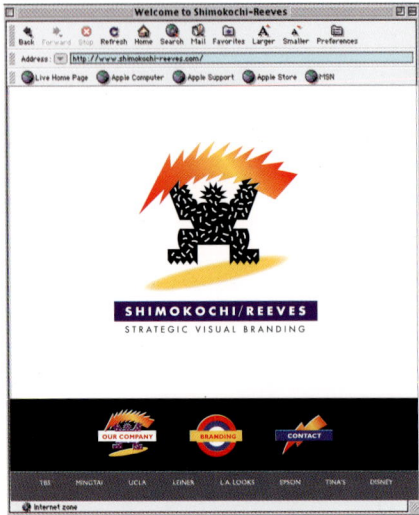

1

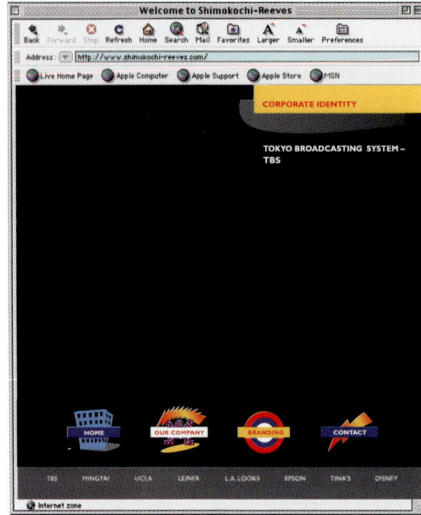

2

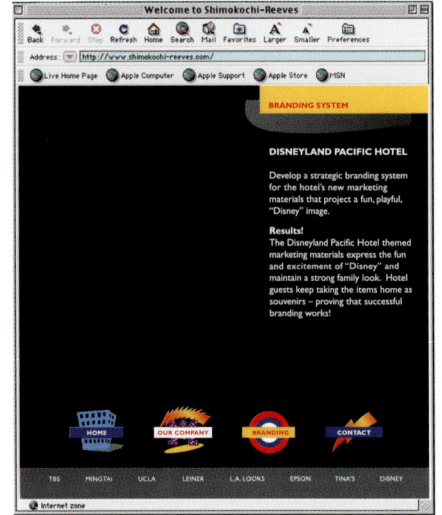

3

1-3. Shimokochi/Reeves: Website design

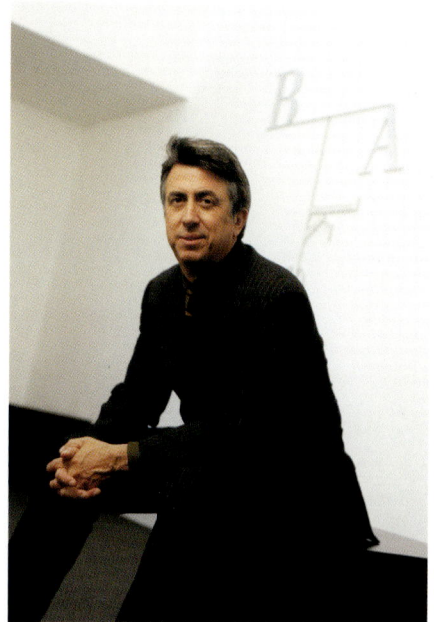

Baker Designed Communications
1411 7th Street
Santa Monica, California 90401
310.393.3993
r.white@bakerla.com
www.bakerla.com

BAKER DESIGNED COMMUNICATIONS

Walk inside Baker Designed Communications, a quiet and spacious building blocks away from the Santa Monica shore, and you'll notice something. Sunlight. Lots of it, flooding in from the skylights overhead. You'll also feel the vibe of creative excellence that epitomizes the company. Founder Gary Baker, a 23 year veteran of the design business, understands the importance of this environment. In his words, "The bottom line is at the end of the day we have to walk out of here and feel extremely proud of what we've done."

Working in teams to deliver the best possible product, the staff at Baker stands ready to take on all comers. Strategic thinkers pair off with creative problem solvers. Project managers support designers. Right-brain befriends left-brain. Carnivores join hands with vegetarians. You get the point. A workplace where creativity and teambuilding are equally important as strategy and service. The result is an impressive client base across Southern California, names like Hilton, Countrywide, K2, Unocal and more. But most importantly, the result is an ability to retain talent. In a marketplace where employers and employees play a constant game of musical chairs, some of Baker's project managers and designers have been on board for nearly a decade.

At Baker, whether you're designing an annual report for QUALCOMM, a web site for Tenet Healthcare, or a holiday card for UCLA, creative energy is a valued resource. In Gary's words, "I try to develop the talent we have and give people a place to grow." That alone makes for an enjoyable workday. The skylights don't hurt either.

1

2

1. Costello Brothers logo
2. Costello Brothers stationery system
3. Costello Brothers capability brochure
4. Hollywood Park annual report
5. Scott Hill packaging
6. USC/Norris annual report

3

4

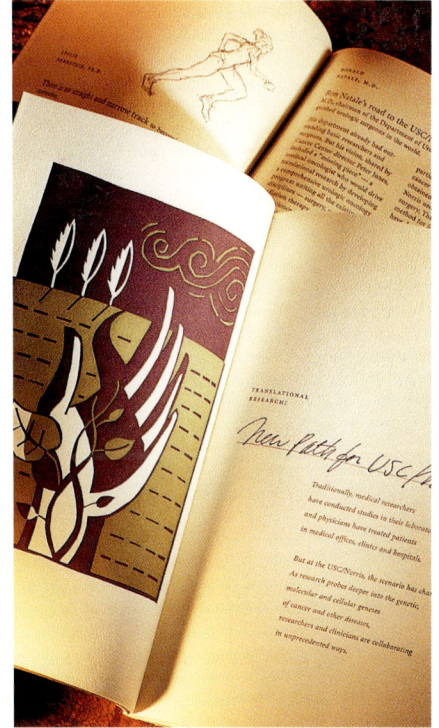

5

6

1

2

3

4

5

guidance

6

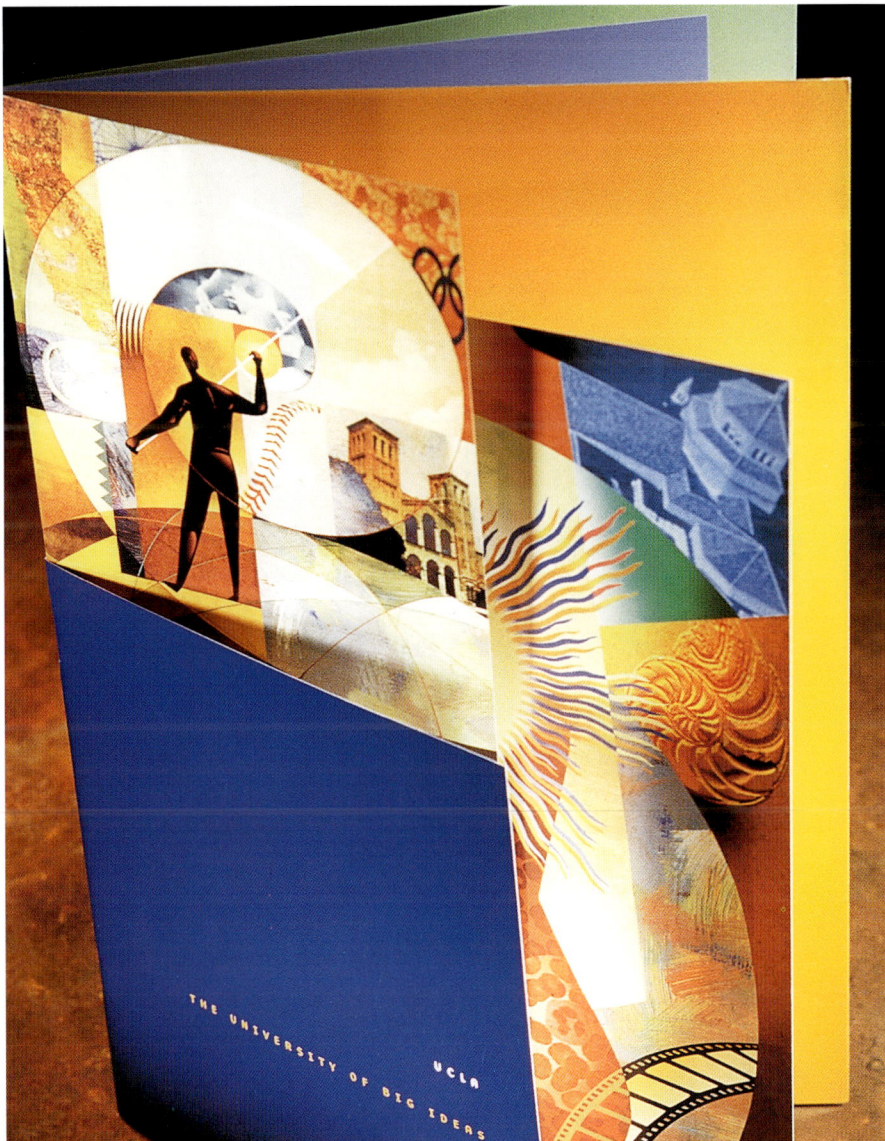

7

1. Music Center capital development campaign
2. Medical Science Systems web site
3. MiniMed annual report
4. Baker Designed Communications calendar
5. Guidance stationery system
6. Guidance logo
7. UCLA image brochure

1

2

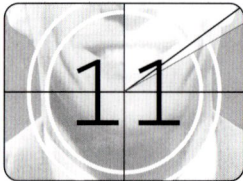

3

4

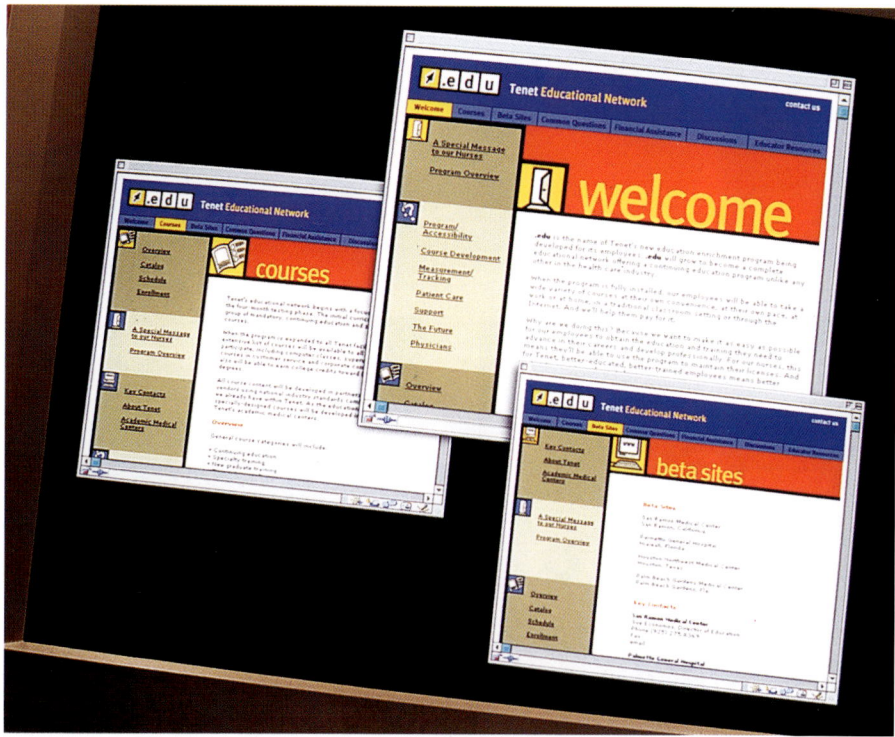

5

6

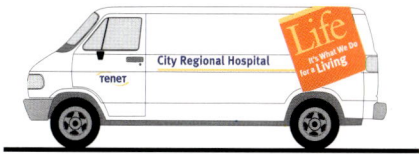  

7

8

1. IndyMac logo
2. IndyMac annual report
3. November Films identity
4. LoanWorks ad campaign

   Tenet Healthcare Branding
5. Tenet edu online
6. Tenet logo
7. Tenet vehicles
8. Tenet banners

215

SafeGuard

1

2

3

1. Safeguard logo
2. Safeguard broker kit
3. STAAR Surgical annual report
4. Unocal annual report

4

Ph.D
1524a Cloverfield Boulevard
Santa Monica, California 90404
310.829.0900 fax 310.829.1859
phd@phd1524a.com

Ph.D

"Ph.D…defined by clean lines, dry wit, deft handling of type and an almost intangible permanence, it is design with a brain, heart and soul. Ph.D design captures the rare moment when form and content merge into a unified whole." *the* David Newman

1

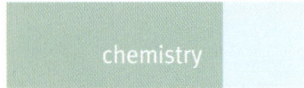

2

3

4

5

6

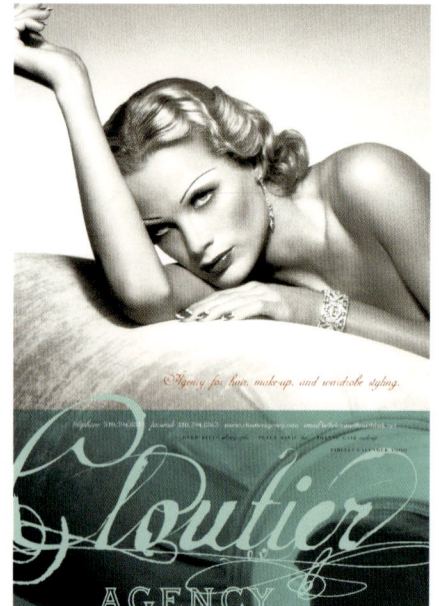

7

1. Rhythm + Hues, commercial production company

2. Commercial production company

3. Restaurant

4. Online dentist referral company

5. Gourmet take-out store

6. Movie advertising

7. Magazine advertisement

1

2

3

4

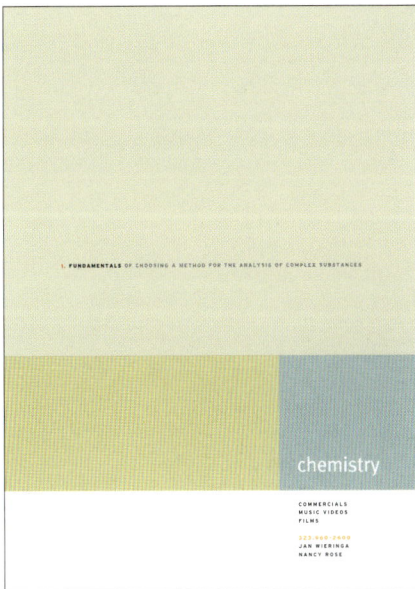

5

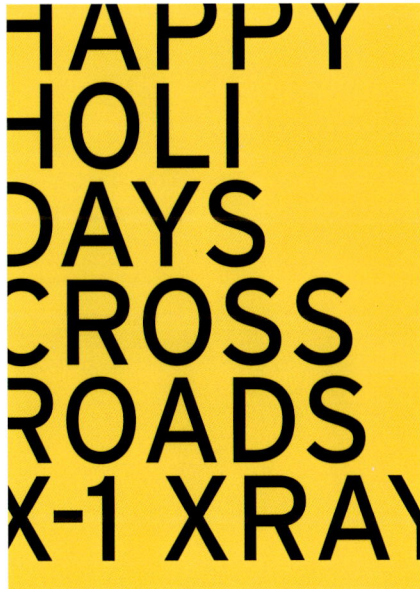

6

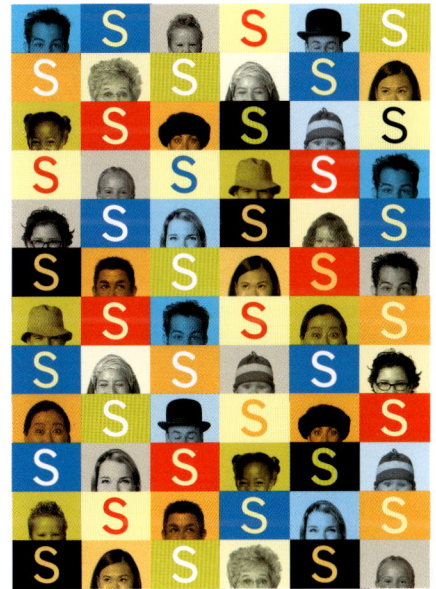

7

1. Editing company
2. Jean Gardner + Associates, photographer reps
3. Restaurant
4. CD Cover
5. Magazine advertisement
6. Crossroads holiday announcement
7. Smileworks announcement advertisement

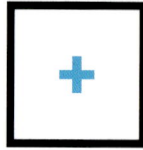

1

2

3

4

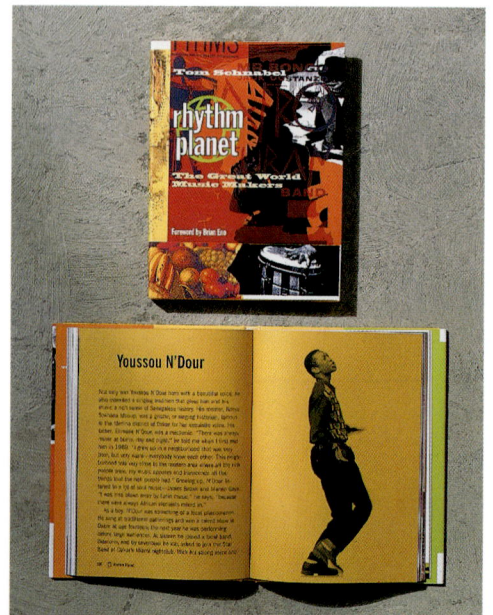

5

6

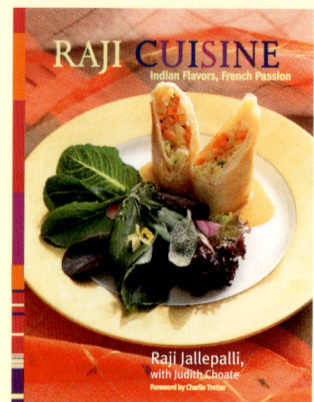

7

1. Foundation Press, printers
2. Food packaging
3. Corporate folder for promotion and marketing company
4. Magazine advertisement
5. Book about world music
6. Astrochef, food packaging system
7. Cookbook
8. Photographer portfolios

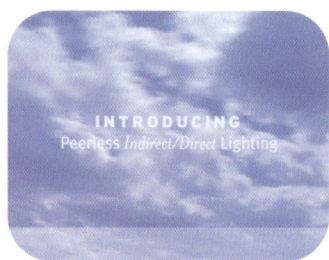

1

2

3

6

7

8

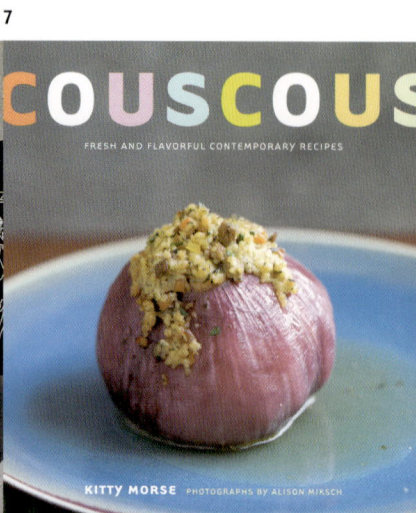

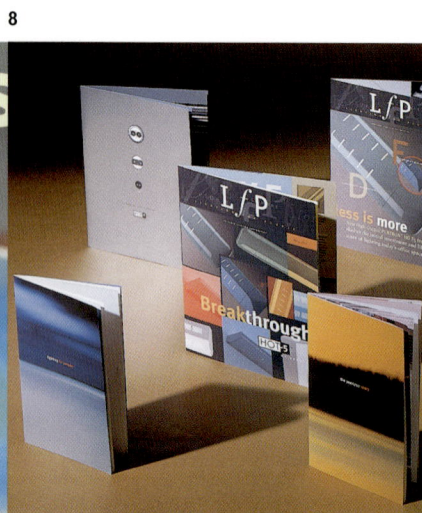

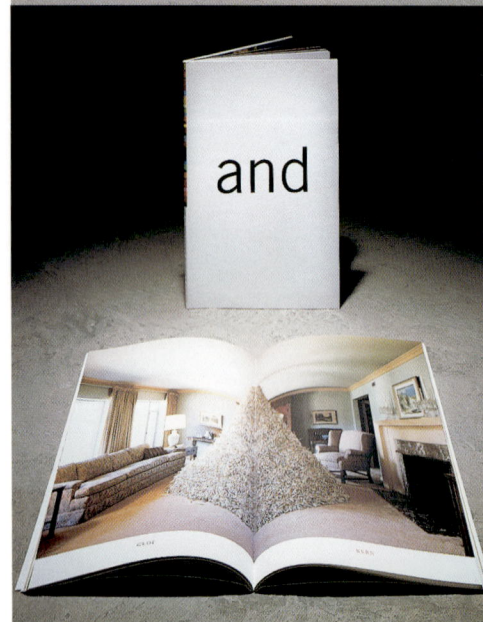

11

12

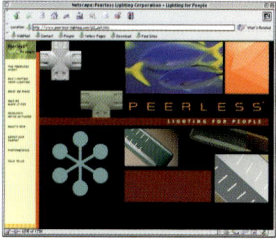

4

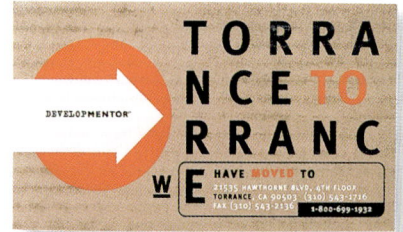

5

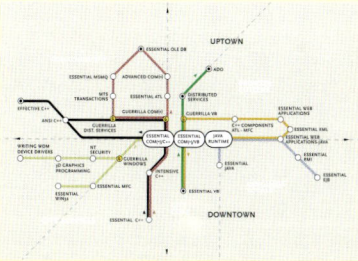

9

10

1-3. Concept video for Peerless Lighting

4. Website for Peerless Lighting

5. Moving announcement

6. Menus and clothing for Border Grill, restaurant

7. Cookbook

8. Brochure series for Peerless Lighting

9. DevelopMentor, course navigation system

10. DevelopMentor website

11. Promotional book for Friend & Johnson, artist reps

12. Business collateral for photographers reps

13. DevelopMentor course schedules

13

1

2

greenroom

3

1-800 PLUMBER

4

inBound

5

1. Identity for local charity 5-10k run
2. Poster series for Santa Monica Aids Project
3. Furniture design company
4. Plumber referral service
5. Custom binder line

4223 Glencoe Ave. Suite A223
Marina del Rey, California 90292
t. 310.305.2565
f. 310.305.2566
www.brightdesign.com

BRIGHT STRATEGIC DESIGN

In the ever-changing global economy, the only constant is change.

And today's marketplace demands rapid innovation and business developing at internet speed. At the core of these new economic forces is the ability to focus on the brand. And how to create and extend a brand. Bright Strategic Design remains at the forefront of this new business model.

Under the direction of its enigmatic leader Keith Bright, their hallmark remains steadfast; business solutions that communicate simply, effectively and with maximum impact.

Developing world brands, and positioning and repositioning companies is Bright's primary challenge.

The traditional concept of spending years to define a company and brand is outdated. New technology advances and thoughtful and impactful design contribute to the new marketing forms.

Concentrating on branding, corporate identity and packaging, Bright Strategic Design leads the way in providing new ideas, concepts, and business solutions in the mass market world.

1.

A fully integrated branding campaign and new business launch for the free internet service provider NetZero, was developed and conceived as a strategic partnership between Bright Strategic Design and Robert Chandler Partners. This creative campaign has at its core the brand message "Defenders of the Free World", and encompassed media including outdoor, print, television and radio.

The NetZero identity and brand were created by Bright to reflect a new attitude about using the internet and home computer. The campaign created by Chandler & Bright showcases a series of images from the 50's as a counter point to the tagline extolling free internet access and e-mail. This paradox heightens the awareness of NetZero's business model and places the company firmly in the mind of the consumer.

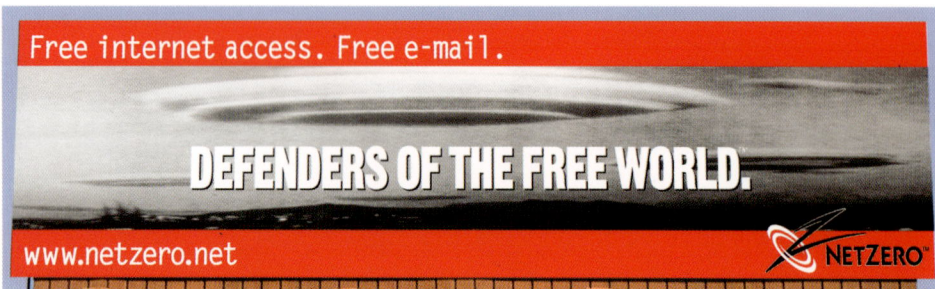

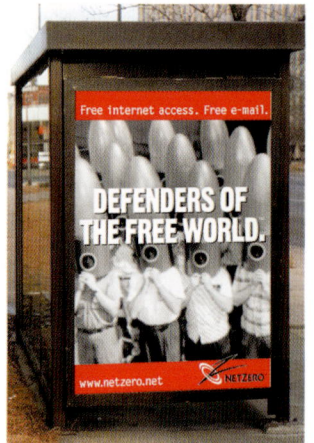

2.

3.

4.

1. Identity for an ISP company.
2. NetZero newspaper ad campaign.
3. NetZero outdoor ad campaign.
4. Bus shelter ad.
5. 1 of 6 10-second TV commercials.
6. NetZero tradead campaign.

6.

She digitizes her grandkids' art, travels by Airstream trailer, and collects ancient Hindu erotica.

Introducing NetZero

In the Free World, we know our audience in unprecedented detail. Because they tell us. Because they stay with us for many hours. And in fact, they show up to stay with them wherever they roam on the Internet. For the entire time they're on. The Free World is the NetZero™ world. A place so attractive that in our first nine months - before any advertising broke - 1.2 million users joined us. What we offer our subscribers is high quality Internet access, including e-mail. For free. In return, when they sign up they give us basic

You might want to know that before you try to sell her something.

undeniable demographic information about themselves. What we offer our advertisers. Is an audience delivered with unprecedented precision. An audience that welcomes your message because we show you how to make it so relevant to their interests. NetZero delivers targeted marketing technology that is destined to utterly revolutionize the way consumers are reached. The ZeroPort™ Ad Missiles™ And Ad Missile Defense Shields™ And more on the way. All things you'll want to know more about before you make your next buy.

Announcing a product so good, no one will pay for it.

Introducing NetZero

Free web access. Free e-mail.

Precision tracking & targeting to millions of subscribers.

No one minds being hit on by someone they want to meet.

Introducing NetZero

Advertise to people who asked you to.

7.

1. Brochure for Samsung Motors
2. 4-page spread from Samsung Car brochure
3. Brochure for Samsung Monitors

1.

2.

3.

1. Brochure for RKS Design
2. Identity for Qorus.com
3. Identity for HealthVest.com
4. Identity for Medschool.com
5. Identity for Nomadix
6. Symbol and consumer ad for Youbet.com

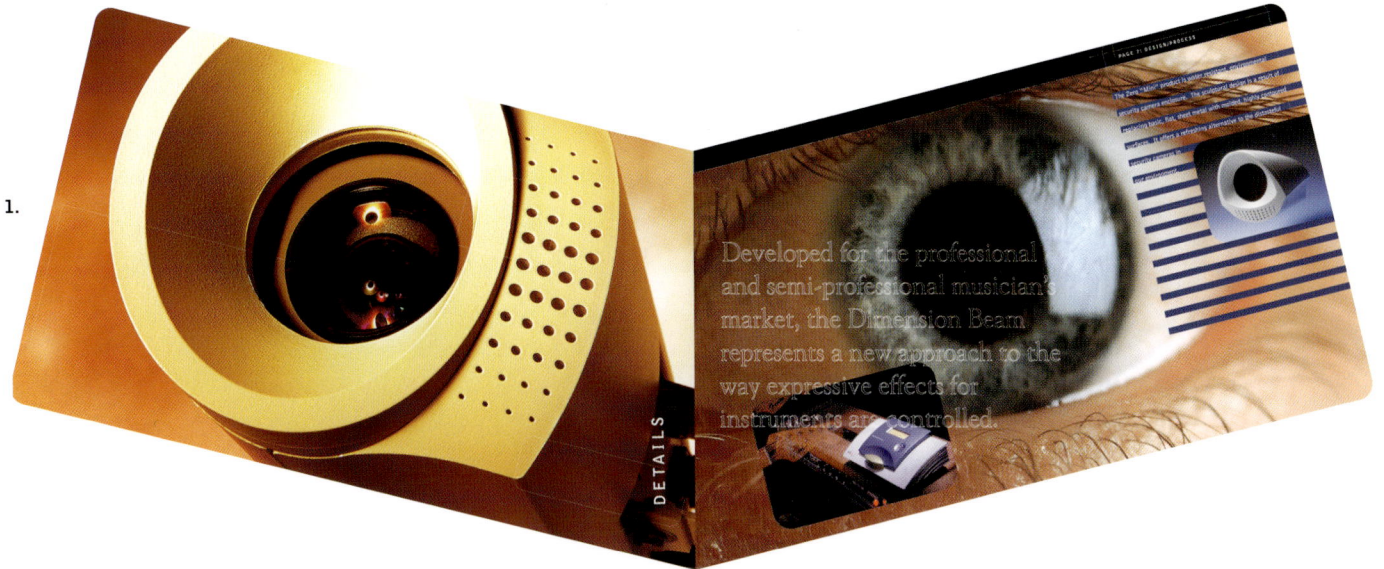

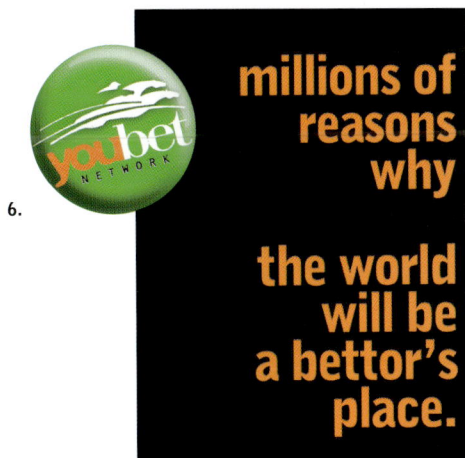

1.

Developed for the professional and semi-professional musician's market, the Dimension Beam represents a new approach to the way expressive effects for instruments are controlled.

DETAILS

2. QORUS.COM

3. HealthVest.com

4. medschool.com

5. NOMADIX

6.

youbet NETWORK

millions of reasons why

the world will be a bettor's place.

millions of stir crazy cyber surfers

millions of occasional players

millions of hat wearing, champagne drinking debutantes

millions of

millions of fanatical pick-six players

millions of wanna be "players"

millions of international playboys

millions of risk taking wall street brokers

millions of martini drinking cigar smoking yuppies.

getting the world on track

1.

2.

3.

4.

5.

6.

7. HIRAM WALKER

1. Packaging for Beverly Hills Farmers Market
2. New bottle design for Virgin Cola
3. Virgin Cola softdrink packaging
4. Identity for Los Angeles 2012 Olympic bid
5. Proposed identity for AT&T
6. Identity for South Park Stadium Group

7. Identity for Hiram Walker
8. Packaging for Hiram Walker Sourballs
9. Packaging system for Hiram Walker Cordials

8.

9.

1.

1. Identity for Nutro Products
2. Packaging for Nutro Dog Food
3. Identity for Hal's Bar & Grill
4. Identity for Shipper.com
5. Logo for Beverly Hills Farmers Market
6. Packaging System for Kirin Beer

2.

3.

4.

5.

6.

Yashi Okita Design
2325 Third Street, Suite 220
San Francisco, California 94107
Tel. 415.255.6100
Fax: 415.255.6300
yashi@okitadesign.com
www.okitadesign.com

YASHI OKITA DESIGN

After arriving in the states in 1968, Yashi Okita spent 15 years working at advertising agencies as an art director and creative director. Not content with overseeing other designers develop his concepts, Yashi felt he could do more as a designer. In 1982, Yashi opened Yashi Okita Design.

For Yashi being a designer isn't just a job its a way of life. You see everything as a project. You're always thinking how do I improve that, or that's a good idea for this project. A true designer lives and breathes design at every moment.

"When you put all your heart and mind into a design, you can never go wrong." This is the belief behind YOD. This philosophy is carried throughout all the projects from small niche market packaging to high end corporate brochures.

Introducing Trixels Media...
The internet, and especially e-commerce has provided new opportunities for design. Wanting to expand his business into this new arena, in May of 1999 Yashi Okita Design formed Trixels Media with Central Graphics Lab of Phoenix. Trixels Media a new kind of web design company, combines the experience of Yashi Okita Design with the cutting edge technology of Central Graphics Lab to create innovative and productive interactive publications.

For over 25 years Yashi has dedicated his life to improving the quality of design. He has a portfolio full of award winning designs to show for his endeavors. Asked when will he retire from the business, Yashi is quick to reply with never. There's just too much to do.

KUNGKUNGAN
BAY RESORT

1

KUNGKUNGAN
BAY RESORT

2

KUNGKUNGAN
BAY RESORT

Fine Diving in the Lembeh Strait

At the Crossroads of the Pacific

ACCOMODATIONS

DIVER S DREAM

LOCAL MYSTIQUE

1. Kungkungan Bay Resort, Indonesia
Tour Guide Brochure
2. Kungkungan Bay Resort Logo

1. Echelon Corporation Corporate Brochure
2. Fujitsu PCMCIA Card Packaging

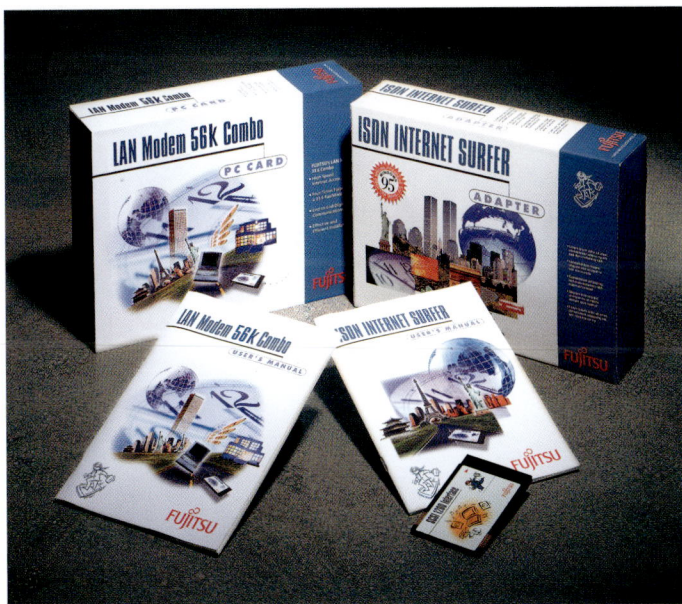

1

2

1. Traditional Medicinals Herbal Tea
   Packaging Series (40 boxes total, 7 shown)
2. Gric Communications Data Sheets

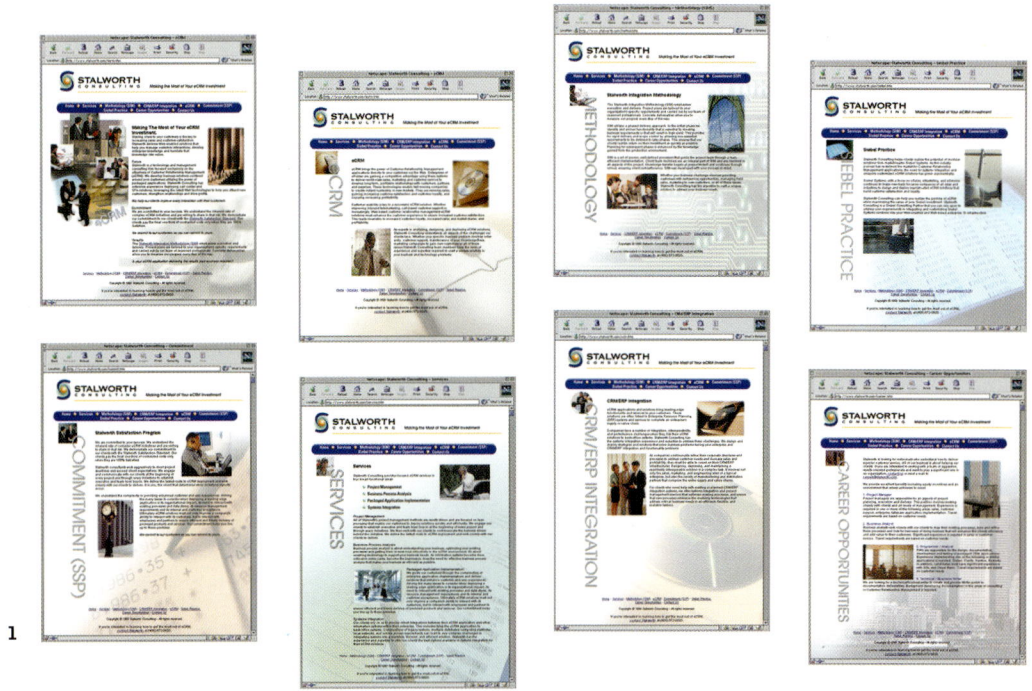

1. Stalworth Consulting Website
2. Stalworth Corporate Brochure
3. Stalworth Logo
4. Stalworth Business System

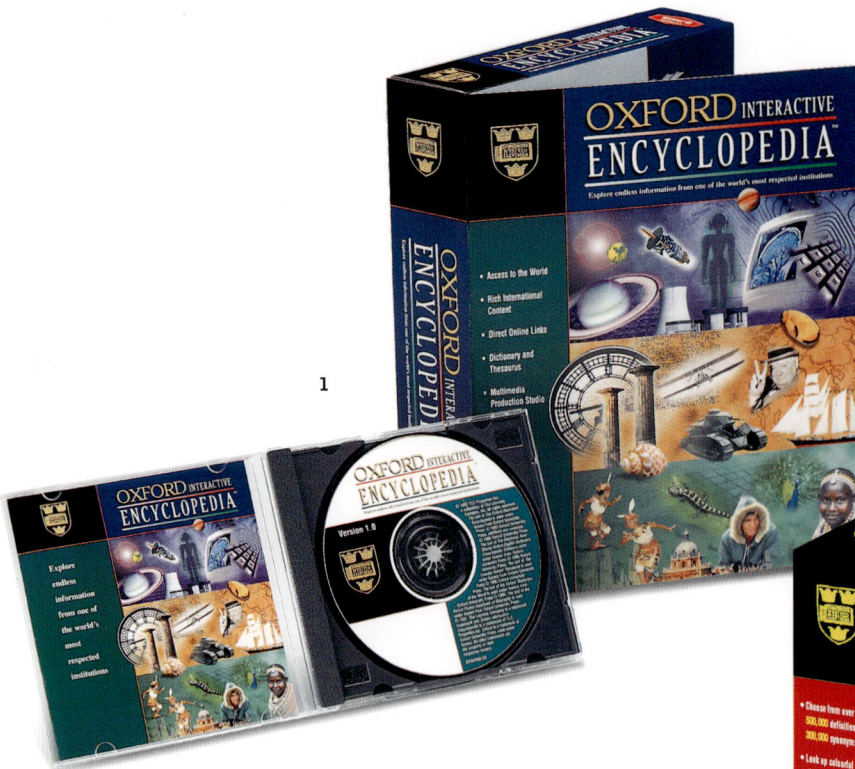

1. The Learning Company
Oxford Interactive Encyclopedia
CD-ROM Packaging

2. Oxford Talking Dictionary
CD-ROM Packaging

1. Amkor Corporate Capability Brochure

2. Hambrecht Quist
IPO Emerging Funds Brochure

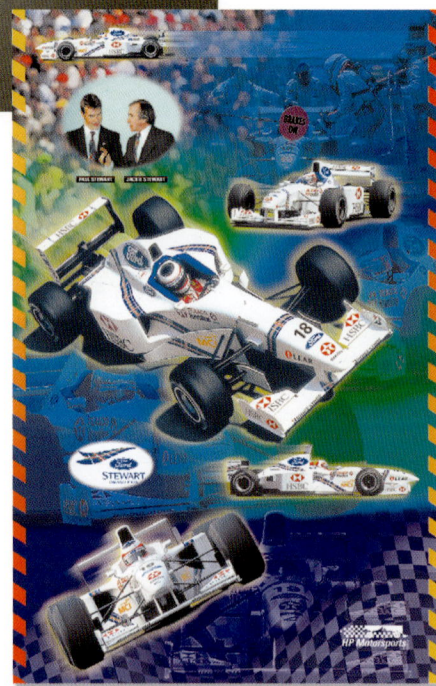

1. Hewlett-Packard, Service and Support
Network Lifecycle Brochure

2. Team Rahal and Team Stewart
Racing Promotional Kit

Sackett Design Associates
2103 Scott Street
San Francisco, CA 94115-2120
Voice: 415.929.4800
Fax: 415.929.4819
www.sackettdesign.com
E-mail: info@sackettdesign.com

SACKETT DESIGN ASSOCIATES

Founded in 1988, Sackett Design Associates has become a highly regarded, award-winning design, product development, branding, and marketing communications company. Headquartered in San Francisco, Sackett Design has a staff of 11 print, retail and multimedia designers, directors, and account management personnel. The firm occupies two buildings in the Pacific Heights neighborhood; which house the company's principle operations, as well as its subsidiaries: Circa Props, antique prop rentals (with its thousands of antique toys, game boards, dolls, packaging, and advertising items); Republic of Sound, the firm's recording label; and Stage 24 Productions, its event production division.

Mark Sackett, principal owner and creative director, and his staff have won over 750 industry awards in national and international design competitions. Their work has been published in numerous design annuals, books, and competitions including The AIGA Communications Graphics Show, Communication Arts, Graphis, American Corporate Identity, California Graphic Design, San Francisco Design, How Magazine, Step-by-Step Graphics, and Print among many others. Additionally, their work is included in the permanent collection of the Library of Congress.

Sackett Design Associates selects assignments where they can collaborate with their clients in the creation of strategic dynamic solutions and integrated brand development. In addition, they have designed and implemented a corporate creativity training program entitled Brainfood,™ for corporations with in-house marketing and creative departments. Brainfood focuses primarily on team building, trends analysis, cognitive skills development, research techniques, and motivational programs, designed to improve individual and team productivity as well as their creative results.

1

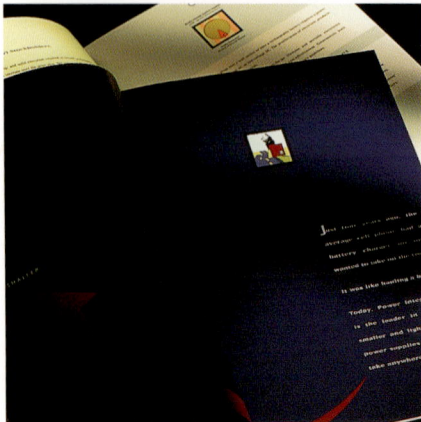

2

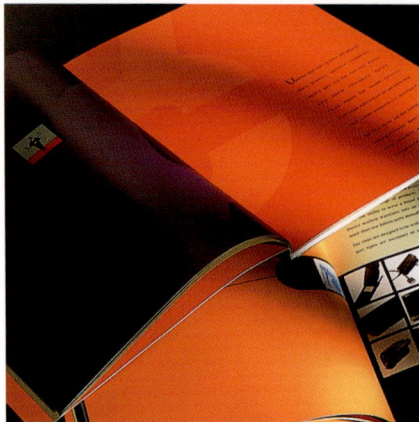

3

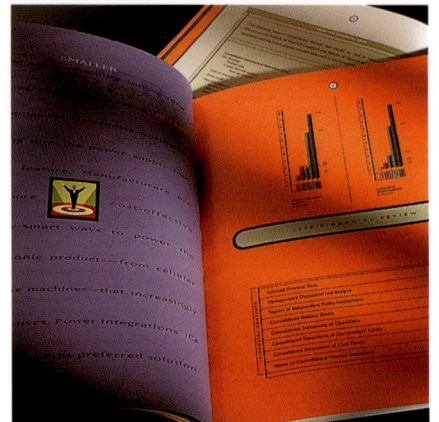

4

1. Annual report for Power Integrations, a leading computer chip manufacturer. (Interior Spreads **2-4**)

5. Debut CD packaging for Jeric.

6. Brochure, promotional launch materials, toy, and puzzle for Charles Schwab & Co., Inc. Institutional Select Funds.

7. Retail identity and signage for Nightshade Restaurant. (Business Cards and Menu Design **8**)

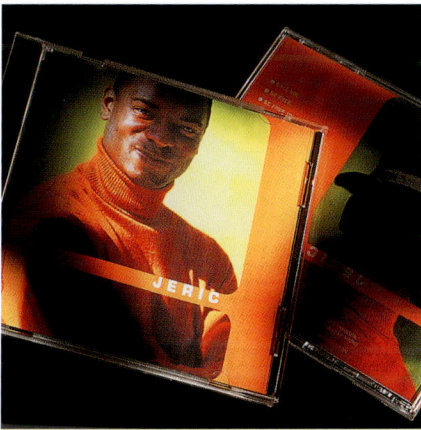

5

6

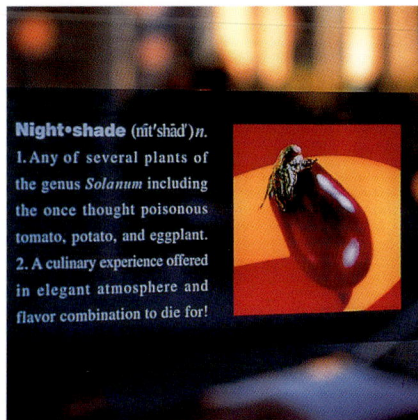

7

8

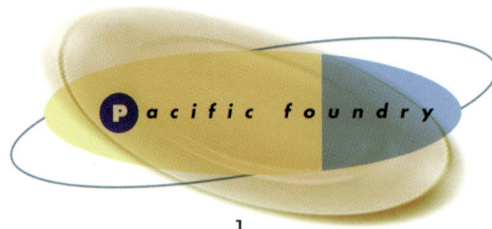

1

2

1. Logo for Pacific Foundry.
2. CD packaging for Grant Taylor.
3. Dinnerware designed for Pacific Foundry.
4. Brochure for the San Francisco Airport Museums, featuring aviation collections displayed at the San Francisco International Airport. (Subsequent Spreads **5-6**)

4

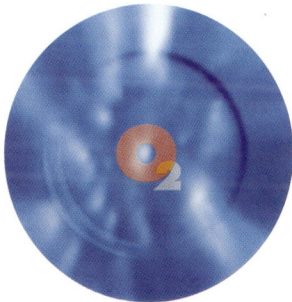

3

5

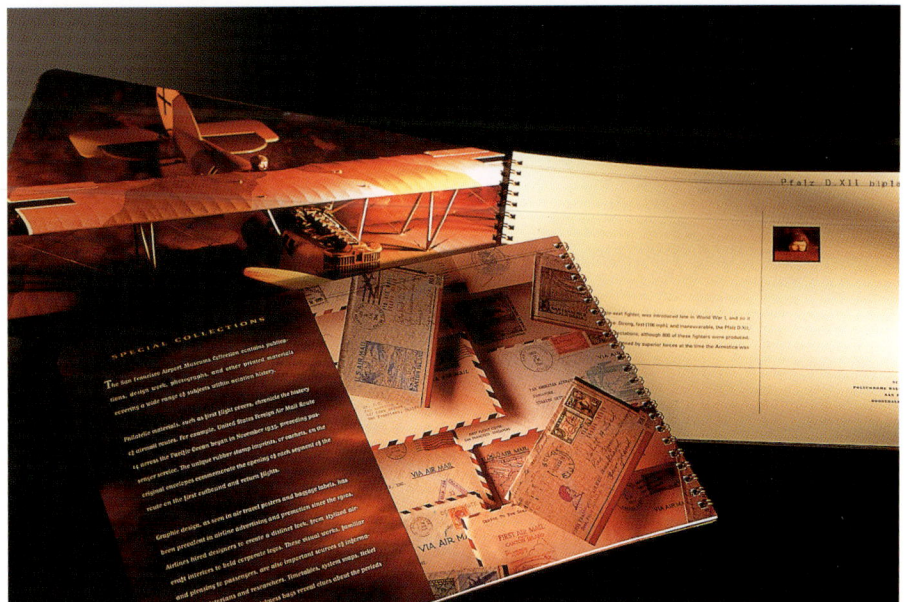

6

245

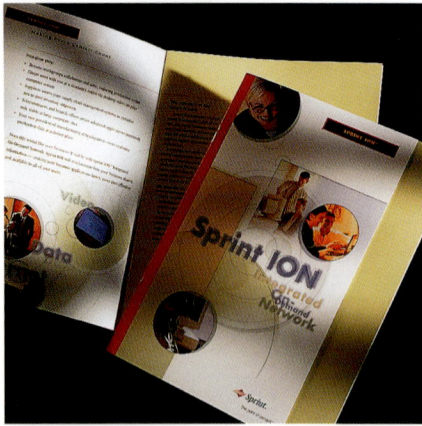

1

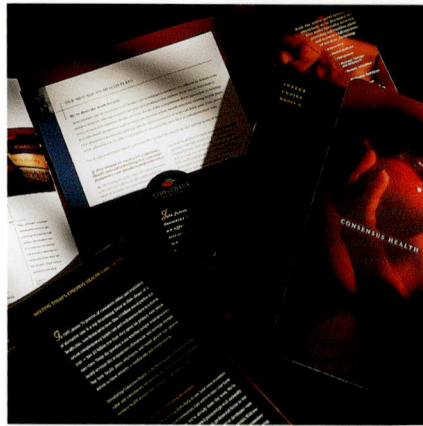

2

3

4

1. Brochure for Sprint ION product launch.

2. Capabilities brochure for Consensus Health, the first alternative health care network in the nation.

3. Pro bono direct mail event materials for the Business Arts Council, Cyril Awards.

4. Brand and corporate identity for Communities.com.

1

2

3

4

5

6

7

8

9

1. Corporate identity for SSA Capital Leasing Corporation.

2. Logo for Biff Henderson of the Late Show with David Letterman.

3. Corporate identity for Azzolino Chiropractic Neurology Group.

4. Personal logo of singer, songwriter Michelle Shocked.

5. Pro bono logo for Fire Fighters in the Schools.

6. Restaurant identity for Nightshade.

7. Corporate identity for Resource and Design interior design consultancy.

8. Corporate identity for Power Integrations.

9. Corporate identity for MindYourBiz.com.

1. Media kit for Spark Online, a company specializing in on-line media buying and negotiating software. (Capabilities Brochure and Brand Identity for Media Mpact **2-4**)

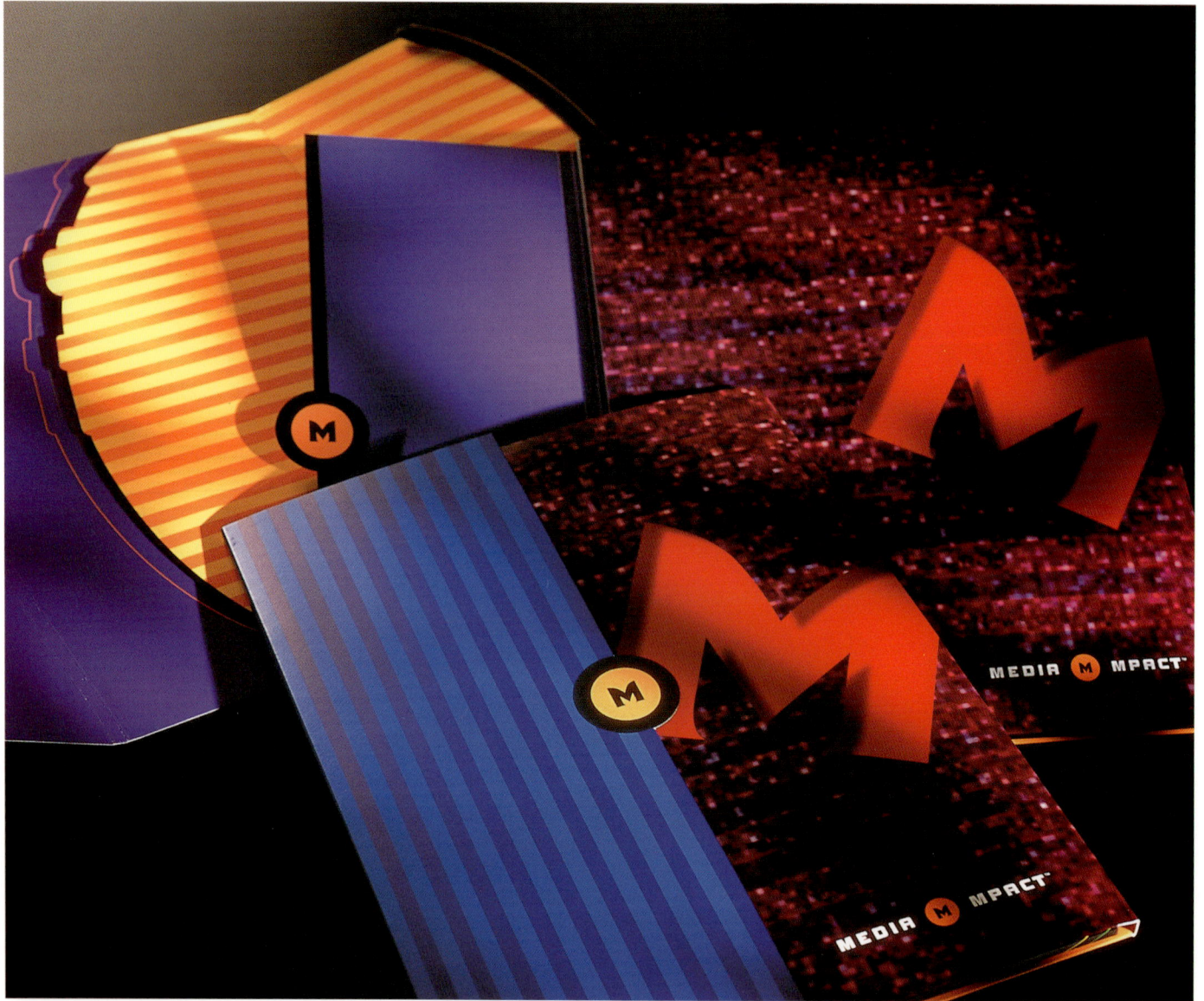

1

2

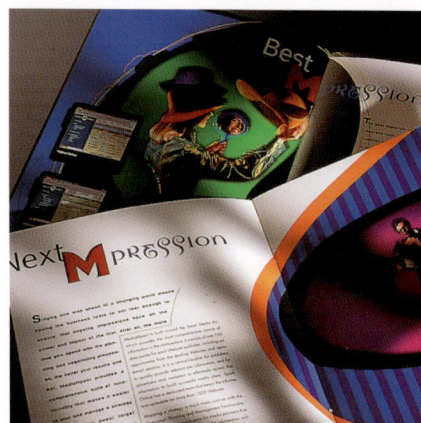

3

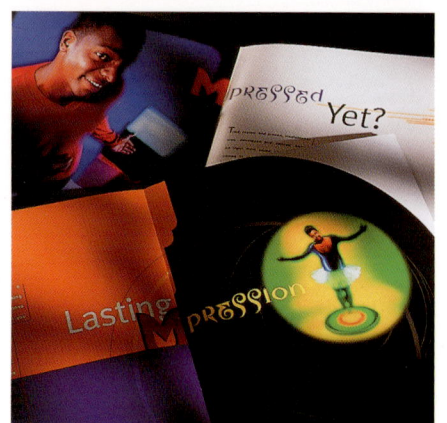

4

CAHAN & ASSOCIATES

Bill Cahan once remarked that his role in the agency was to "create tension." As founder and creative director of Cahan & Associates, a San Francisco integrated communications design agency, he leads, and often pushes, both his team of designers and his clients to a higher plateau of conceptual creativity and breakthrough design solutions.

Founded in 1984, Cahan & Associates' portfolio consists of identity, collateral, annual reports, brochures, advertising, packaging, web sites, and more—each project reflecting the opportunity to create, strengthen, or reinforce a client's brand image.

The diversity in work is also reflected in the range of clients—from high tech, biotech, banking, sporting goods to Fortune 500 and internet start-ups. Each client presents a unique problem to be solved. Through extensive research and the agency's trademarked Visual Rorschach Test[SM], each clients' vision of their company is uncovered, both visually and strategically.

Through the years, Cahan's work has earned numerous accolades for design excellence, nationally and internationally, from magazines, museums, and award shows. However, Cahan feels the true measure of success is the performance of the piece and the client's satisfaction.

The work of Cahan & Associates is different and smart. It's through the collaboration of a talented team of designers and clients, infused with the tension of both strategy and design, that great work is produced.

1. Cover & spreads from Collateral Therapeutics
1998 Annual Report. Art director: Bill Cahan;
designer: Kevin Roberson; photographers:
Christine Alicino, Bill Phelps, Robert Schlatter,
Ken Probst; copywriter: Thom Elkjer.

2

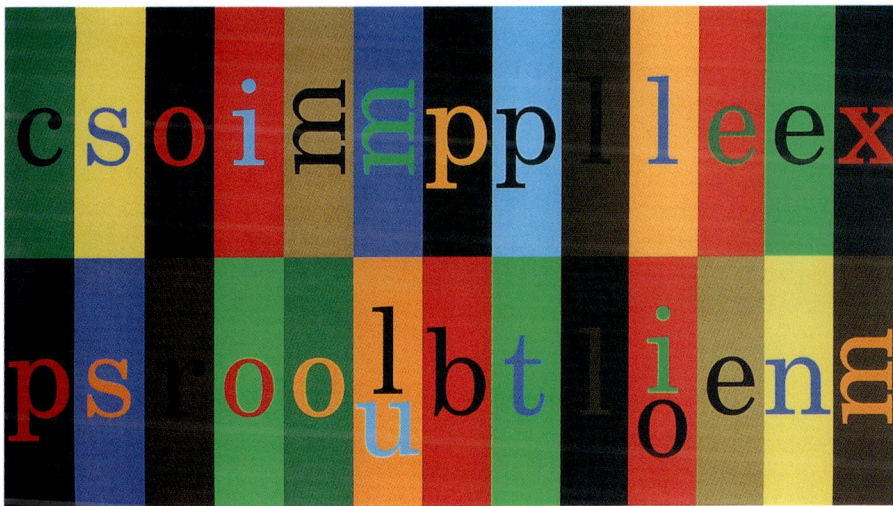

3

2. General Magic 1998 Annual Report. Art director: Bill Cahan; designer: Bob Dinetz; photographer: various; copywriters: Thom Elkjer, Bob Dinetz.

3. Poster for Cahan & Associates lecture sponsored by San Francisco Creative Alliance, Artists in Print, and the WADC. Art director: Bill Cahan; designer: Sharrie Brooks.

sample works 1

lise metzger

4

4. Cover & spreads from Sharpe & Associates
Sample Works, a photographer's promotion.
Art director: Bill Cahan; designer:
Sharrie Brooks; photographers:
Lise Metzger Hugh Kretschmer,
Jamey Stillings, Neal Brown,
Everard Williams, Ann Elliott Cutting.

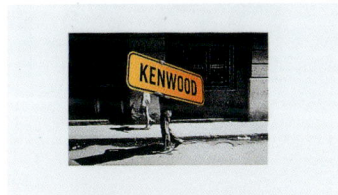

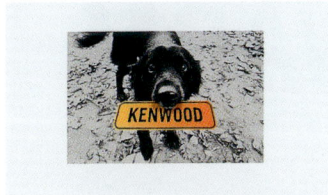

ALCATRAZ
L A G E R

7

8

9

10

11

5. Inquizit Logo. Art director: Bill Cahan;
   designer: Michael Braley.

6. Sound Blaster Logo. Art director: Bill Cahan;
   designer: Sharrie Brooks.

7. Alcatraz Logo. Art director: Bill Cahan;
   designer: Kevin Roberson.

8. Mission Towers Logo. Art director: Bill
   Cahan; designer: Michael Braley.

9. Yerba Buena Logo. Art director: Bill Cahan;
   designer: Stuart Flake.

10. Portal Player Logo. Art director: Bill Cahan;
    designer: Michael Braley.

11. Identity System for the Kenwood Group. Art
    director: Bill Cahan; designer: Sharrie Brooks;
    photographers: various.

MATTER

SOUND   VAULT

WARM   BOTH

12. Cahan & Associates Identity System. Art
director: Bill Cahan; designers: Bob Dinetz,
Kevin Roberson; copywriters: Cahan &
Associates.

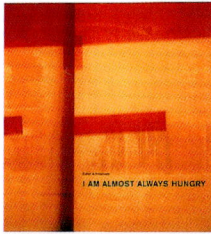

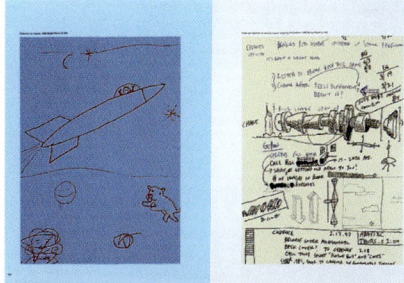

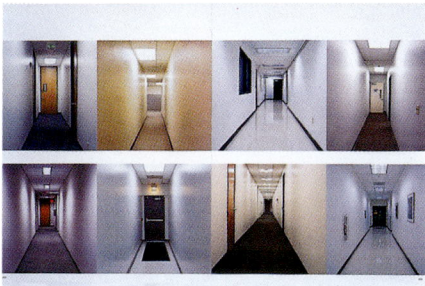

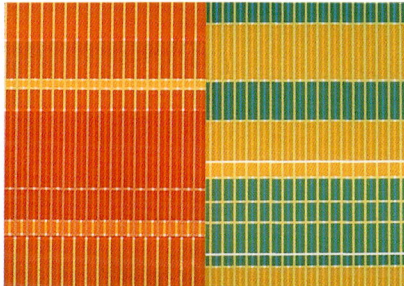

13. "I Am Almost Always Hungry", monograph on Cahan & Associates published by Princeton Architectural Press. Art director: Bill Cahan; designer: Bob Dinetz.

14. Packaging for Caffé Roma. Art director: Bill Cahan; designer: Kevin Roberson; illustrator: Kevin Roberson.

15. Cover of the Pottery Barn Kids Premier Issue Catalog. Art director: Bill Cahan; designer: Ben Pham; photographer: various; copywriter: Pottery Barn Kids.

14

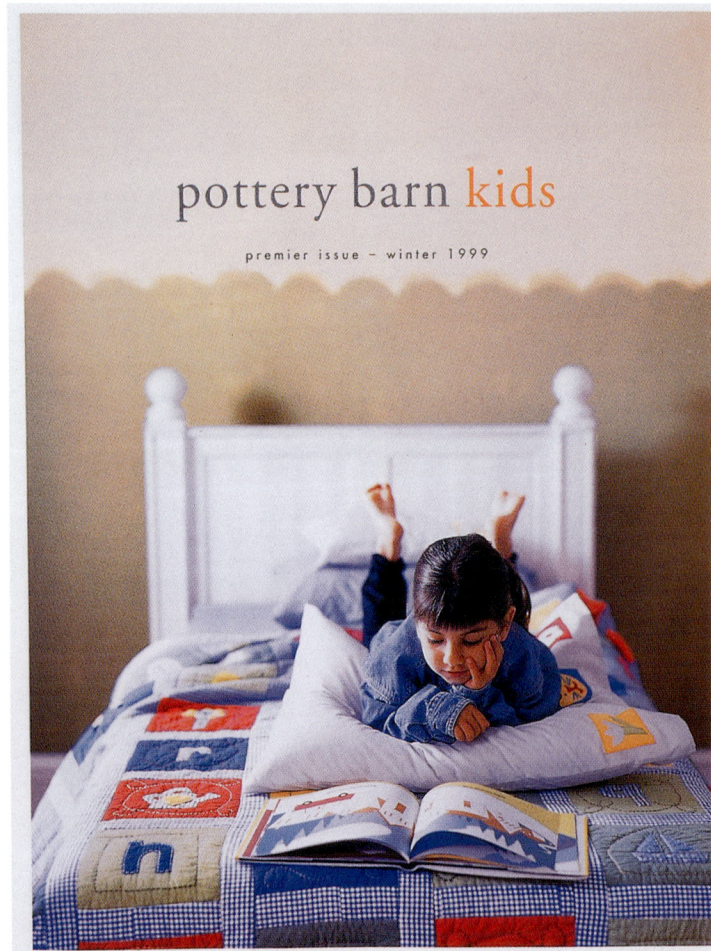

pottery barn kids

premier issue – winter 1999

15

Sussman/Prejza & Company, Inc.
8520 Warner Drive
Culver City, California 90232
310.836.3939
www.sussmanprejza.com

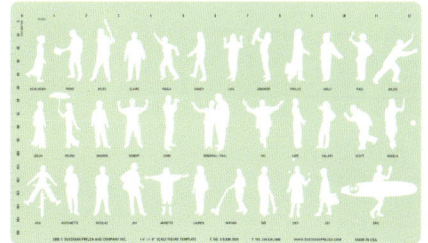

SUSSMAN/PREJZA & COMPANY, INC.

Sussman/Prejza's work has recently been described as "urban poetry". Our practice merges graphic design with architecture and the urban cityscape. Our truly multi-cultural staff brings depth to the problems we are asked to solve, and we relish those opportunities that challenge us to explore new territories. The design of an icon which becomes a sculptural fountain embroidered with stories, is an example; towers and street furniture informed by the Bauhaus in the middle of a Theme Park, is another.

For a long time our work has been intensely contextual to the region if not the locale (as Charles Moore put it) in which it is to be built. S/P's designs have always been informed by immersion into cultures that shaped the communities we serve.

In our increasingly themed world, public gathering places are proliferating that repli-cate the famous past and even the familiar present. "Entertainment" is to be found everywhere in the built environment, in the form of recognizable images, icons, brands.

All of this makes a "pure" solution look better and better. The essence of modernism, which, in its golden years celebrated lean-ness, absence of gratuitous decoration and a minimalist ethic, has returned. At this time, S/P is drawn to abstraction, to make things equally readable in any culture.

Sussman/Prejza is well known to the retail development community and continues to receive commissions for such work. In everything that we do-whether corporate or global (several such projects are on our boards), institutional, or civic, we strive for the best possible product with equal enthusiasm and effort. We try to give the "mundane", even the "profane", as much meaning and quality as we do to the sacred, sharing our knowledge of the arts with collaborators, clients and the public.

Sussman/Prejza & Company, Inc.

1

2 *(above, photo:Kristen Finnegan)*, 4

3 *(above)*, 5

All photographs by Jim Simmons/Annette Del Zoppo
Productions or S/P, except as noted.

Time and Motion in 3D

1. Pioneer Place, phase 2; Portland, Oregon. Full scale models with exhibitry about the rose, symbol of Portland. Spring 2000

2. Pioneer Place, phase 1; Portland, Oregon (now a mixed use project on 3 city blocks). 1990

3. Pioneer Place, phase 2; Portland, Oregon. Model of rose fountain/sculpture. Spring 2000

4. Model showing rose sculpture and its shadow.

5. Detail of petal and stem showing collar. Water will rise through and spill over each metal column.

6

6. Universal CityWalk; Orlando, Florida. Light and sound fixtures with banner poles. 1999

7. Universal CityWalk; Orlando, Florida. Axonometric view of abstract urban icons, signs, street furniture. 1999

8-9. Universal CityWalk; Orlando, Florida. Cineplex signs. 1999

10-12. Universal CityWalk; Orlando, Florida. Shade structures, light and sound armatures, iconic towers with animated lighting. 1999

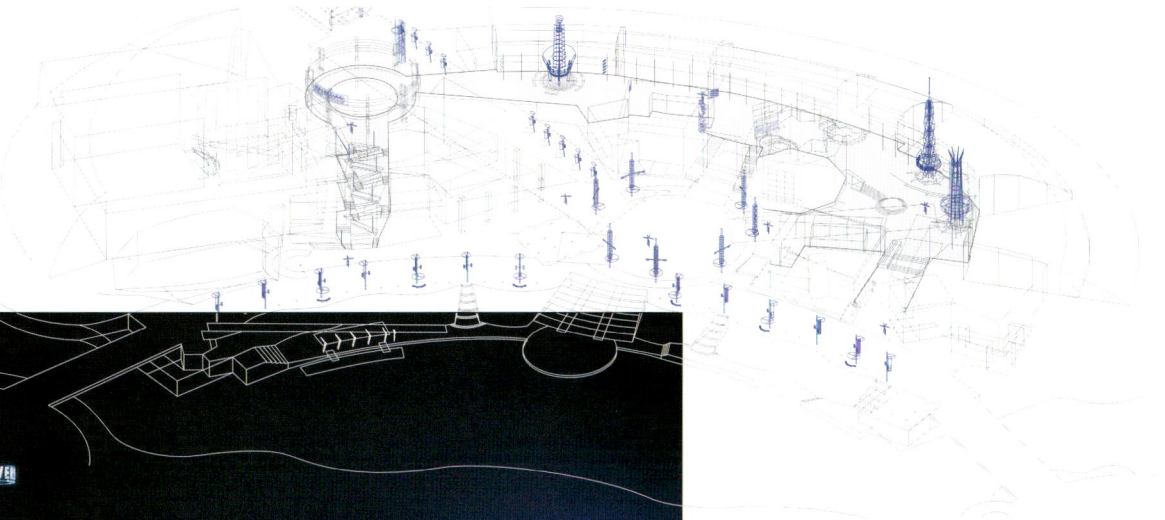

7

8

9

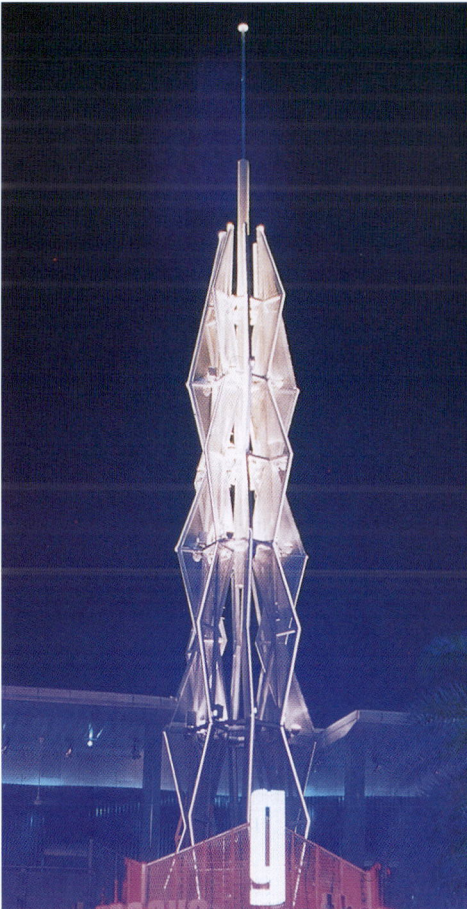

10

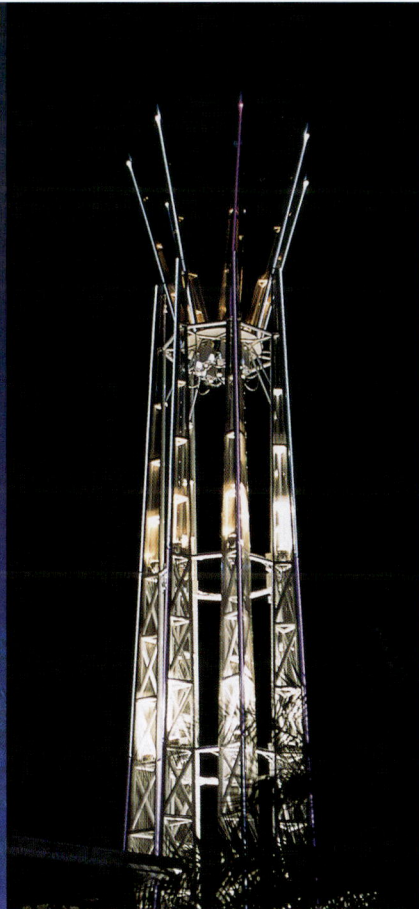

11

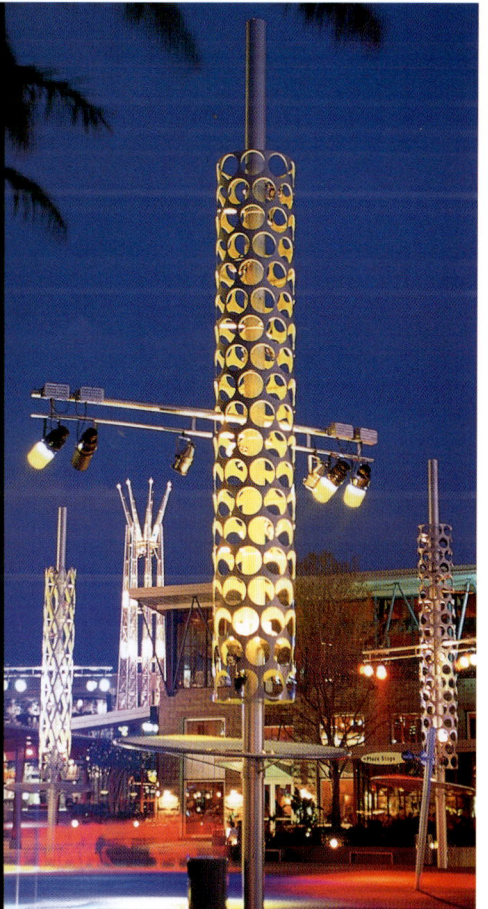

12

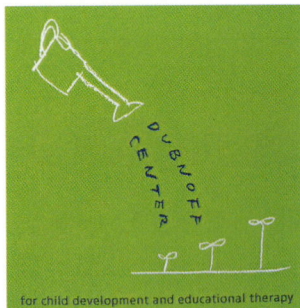

1

2

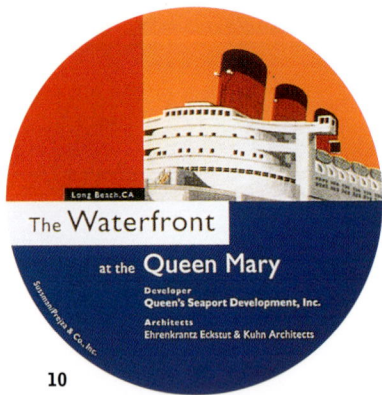

3

4

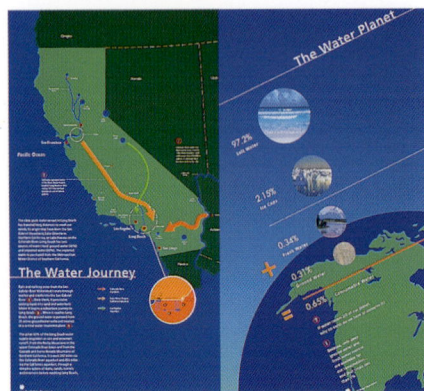

5

10

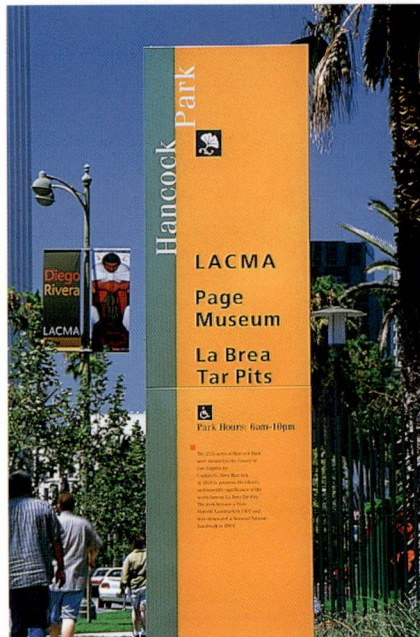

11

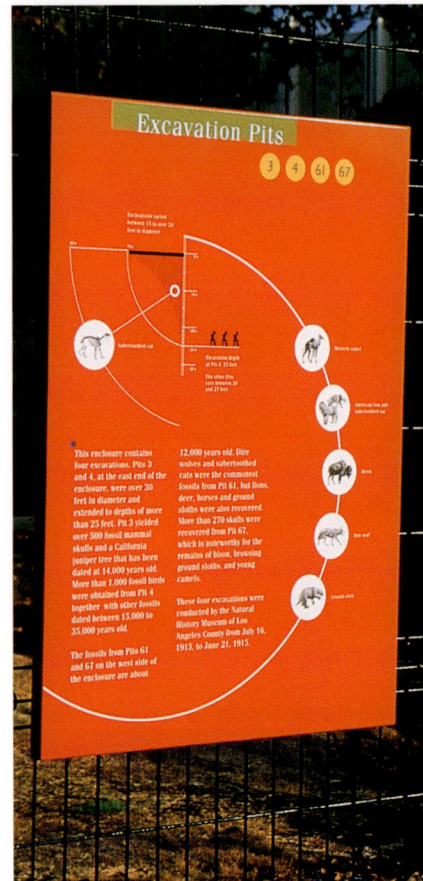

12

13

14

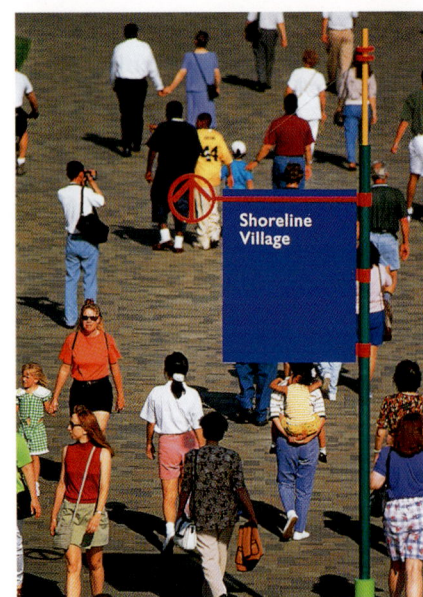

15

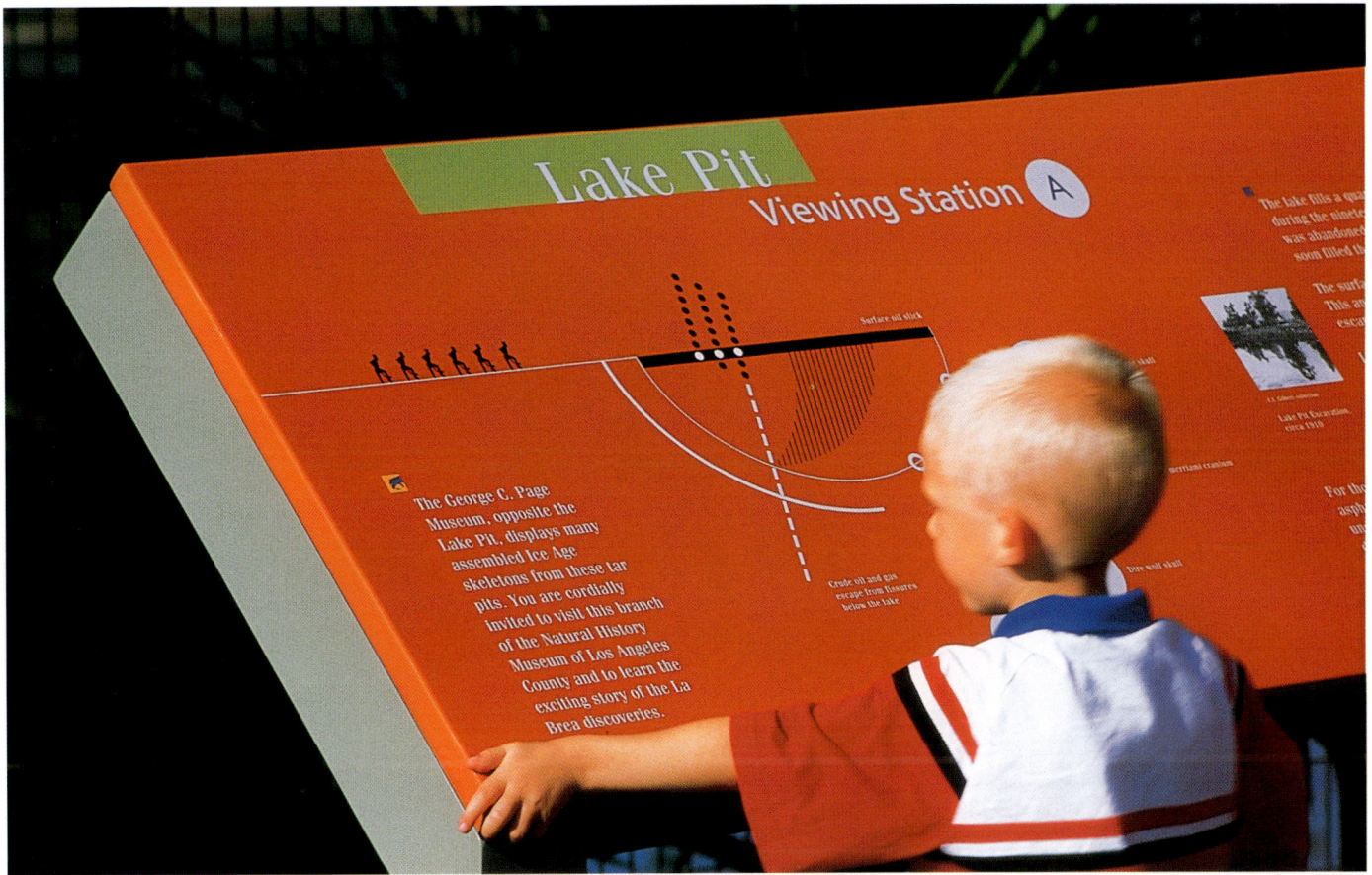

6

7

Information and Identity

1-2. Logo and identity program; Dubnoff Center for child development and educational therapy; Los Angeles, California. 1999

3-9. Hancock Park is home to the Los Angeles County Museum, the Page Museum and the La Brea Tar Pits. Exhibitry and wayfinding, shown, form part of an extensive future program. Los Angeles, California. 1999

10-15. Rainbow Harbor at Queensway Bay; Long Beach, California. A system of graphics, color, wayfinding, pageantry and exhibitry unifies this 60 acre development. 1999

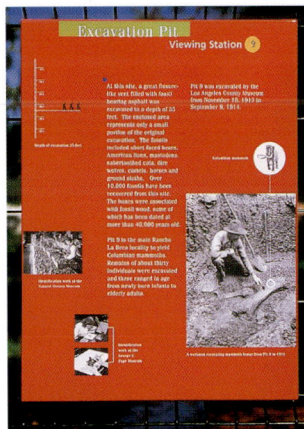

8

9

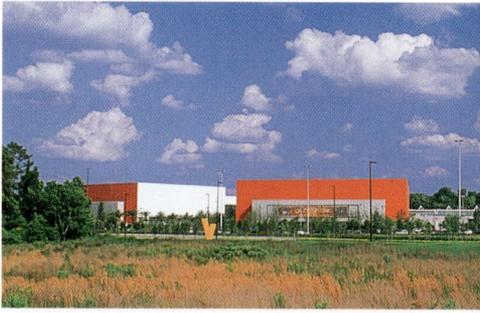

1

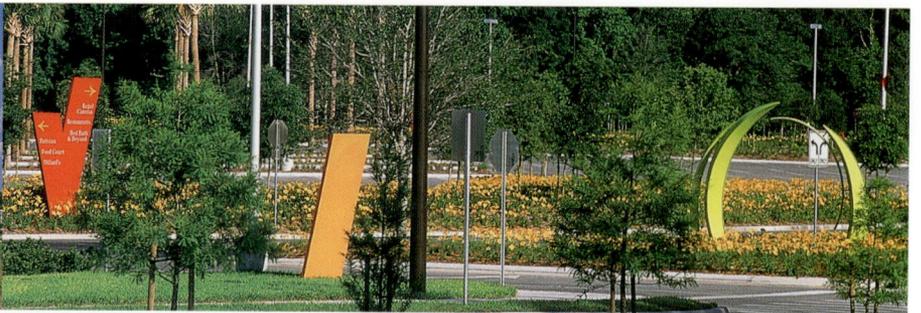

2

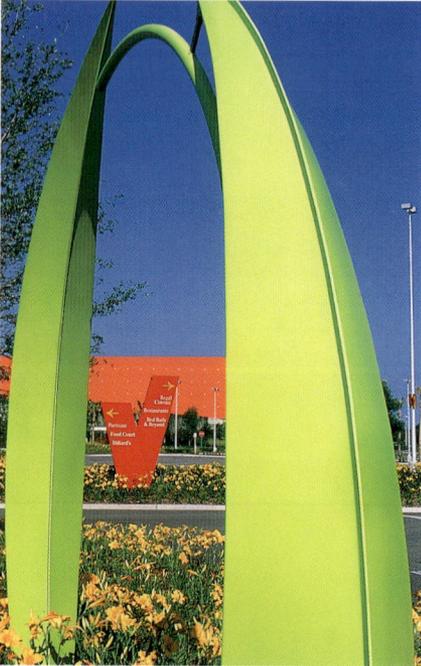

3

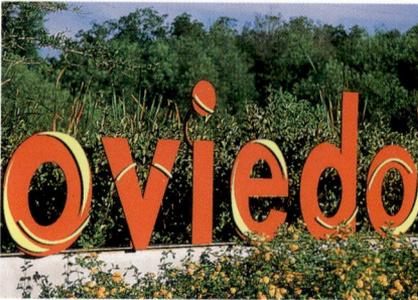

4

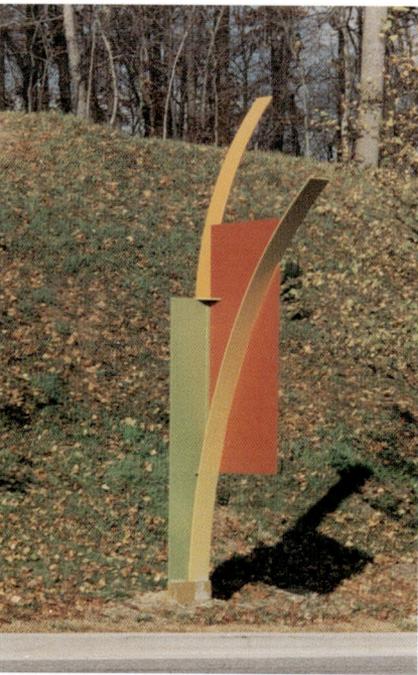

5

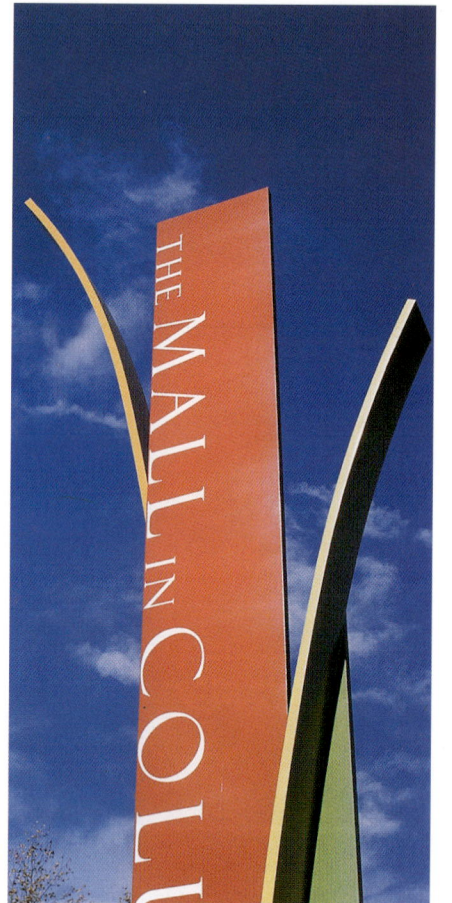

6

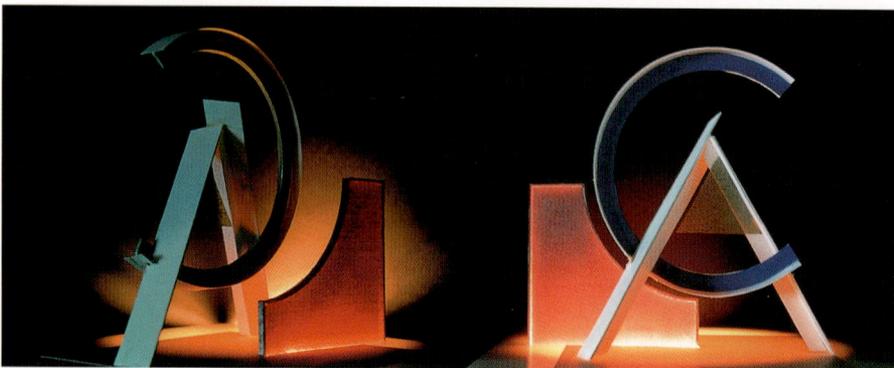

7

Messages as Sculpture

1-4. OviedoMarketplace; Orlando, Florida. Program includes identity, wayfinding, interior and exterior color, amenities and paving. 1998

5-6. Mall at Columbia, Maryland. New iconography, graphics and major interior and exterior renovation. 1998-1999

7. Model of identity sculpture for Azrieli Center. Tel-Aviv, Israel. 1998

8

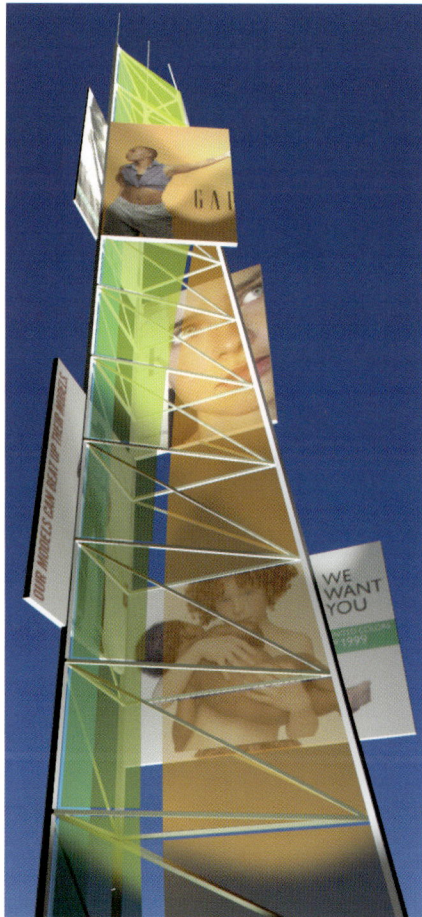

9

10

photo:Peter Bellanger

11

12

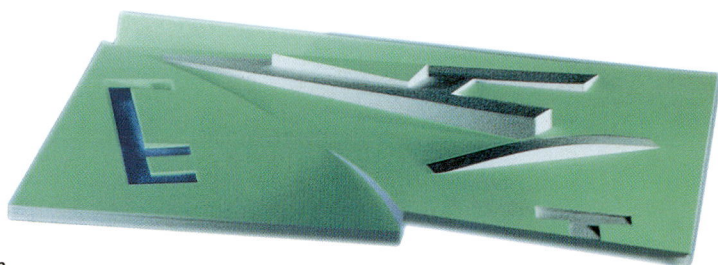

13

8-9. Studies for an identity and advertising tower structure for a mixed use project. Budapest, Hungary. 1998

10. Prototype sign for a global signing program designed for sgi; Mountain View, California. The cut-out logo creates constantly changing light and shadow effects on the rear surface, symbolizing sgi's innovations. 1999-2000

11. Selection of components in the sgi system.

12,13. Birds-eye view of models for a playground, and park seating. 1999

2

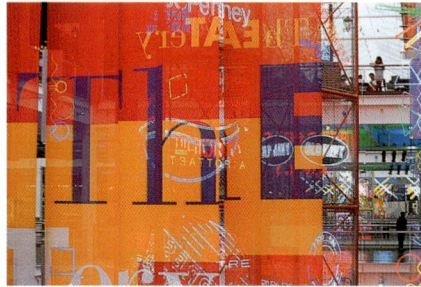

3

4

1

Emotive Graphics Layered Inside and Outside

1-4. Symbolic roller coaster, graphic scaffolding and scrims. Elements from an extensive remodeling for Palisades Center, New York. 1997

5. Millennium pageantry program, "shimmering zodiac"; Beverly Hills, California. 1999-2000

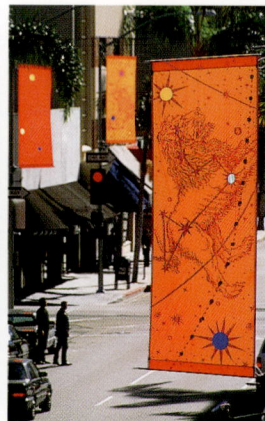
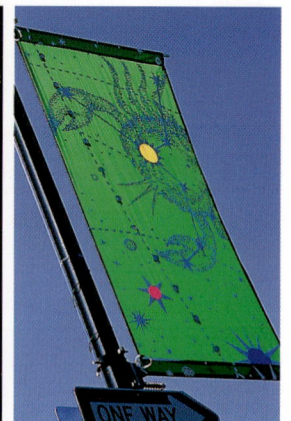

5

Curtis Design LLC
3328 Steiner St.
San Francisco, California 94123
415.567.4402
info@curtisdesign.com
www.curtisdesign.com

CURTIS DESIGN LLC

Founded in 1989, Curtis Design has earned a national reputation as a leader in graphic design, corporate identity, branding, print, packaging technology and project management.

Adhering to the axiom that quality design is the product of in-depth research, strategic vision, talent and forward-thinking project execution, Curtis Design effectively bridges the gap between compelling design and assisting our clients in resolving their business issues in the most expeditious manner.

Our expertly choreographed design approach is thorough and accurate. We believe comprehensive research leads to focused design. Thoughtful project planning yields streamlined project execution and a clear understanding of our customer's perspective ensures highly satisfied clients.

1

2

3

4

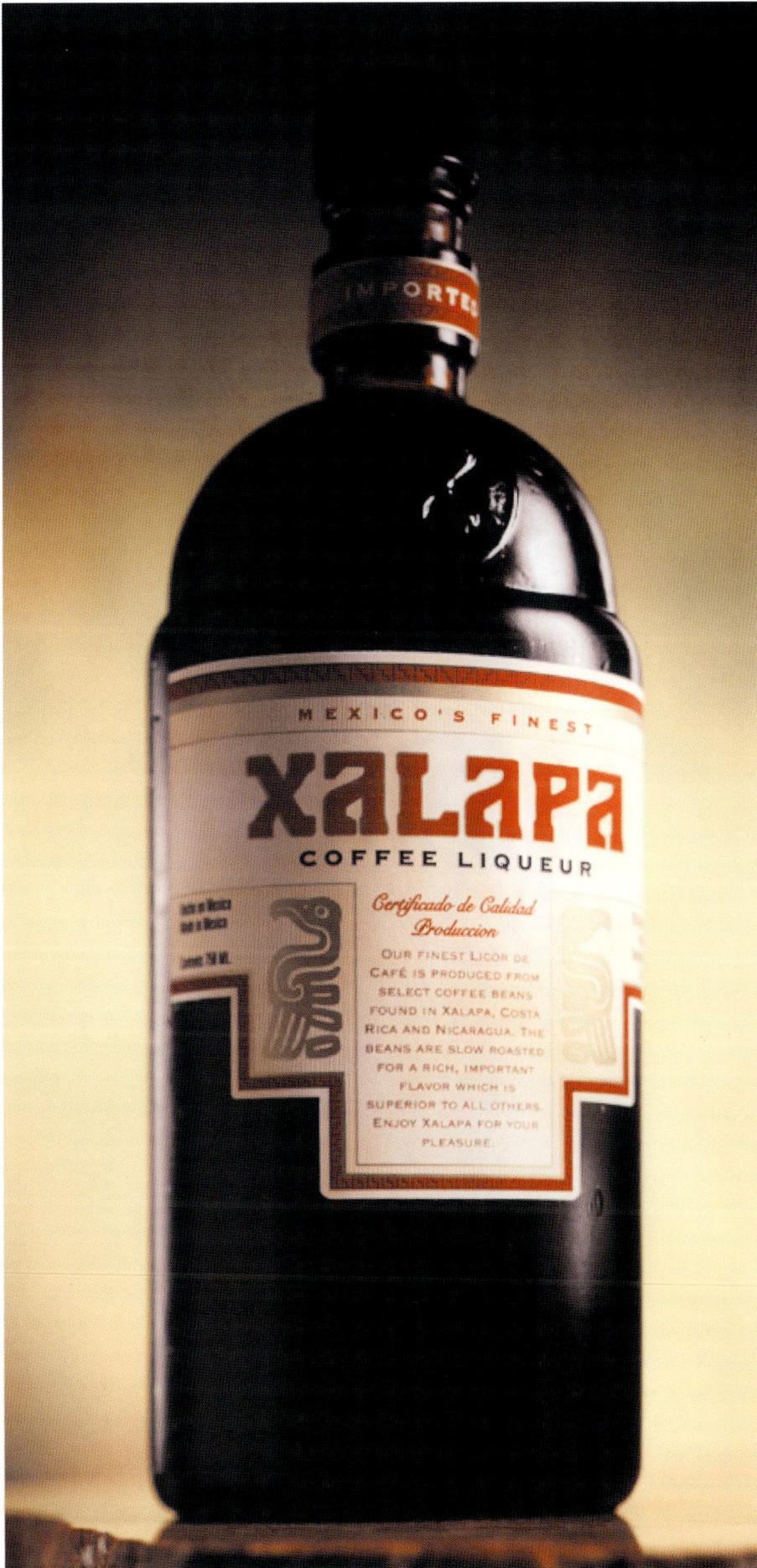

5

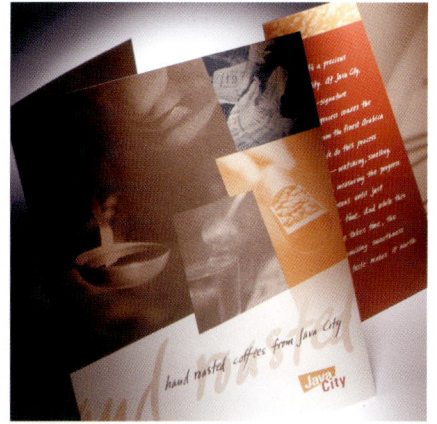

5

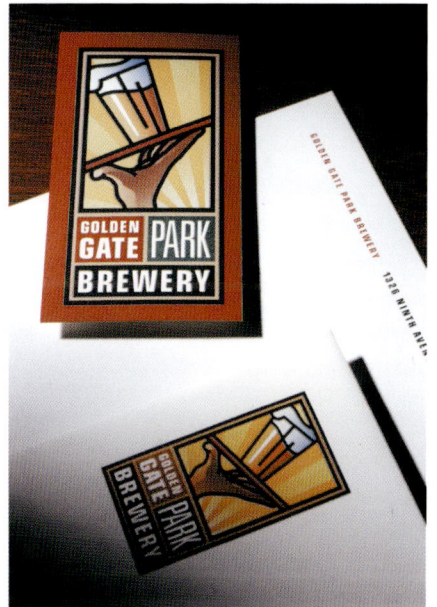

6

1. World Wide Welding identity.

2. Branding and product line design for Garden of Eatin', the category leader in all-natural chips.
   AIGA Brand 50 Award winner

3. Vinomex S.A. de C.V. Hacienda de Chihuahua Sotol brandmark and package design.
   AIGA Brand 50 Award winner

4. Seagram America, packaging for Jimmy Buffet's Margaritaville line of tequila products.

5. Casa Rockefeller S.A. de C.V. brandmark and package design for Xalapa coffee liqueurs.

6. Identity for Golden Gate Park Brewery.

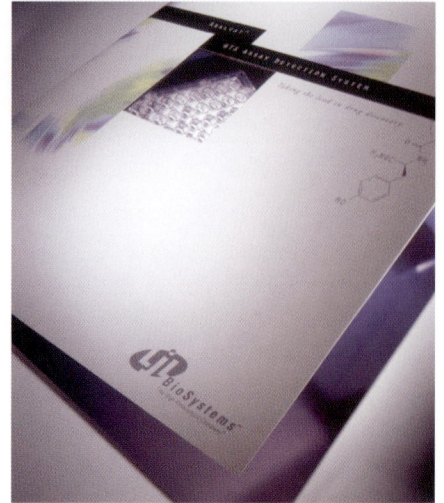

1

3

2

4

1. Xerox New Enterprise Company, Uppercase brandmark.

2. Identity program for Mailwave, an internet mail company.

3. LJL Biosystems product brochure.

4. brandmark and corporate identity manual for Norian Corporation, a biomedical company.

5. Kensington trade show booth. Finalist, best-of-show, Comdex.

6. San Francisco Film Centre identity.

7. Brochure for n&k Technology Inc., a producer of thin film characterization systems for the semiconductor industry.

8. Hewlet-Packard Global Partnerships, interactive style guide.

5

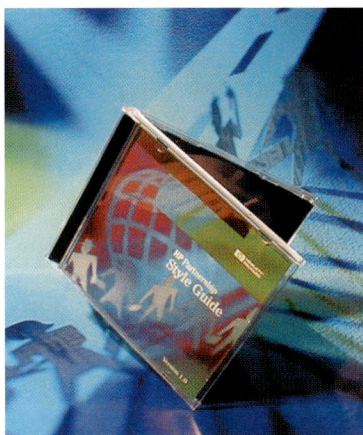

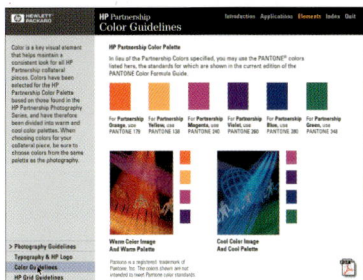

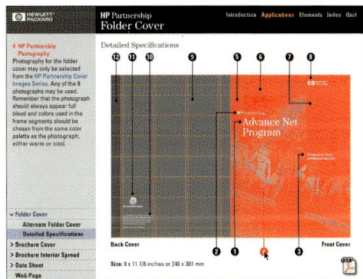

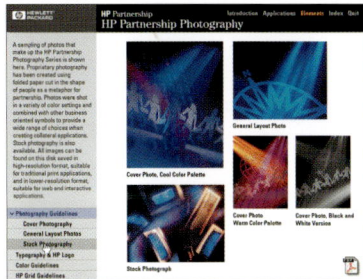

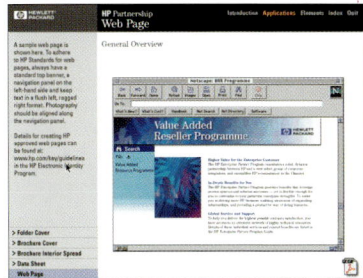

SAN FRANCISCO **FILM** CENTRE

6

8

7

1

2

3

1,2. Sudwerk Privatbrauerei Hübsch, brandmark and package system design.

3. Turtle Mountain Foods, package design for Soy Delicious line of frozen desserts.

4. Caravali Coffee Company, brandmark and package system design.

5. Identity for KLA-Tencor Corporation.

4

5

1

1. Fantastic Foods. Packaging system
design for Natural Entrées, a product
line consisting of over forty SKUs.
AIGA Brand 50 Award winner

2525 Main Street,
Suite 204
Santa Monica, CA 90405
310_396_7724>voice
310_396_1686>fax
studio@loueyrubino.com
New York_Hong Kong

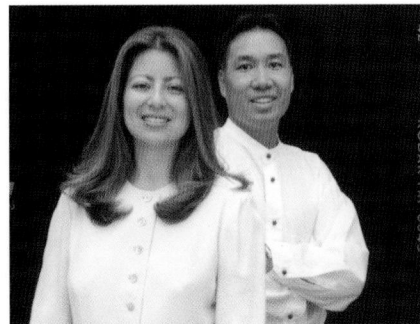

LOUEY/RUBINO DESIGN GROUP

Louey/Rubino's Design Group's philosophy and corporate strategy has always been to work closely with their clients to visually realize their business and image goals through design driven, powerful and effective communications. "Knowledge is power and power lies in the ability to communicate" says Robert Louey, President and Creative Director of the Santa Monica based firm with offices in New York and Hong Kong. "The early alchemists sought to transform ordinary metals into precious gold. Modern communications is 'Image Alchemy'. By mixing emotion, culture and beauty: Intelligence directed towards a specific audience and goal; Design and communications can have an immediate and positive effect on a company's bottom line".

Founded in 1984 by Robert Louey and Regina Rubino, Louey/Rubino Design Group Inc. is a full service marketing communications firm specializing in corporate communications, strategic marketing, and related promotional and advertising programs.

The company has had the pleasure to serve many leading corporations, on an international scale, for over 15 years, including Fremont General, Grand Hyatt, Hearst Communications, homestore.com, Kaufman and Broad, Mandarin Oriental, Marriott, PacifiCare Health Systems, MCI/Worldcom, Rand, Rockwell International Corp. and SunAmerica.

Louey/Rubino Design Group's work is included in the Library of Congress Permanent Collection and has appeared in The Mead Show, AR100, Print, How, Graphis, Communication Arts, AIGA, The Type Director's Club and Interiors Magazine.

We'll continue to accelerate Growth.

THINK BIG
think big
BIG
BIG
BIG
thinkbig
BIG

OUTSTANDING PERFORMANCE

59%
its GROWTH

Outstanding
Long Term Value

Kaufman and Broad Home Corporation

architecture
is an international
language with
few barriers to
communication.

By 2008, i think
everything will change.

And
hopefully, there
will be a lot more
peace.
That's cool.

FIGURE XIII.

FREMONT GENERAL
Stock Performance vs. S&P Indices
(in dollars)

INDEX: 12/31/90 = $100

$1,068 FREMONT GENERAL

$681 FINANCIAL INDEX

$485 SAVINGS & LOAN INDEX

$323 PROPERTY-CASUALTY INDEX

90 91 92 93 94 95 96 97 98
CAPITAL APPRECIATION PLUS DIVIDENDS

SOURCE: BLOOMBERG

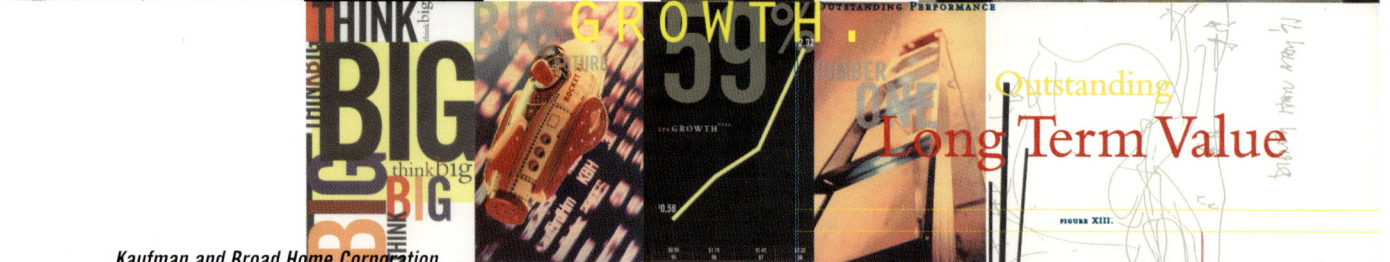

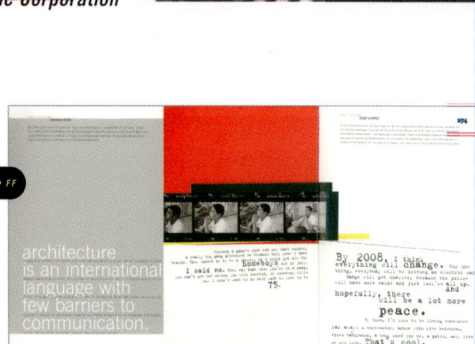

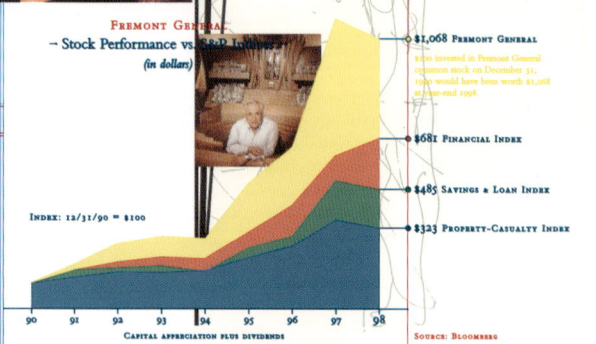

Fremont General Company Highlights — *Forbes Magazine* "Forbes Platinum List 400" named Fremont General as #103 out of its pick of the 400 best-performing companies in the United States over the past 5 years and last 12 months.

FORBES MAGAZINE, JANUARY 1999

Kaufman & Broad Home Corporation
Rand
Fremont General Corporation
Rockwell International Corporation

THINK

react

homestore.com
Reliance Steel & Aluminum
Cast Consulting
SunAmerica Inc.
X/Games S.F.

Reliance boasts product lines of over 20,000 various metal products spread our over 33,000 customers.

of goods and services, as well as enable a participatory
new social and economic
the imperative to know

dot.com guy

I.M>THE//REVOLUTION

ROAD TRIP 99

Other 5%

Valex 7%

Carbon Steel 45%

Stainless Steel 15%

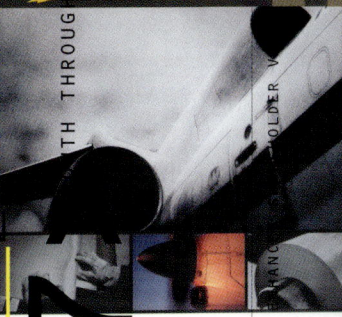

Seasons

1997

RELIANCE STEEL & ALUMINUM CO. annual report for the year ending 1997

NATIONAL PRESENCE + PRODUCT DIVERSITY + PERFORMANCE EXCELLENCE +

ACQUISITION

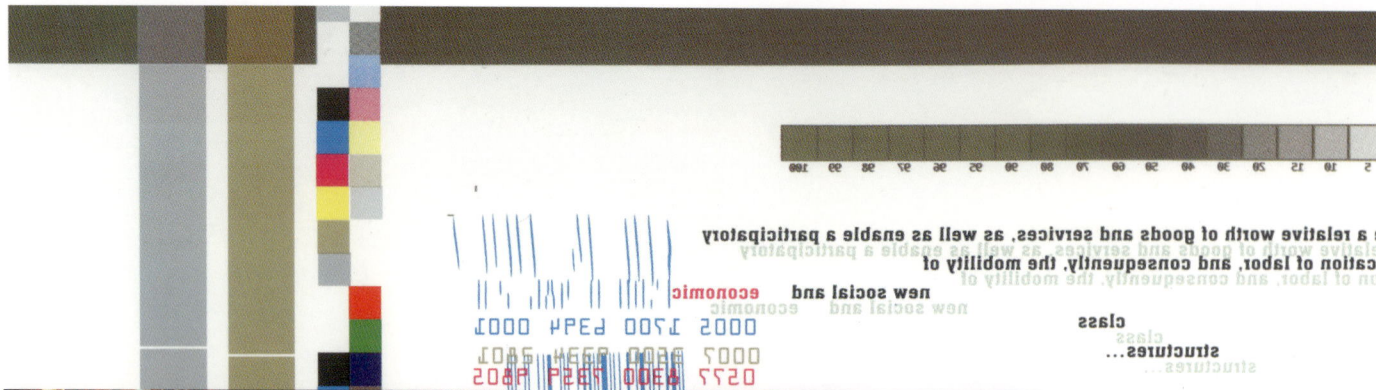

V 1 3 V O D K A B A R

V13 Vodka Bar/Hong Kong
Intuit Solutions
Red Pagoda International LTD.
Primal Piercing & Tattoo Studio

create

COMMUNICATE

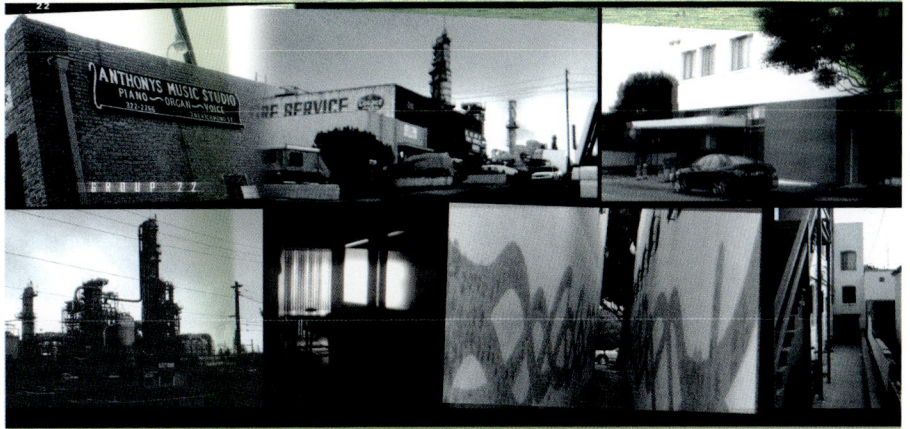

Group 22, Inc.
200 West Grand Avenue
El Segundo, California 90245
310.322.2210
studio@group22.com
www.group22.com

GROUP 22, INC.

A scant year and a half after opening its doors, what had originally begun as a one-man studio operating out of the converted front bedroom of a house had incorporated, moved into a deconstructivist 3,300 square foot work-in-progress studio and commanded a full-time staff of eight.

Group 22 fosters a collective atmosphere with all employees taking a part in the design of any particular project as well as the direction of the company. There are no titles or hierarchy here; just a family.

Though Group 22 is a young firm, the principal designers shared a combined experience in the field of over thirty years. The firm's philosophy is as simple as it is true; less is more. Design should first and foremost communicate and should never get in the way of the message.

At any particular G22 gathering you'll likely find a mix of vendors, clients and employees. The reason is because Group 22 likes to work in close partnership with clients. Instead of doggedly presenting comps and sketches for approval or rejection, we feel that clients should be an integral part of the design process. G22 prefers to make its clients into friends and often enough ends up with friends becoming clients.

Whether you pass by the studio at two in the morning or eight o'clock at night, seven days a week, you will always find the lights on and at least one of us hard at work. Why? Quite simply put: We love what we do.

1

GROUP 22

2

1. Group 22, Inc. corporate identity system
2. Group 22, Inc. corporate logo
3. Ford ZX2-S/R poster

3

1

4

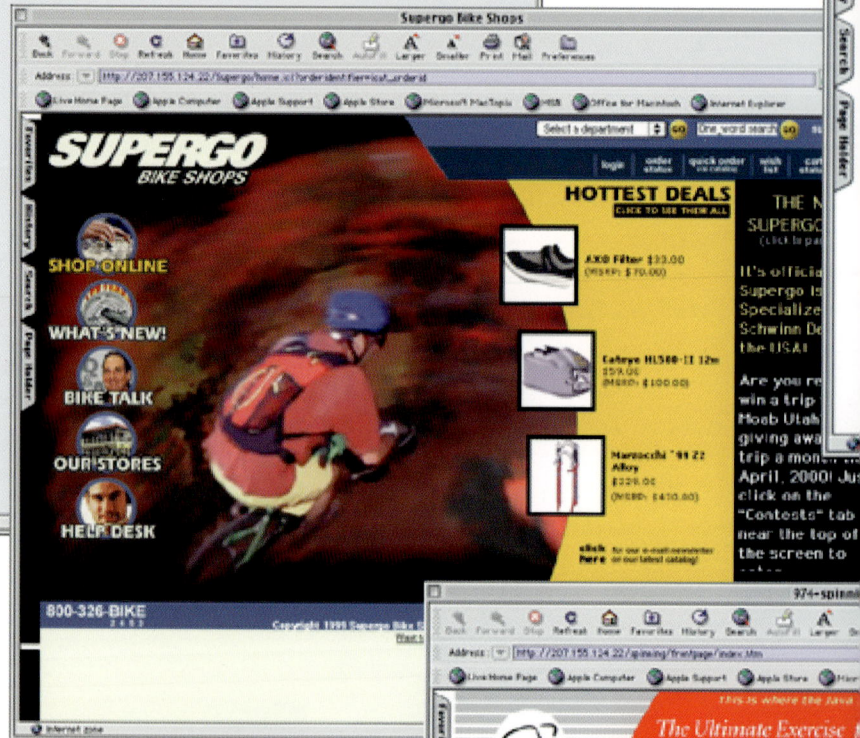

5

2

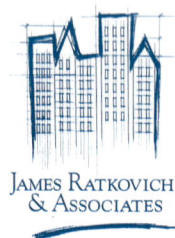

3

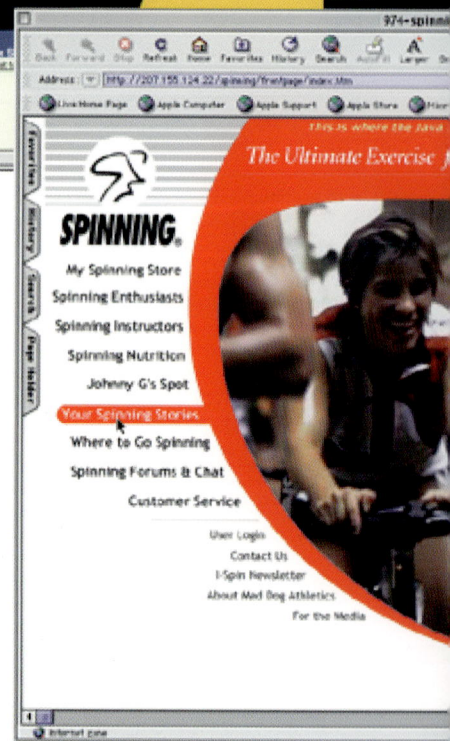

6

1. Interval™ corporate logo

2. Dish Handcrafted Bath & Body Stuff
brand logo

3. James Ratkovich and Associates corporate logo

4. The CO-OP Network Intranet

5. SuperGo Bike Shops web site

6. Spinning© web site

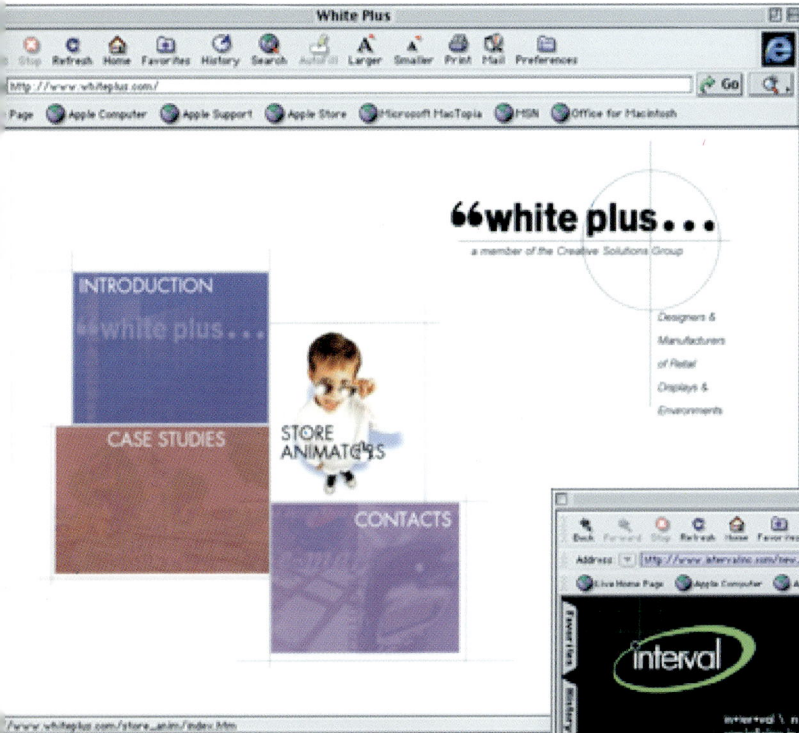

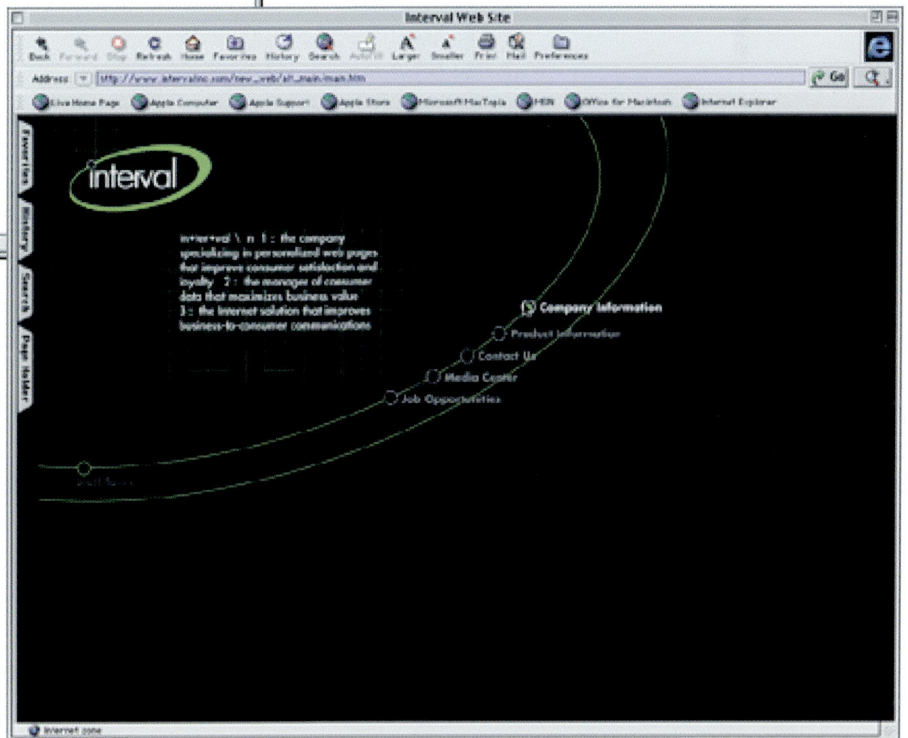

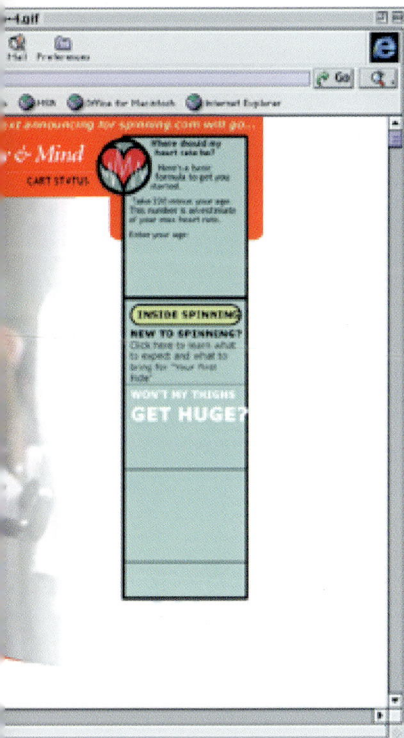

7. White Plus web site

8. MyCarPage.com brand logo

9. Hunter Recruitment Advisors corporate logo

10. Interval™ corporate web site

1

2

3

4

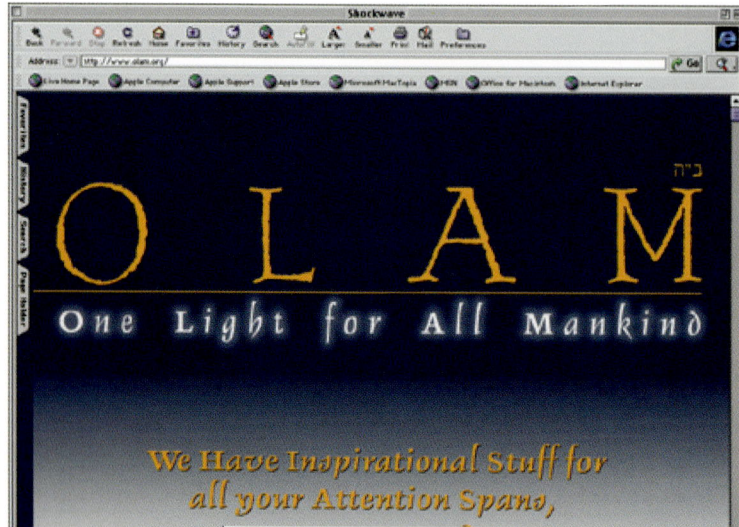

5

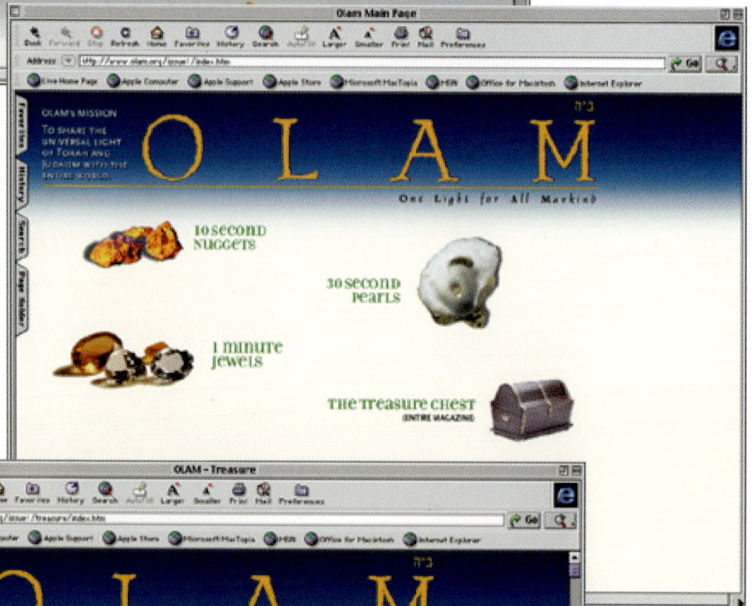

1. Wham-O BALZAC® brand logo
2. Civilian Pictures, LLC corporate logo
3. Mesa Microwave, Inc. corporate logo
4. Life Insurance Legacy brand logo
5. OLAM online magazine

6. Ford Cougar marketing promotion
7. Wham-O Boogey Board product designs
8. Morey Boogie Custom product line catalog

7

8

1. Wham-O BALZAC® packaging
2. Wham-O WATER product packaging

Sapient
Atlanta
Cambridge
Chicago
Dallas
Denver
Houston
London
Los Angeles
Milan
New York
San Francisco
Sydney
Washington, D.C.

SAPIENT

Sapient is a leading e-services consultancy providing Internet strategy consulting and sophisticated Internet-based solutions to Global 1000 companies and start-up businesses. Sapient helps clients identify successful business strategies for the digital economy, then designs, architects, and implements solutions to execute those strategies.

Known for thought leadership in the fields of technology, creative, experience modeling, digital business strategy, and integrated engagement leadership, the company has helped create and continues to shape the digital economy.

Of note is the company's leadership in the area of user-centered design. A champion of simplified communication and design across a variety of media, Sapient is a recognized thought leader in the field of interactive design.

Founded in 1991, Sapient is headquartered in Cambridge, Mass., and employs more than 2100 people around the world. More information on Sapient can be found at www.sapient.com or by calling (617) 621-0200.

1

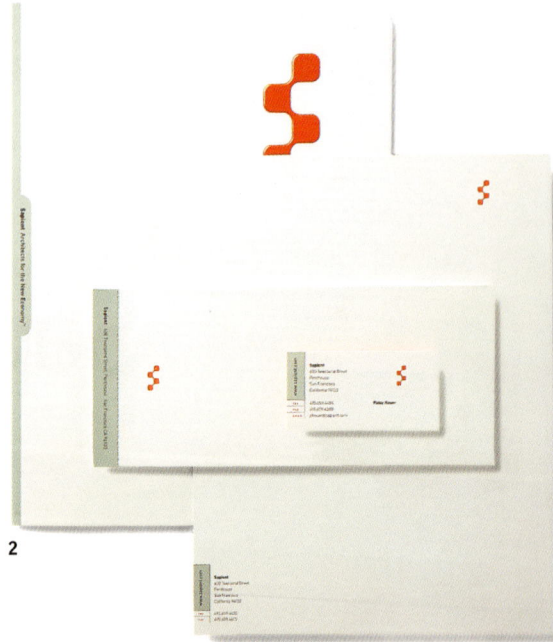

2

3

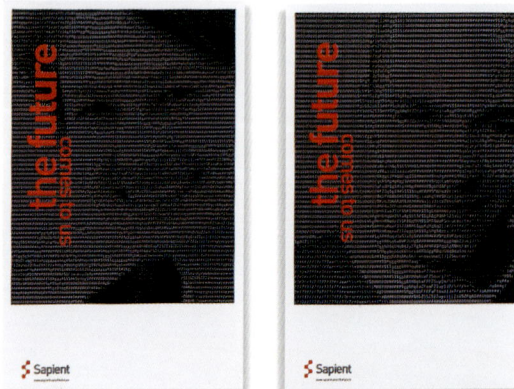

4

The Sapient visual identity is centered around a
stylized "s" symbolizing one entity made up of
smaller parts; it is fluid, digital, and ascendant.
The site design and recruiting campaign portray
people and their stories as a way to illustrate the
impact that our services deliver.

1. Sapient logo

2. Stationery

3. Promotional recruiting postcards

4. Recruiting posters

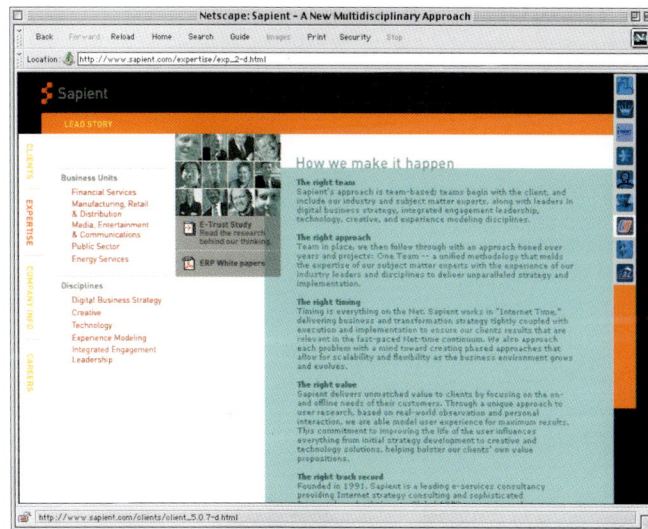

5. Sapient Web site homepage and lead story
pop-up window

6. Expertise section

7. Company Info section

1

2

3

4

5

This online apartment location service was revitalized by an elegant new visual identity and a smart Web site design, which make moving a simple pleasure. SpringStreet gives people an easy way to find and move into the perfect new home.

1. SpringStreet stationery

2. Logo

3. Homepage

4. Manager's & Owner's Corner

5. "Find your place" section

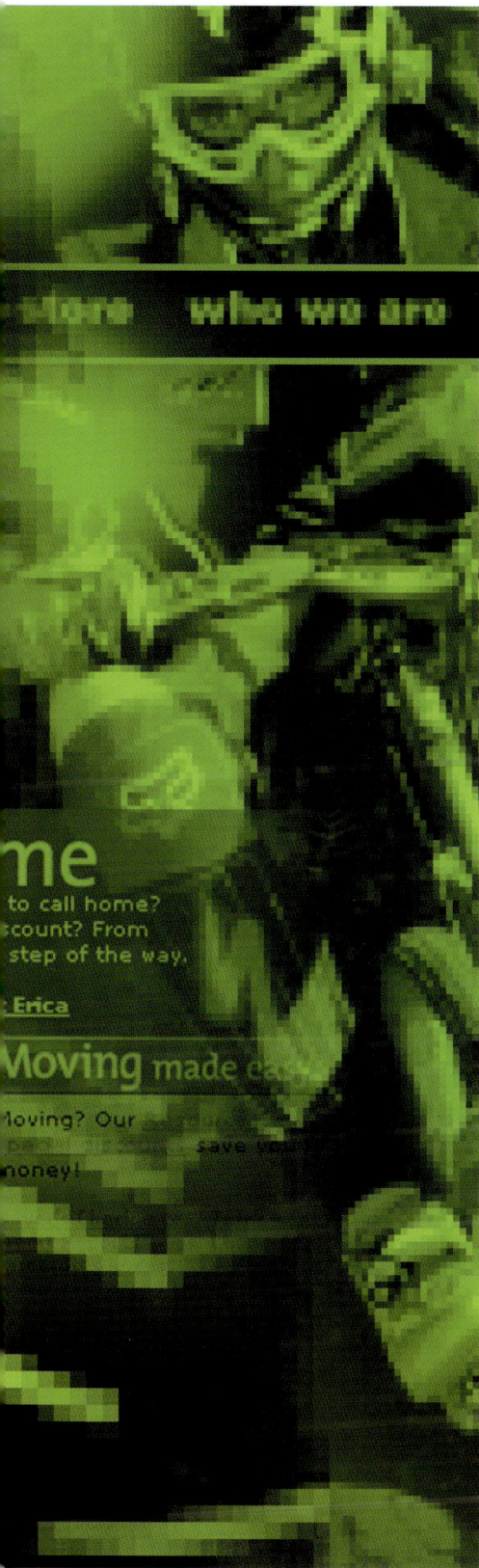

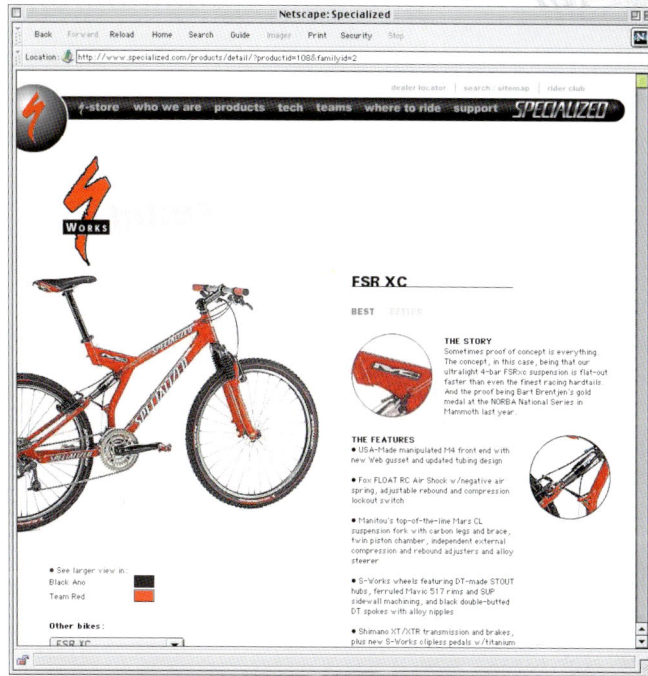

1

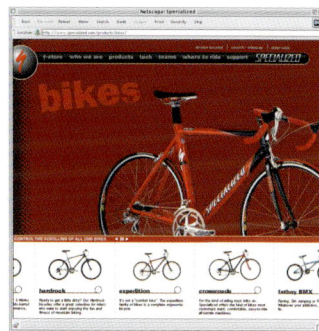

2

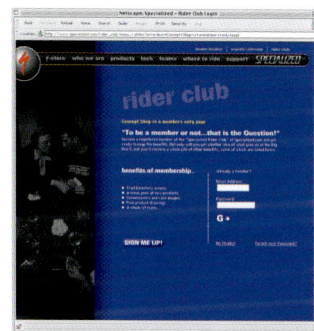

3

4

Specialized's Web site goes beyond static marketing communications. The site truly engages its online customers, captures their contact information and preferences, and offers strong justification for regular repeat visits.

1. Specialized product specifications

2. Product line

3. Rider Club membership section

4. Homepage

1

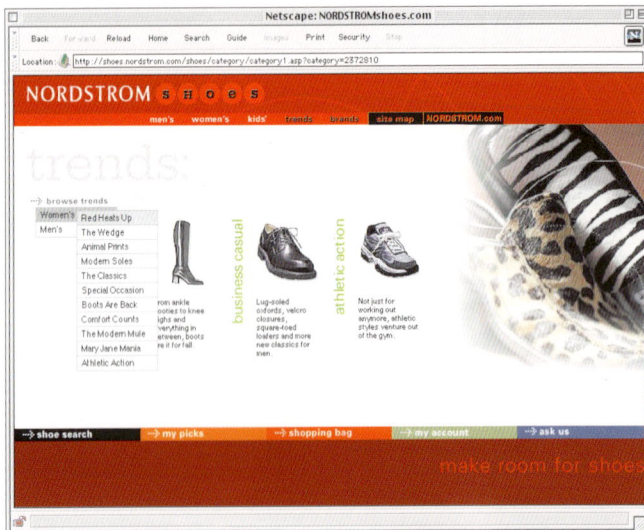

2

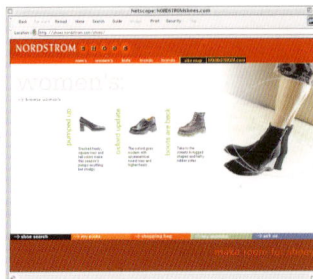

3

By launching nordstromshoes.com, Nordstrom became the biggest shoe store on the Web, while also reinvigorating its brand and appealing to a younger market demographic.

1. Nordstrom shoes homepage and pop-up window

2. Trends section

3. Women's section

1

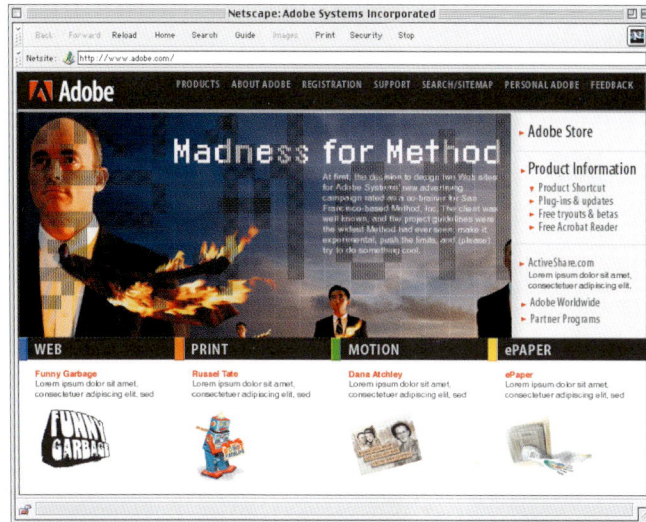

2

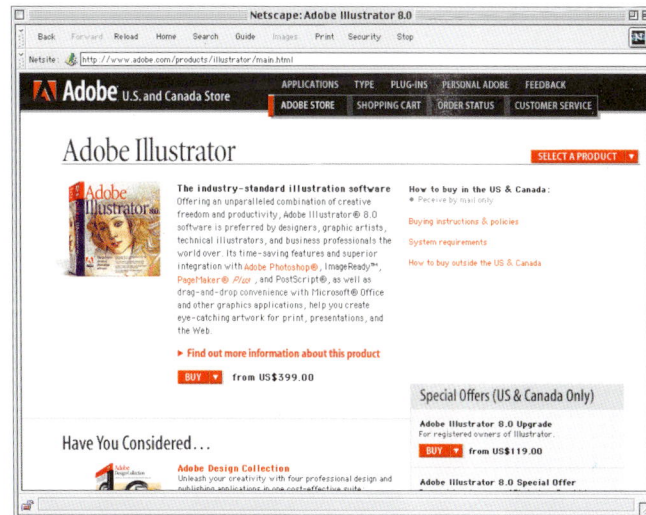

3

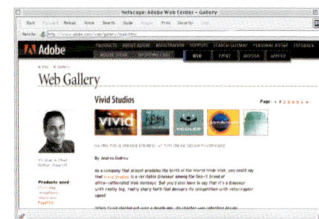

4

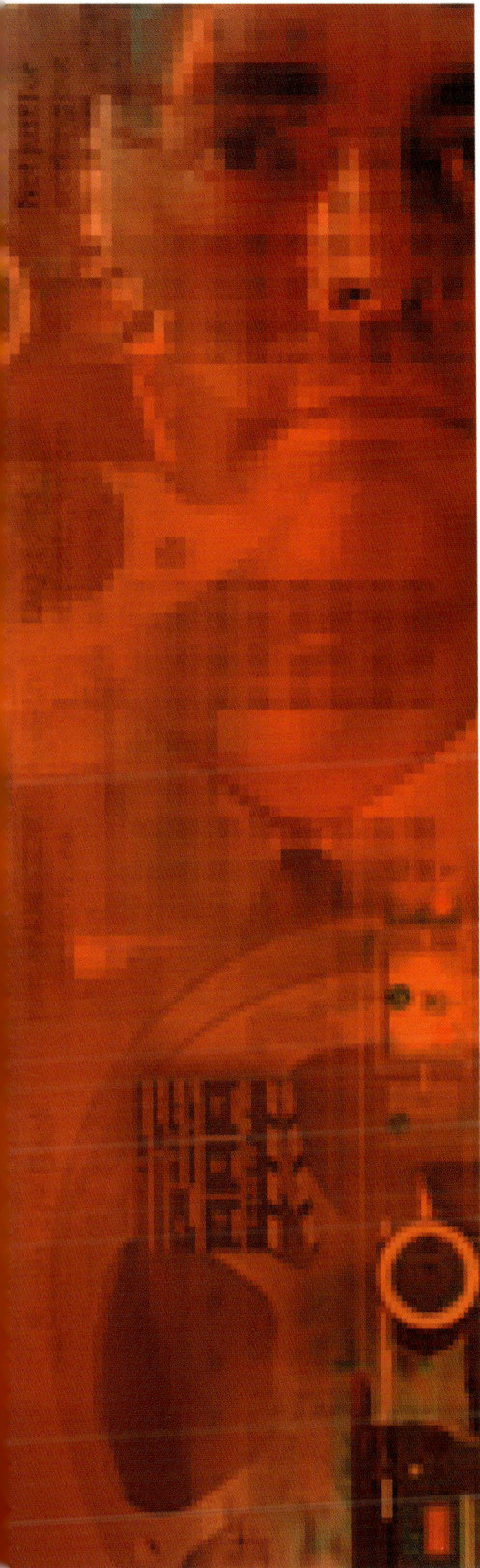

The new Adobe.com site provides a wide mix of editorial content, product information, and customer support information targeted at the graphic design professional.

1. Adobe Web site homepage

2. Homepage with alternate primary feature

3. Product detail

4. Web Gallery

1

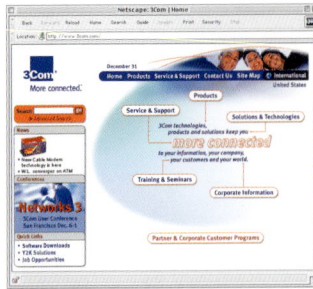

2

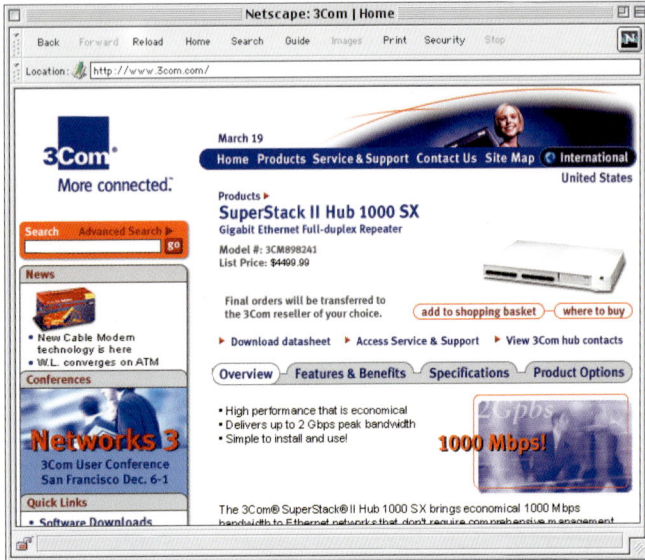

3

4

5

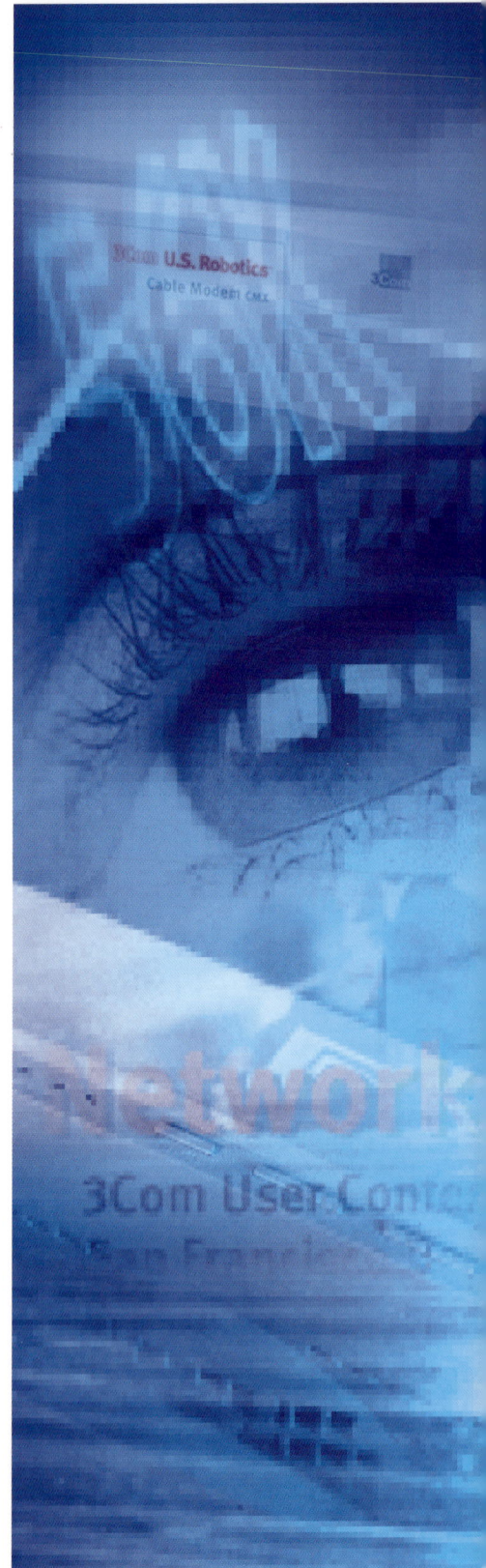

3Com's Web site organizes vast amounts of technical and product information, to quickly connect 3Com's diverse customer base and product divisions to the information they need. The site's visual design and 3Com's identity system reflect the networking company's status as a premium brand.

1. 3Com logo

2. Homepage

3. Product detail

4. Stationery

5. Cable modem packaging

Joan D. Libera
Libera Design Inc.
Los Angeles, California 90064
San Francisco, California 94105
310.477.2027
libera@gte.net

LIBERA DESIGN INC.

Libera Design Inc., a leading design and marketing communications firm, provides a full spectrum of integrated, value-added services to corporate and financial customers. Over the past 20 years, we have produced superior custom designed products that communicate each client's unique positioning.

At Libera Design, our goal is to become an integral part of our customers' visual communications program to build their image, and ultimately assist with creating their success.

To accomplish our goal, we take a business approach to design. We recognized that quality, value and responsiveness – driving factors in business – are essential in our service to corporate clients. We also understand the importance of visual message continuity and corporate branding.

We use our service orientation and business acumen together with cutting-edge, functional designs to develop integrated strategies that support our clients' total communications objectives.

As the business environment becomes increasingly dominated by technology, design is lending itself to standardization, thus losing impact and viewers attention. Libera Design is committed to finding attention grabbing design solutions for each communications project. Every job is approached as a singular creative opportunity.

Libera Design also operates like the businesses we serve. Once designs are client approved, we use cutting-edge technical support to produce work that is on schedule and within budget.

Our efforts have been well rewarded.

We have the proven ability to develop long-term client relationships. We also have received recognition within the financial and design communities, as evidenced by our multinational awards for design communication excellence.

Starwood Lodging

Intellect Capital Corp.

Kaufman △ Broad

S

Sun Life USA

KOLL ANAHEIM CENTER

1999
AVENUE OF THE STARS

Managing the Dynamics of Change
Over a 20 Year Span.

Kaufman & Broad, Inc, began as a small
housing corporation and grew into the
largest housing developer in California and
France. In 1986, the company restructured,
separating its two businesses: Sun Life USA,
a rapidly growing life insurance company,
and Kaufman and Broad Home Corporation.
Our objective was to design one package
for both companies, rather than duplicating
shareholder reporting efforts. The 1989
Annual Report was the first to introduce
the "new" Broad, Inc.

The theme of this report was "Change,"
reflecting both the public offering of a
$7 billion financial services organization and
the company's rapid transformation from a
traditional life insurer (Sun Life Insurance
Company of America) to a marketer of
investment-oriented products addressing
the fastest growing market segment.

As communicated in the Annual Report,
Broad, Inc. shareholders approved a
new corporate name for the company –
SunAmerica – to capitalize on the strong
brand identification we built through recent
years under the Sun Life USA banner.
In 1998, the company was acquired by
American International Group (AIG).

1. Real Estate Developers and Investors
2. Home Builder and Financial Services Company

1

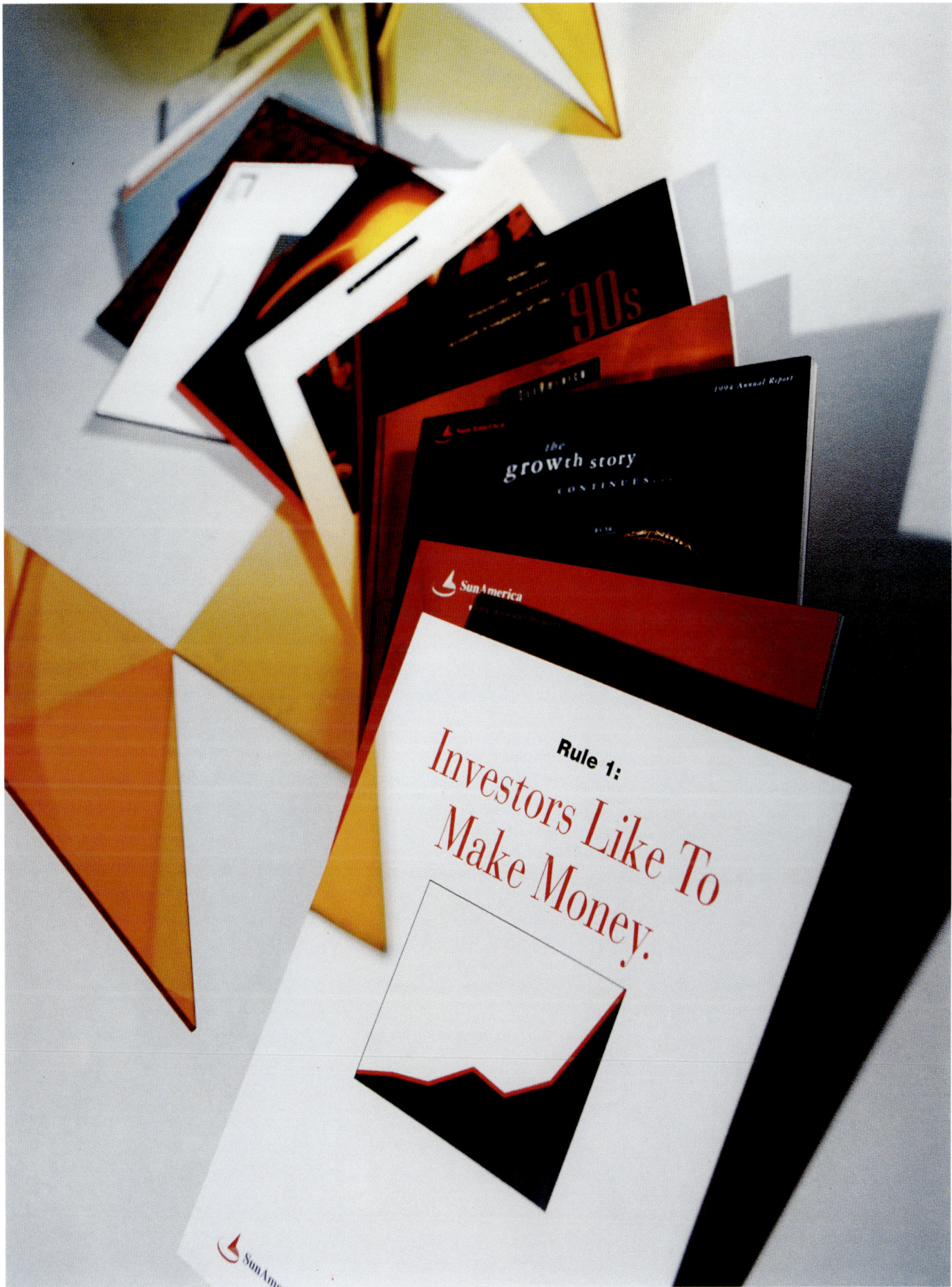

'90s

1994 Annual Report

the
growth story
CONTINUES...

SunAmerica

Rule 1:
Investors Like To
Make Money.

SunAmerica

Libera Design Inc.

A Growth Company Has to Grow.

Sanmina is a leading contract manufacturer
serving the fastest-growing segments of the
$95 billion global electronics manufacturing
services market.

Since Sanmina went public in 1993,
Libera Design has produced annual report
artwork that has served as a total system of
designed communications tools to reach
customers and the investment community.
As Sanmina has expanded, the market it
serves has itself grown and changed. Our
challenge has been to create encompassing
concepts that support the company's visual
presentation for shareholder and marketing
documents, continue to build the company's
brand, and keep the company's image
current and relevant to customer needs.

Sanmina is proficient at integrating new
acquisitions, while maintaining its high
standard of customer service. This is evident
in the company's financial performance,
as well as in its innovative new image and
communications documents.

1. Electronic Contract Manufacturer
2. Software / Hardware Companies

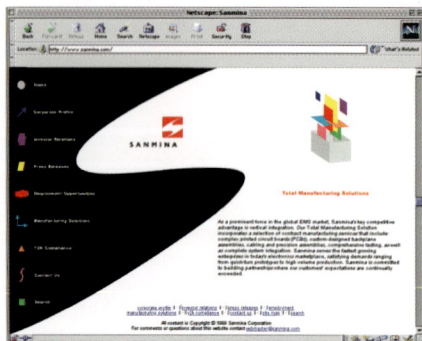

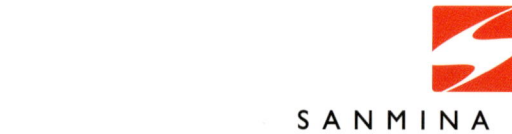

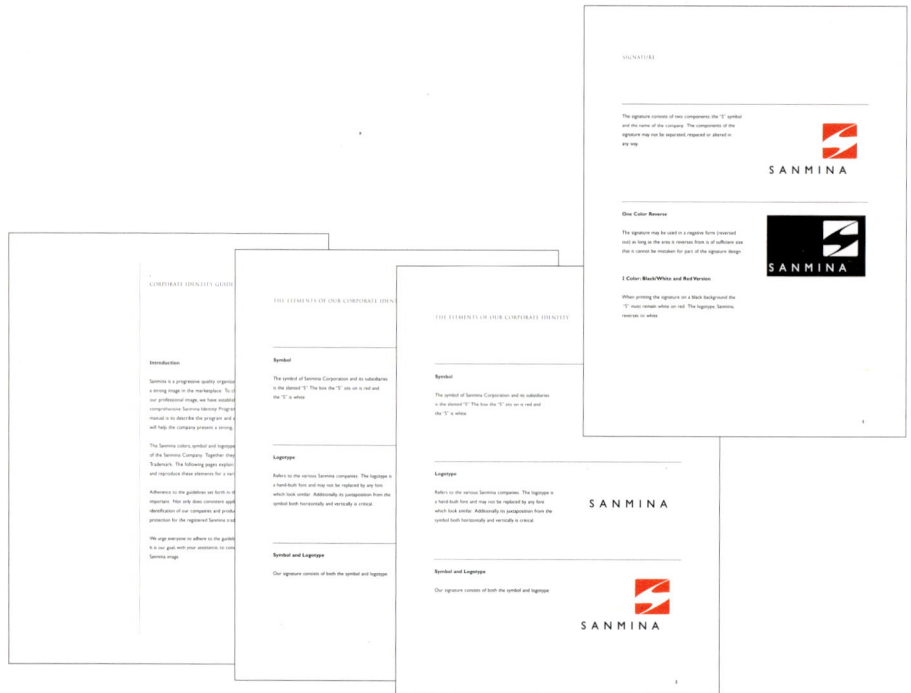

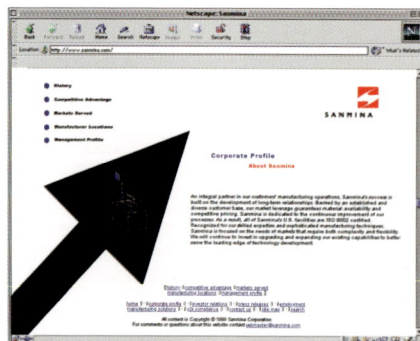

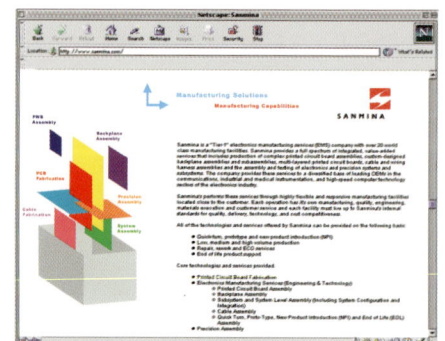

1

2

Libera Design Inc.

1

It's All in the Balance.

From basic industries such as aluminum ingots, steel, pipelines to new emerging technologies in medicine and "the .coms," each Libera Design is tailored to the precise needs of the client.

A design firm is a third-party resource. We see things from an outside perspective more like the audience with whom it needs to communicate.

The design firm and the client, we find need to "co-produce" each project. The fundamentals of co-production are partnership, mutual trust and effective communication. These are the keys to balance.

1. Medical and Financial Service Companies
2. Industrial Corporations
3. Emerging Technology Companies

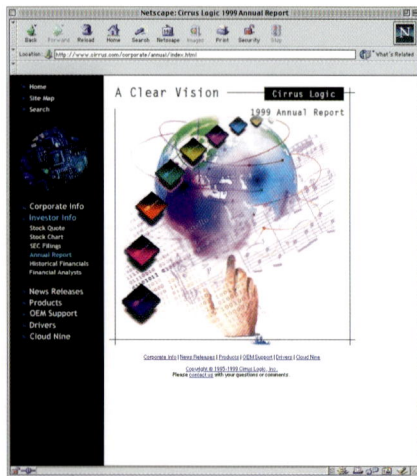

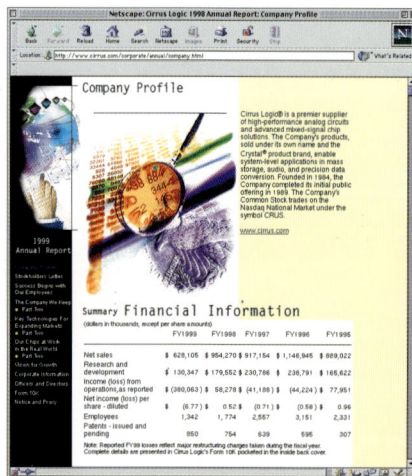

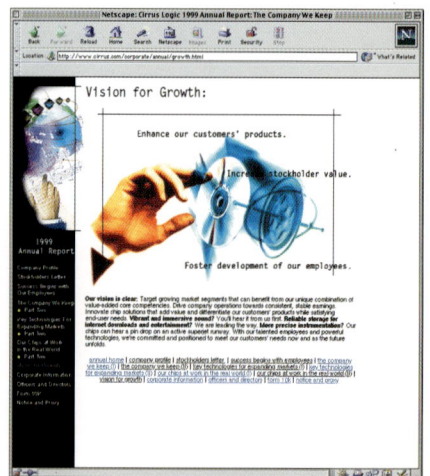

PharmaPrint

SIGMA

Xerox Electronic Printing

2

3

KAISER RESOURCES INC.

1

2

3

Image is Everything.

With a client base ranging from Borland to Litton Industries, Spelling Productions to SunAmerica / Kaufman & Broad, the Los Angeles International Airport to OnSale.com, ARCO to UCLA Extension, the audience for Libera's projects is quite diverse. Whether the project is an annual report, web site, brochure, announcement, or corporate identity program, it invites audiences to interact with the visual.

Libera Design has won numerous national financial and design awards, including honors from Financial World, NIRI, the Mead Annual Report Show, the New York Art Directors Club, American Institute of Graphic Arts, The American Center for Design and the Art Directors Club of Los Angeles. Joan Libera is a member of the American Institute of Graphic Arts, The American Center for Design, NIRI and has served on the board of directors of the Art Directors Club of Los Angeles. She also has addressed and hosted groups from such institutions as USC and Pepperdine University.

1. Banking, Foundations, Universities and Airports
2. Promotional Calendars
3. Branding and Packaging

Hilton
International
Hotel

SUSHI GIRL

VENICE
ART WALK

Madeleine Corson Design
25 Zoe Street
San Francisco CA 94107
415-777-2492
415-495-6495 fax

MADELEINE CORSON DESIGN

Madeleine Corson creates graphic communications that are as intellectually precise as they are visually distinctive. Her attention to every element – typography, color, line – results in meaningful solutions characterized by an immaculate elegance. Corson also manages to imbue her impeccable solutions with a liveliness and warmth – traits that further distinguish her portfolio.

Having gained early experience working with some of San Francisco's leading design and architectural firms, Ms. Corson opened Madeleine Corson Design in 1985. As principal, she has continually broadened the scope of the firm's work to include book and poster design, marketing collateral, packaging for both retail and software products, and comprehensive image programs.

Since its inception, Madeleine Corson Design has received national and international recognition and has satisfied a wide range of clients, producing highly effective communications for both corporate and non-profit companies alike. Recent clients include National Geographic, Cantor Arts Center at Stanford University, Frog's Leap Winery, and Oracle Corporation.

Ms. Corson believes that strong graphic solutions evolve from keen, intuitive observation. This highly committed firm takes a hands-on approach, beginning each project with only one assumption: that everything matters. The information gathering process is meticulous, and with Ms. Corson creatively driving every project, the quality of the design is consistently high. The resulting communication, whether it be an identity system, product packaging, or an environmental signage program, is wholly engaging and never fails to convey an insightful (and often times inspiring) point of view.

CALIFORNIA
DESIGN LIBRARY

CALIFORNIA
DESIGN LIBRARY

B E D R O O M S

Diane Dorrans Saeks

B A T H R O O M S

Diane Dorrans Saeks

CALIFORNIA
DESIGN LIBRARY

CALIFORNIA
DESIGN LIBRARY

K I T C H E N S

Diane Dorrans Saeks

L I V I N G   R O O M S

Diane Dorrans Saeks

1

SACRED
BOND black
men and their mothers
by keith m brown

2

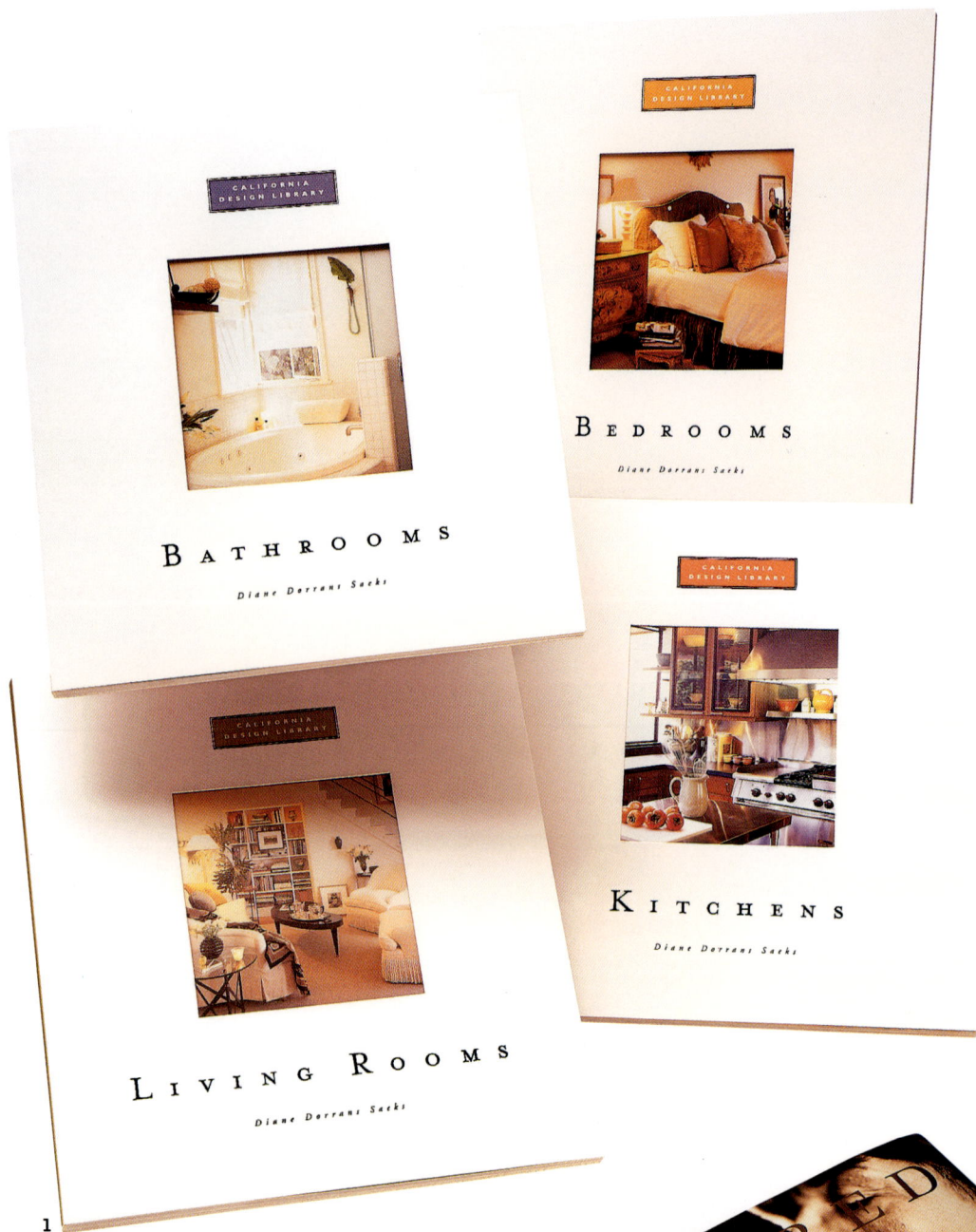

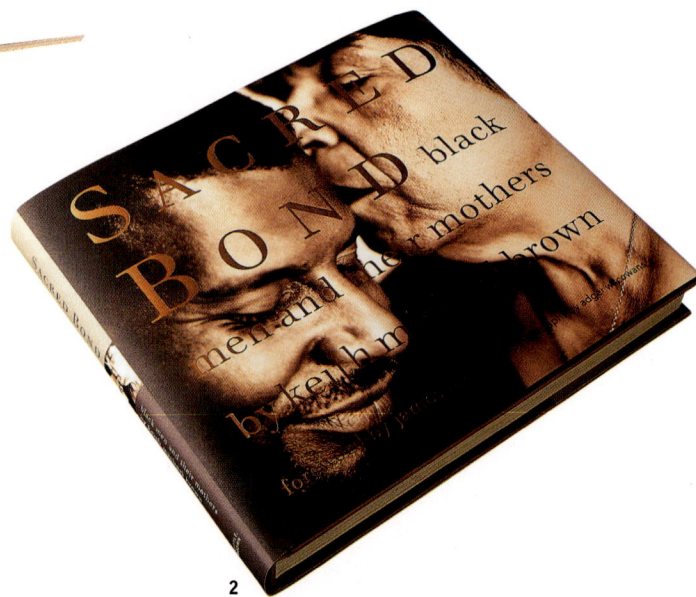

1. A contemporary West Coast style series entitled *California Design Library Series: Kitchens, Bathrooms, Living Rooms, Bedrooms.*

2. *Sacred Bond,* a book revealing the personal histories of black men and their relationships with their mothers.

3. *The Art of National Geographic: A Century of Illustration,* a 240-page collection featuring works from the Society's archives.

4. Brand packaging for a line of sport towels.

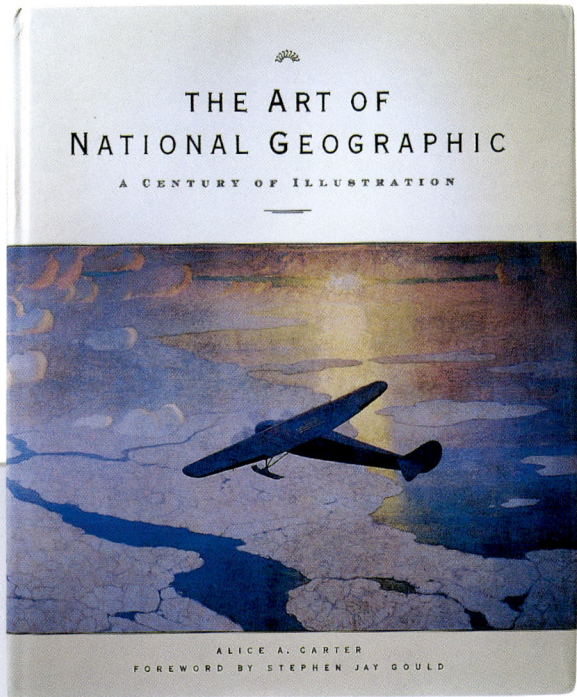

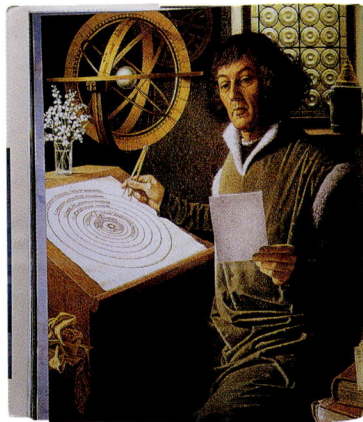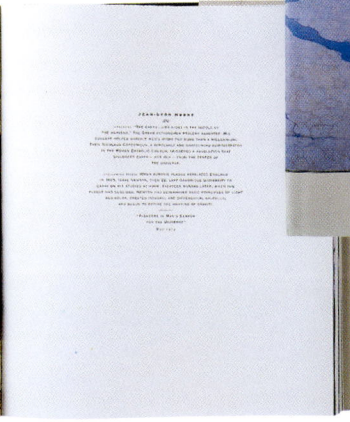

3

4

1

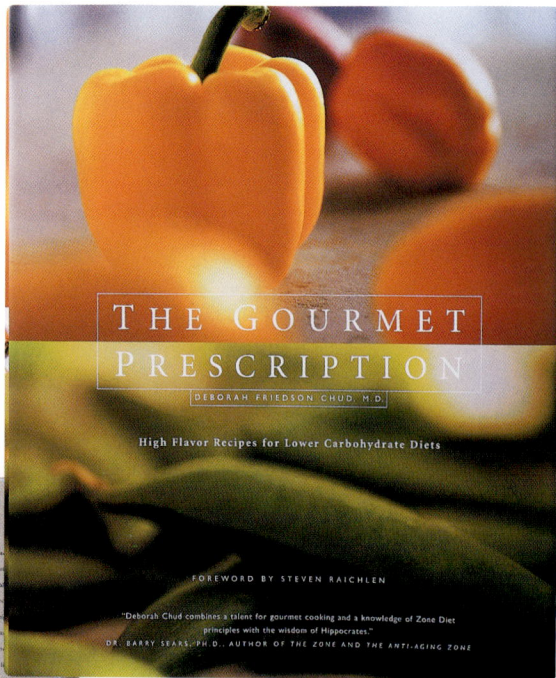

2

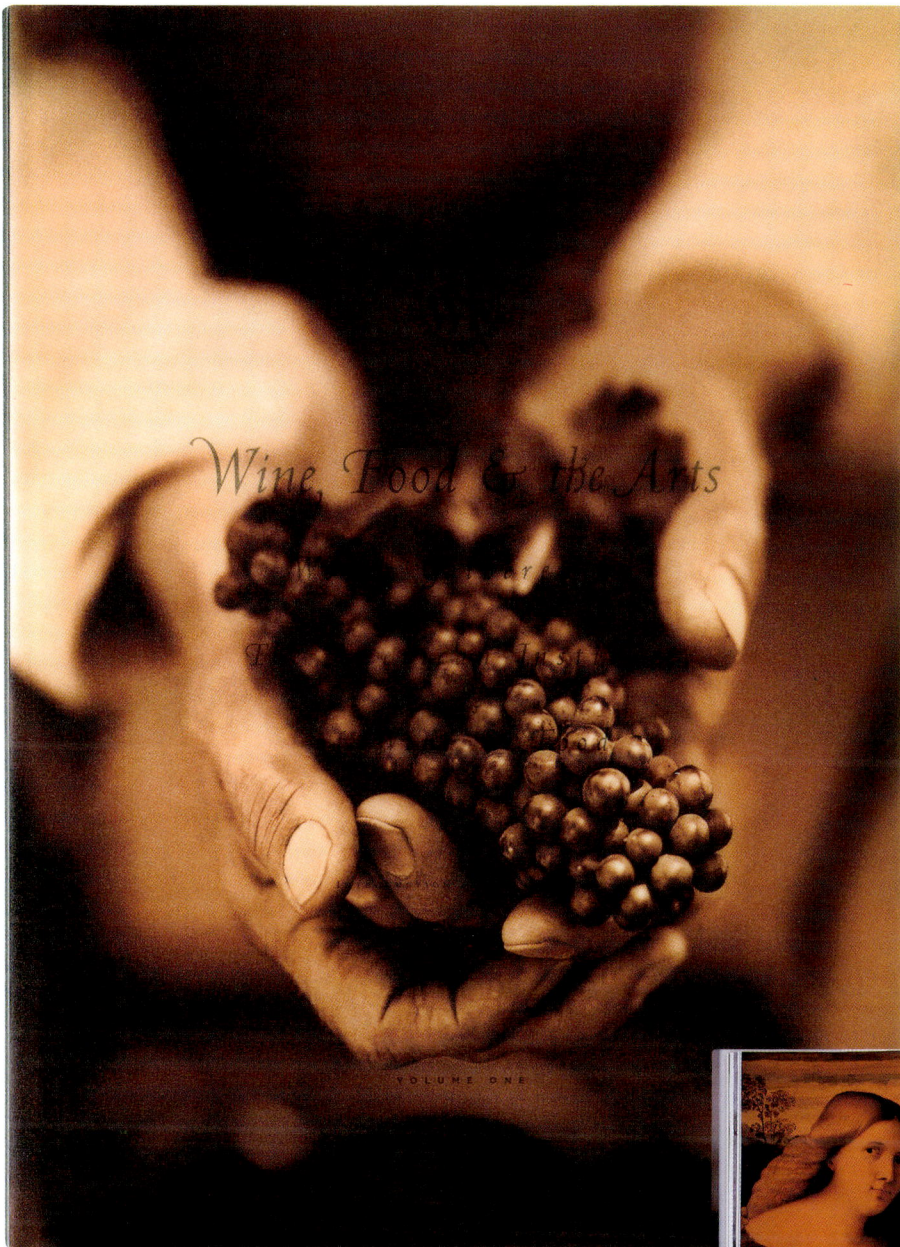

3

1. A book of recipes entitled *The Gourmet Prescription*.
2. Chalk Hill's Estate Vineyard Selection engraved bottle label and shipping carton.
3. The American Institute of Wine, Food & the Arts' 112-page annual featuring the fare of writers, artists, chefs and food historians.

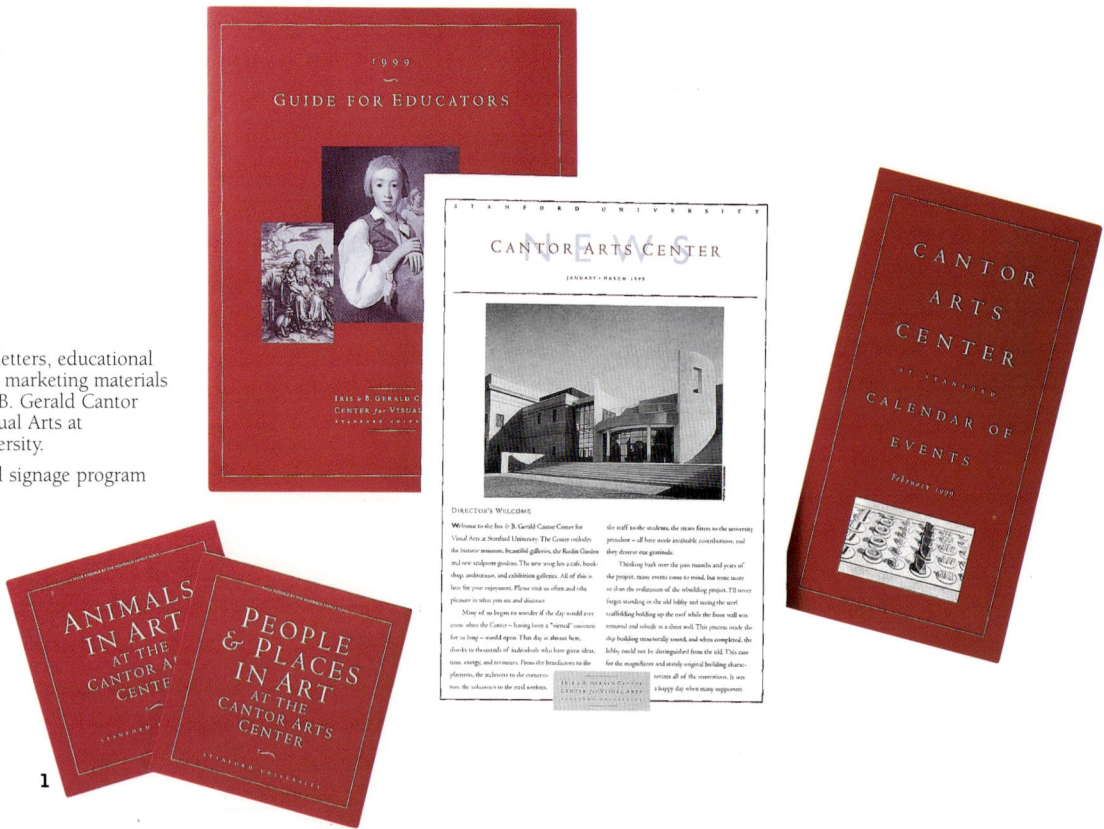

1. Identity, newsletters, educational brochures and marketing materials for the Iris & B. Gerald Cantor Center for Visual Arts at Stanford University.
2. Environmental signage program for the Center.

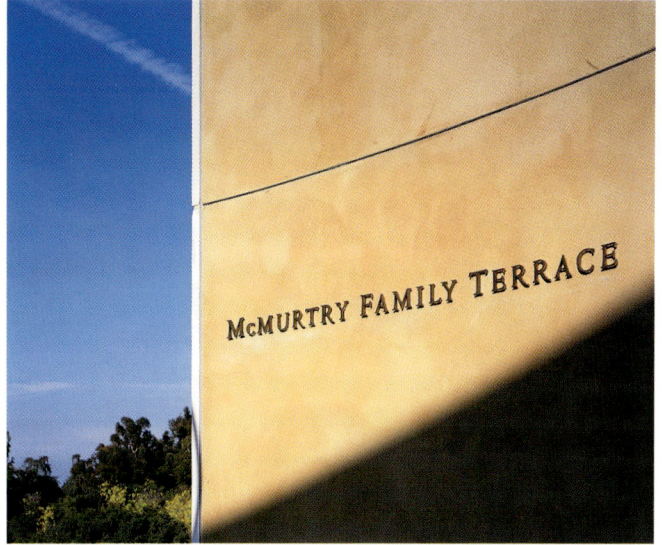

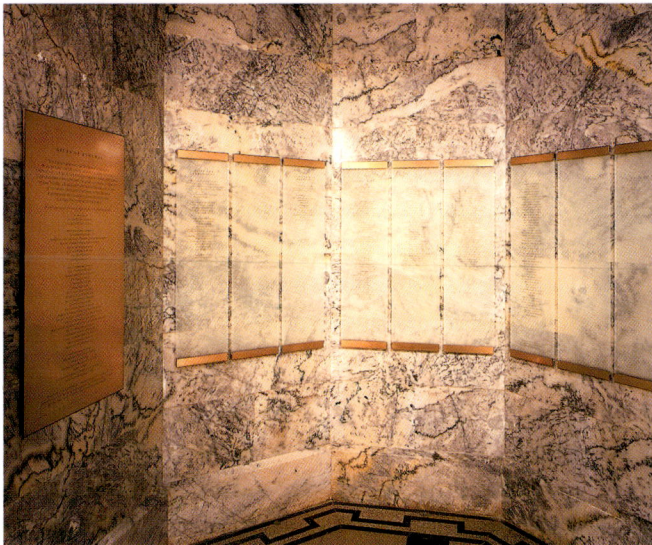

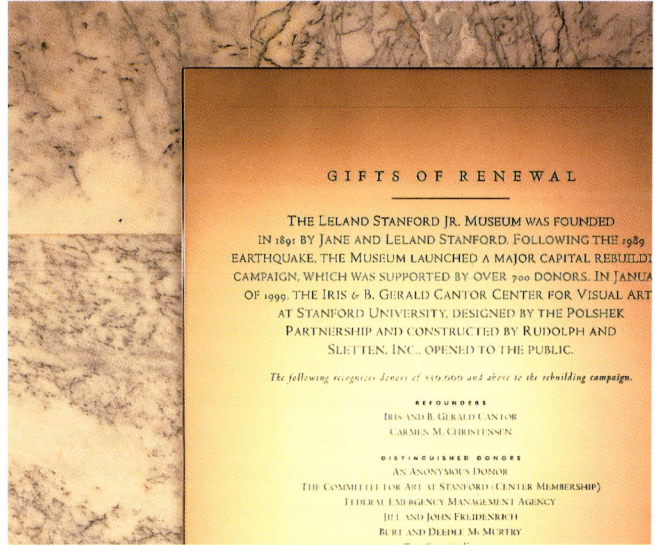

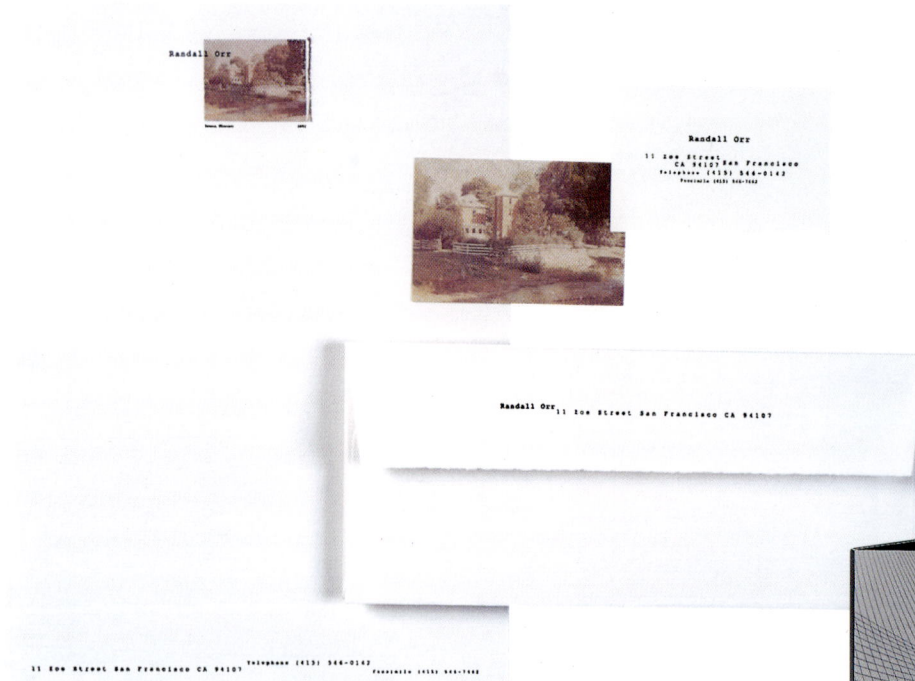

1

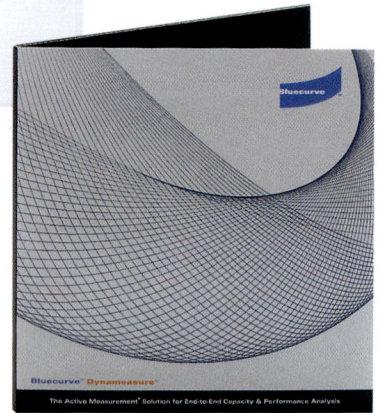

2

3

1. Letterhead system for a fine arts photographer.
2. Identity and product packaging for Bluecurve, Inc., a software company.
3. Event calendar series for Theater Artaud, a performing arts organization.

Follis Design
927 Weimar Avenue
Altadena, California 91001
626.792.3590
follisdesign@earthlink.net

FOLLIS DESIGN

One of the oldest architectural graphic design firms in Southern California, Follis Design has contributed to the design and development of architectural signing and environmental graphics since 1960.

The firm was originally established by John Follis as John Follis and Associates, and today is headed by his son, Grant Follis. They are considered pioneers in the field, and continue to specialize in graphic design for architectural environments.

Consulting services are offered for all phases of work associated with architectural signing, as well as special projects. Services include: image/identity development, analysis and communication planning, way-finding, sign programming, ADA sign code issues, building and life safety signing, conceptual design, design development, design documentation, obtain bids for fabrication, preparation of final art and inspection during fabrication and installation.

Their experience is diversified among projects ranging from museums to cathedrals to convention centers. The following images illustrate this diversity and the ability to successfully meet the unique requirements of each client.

The firm's dedication to fine architectural signing and environmental graphic design is founded in the philosophy of recognizing the individual challenges of each client and responding to individual needs. Respect for architecture is given foremost consideration, complementing the design with appropriate form and color, yet avoiding certain elements for the sake of current trends.

Follis Design strives for a fresh and contemporary solutions that enhance the environment with stated restraint, functionality, and endurance over a given period of time.

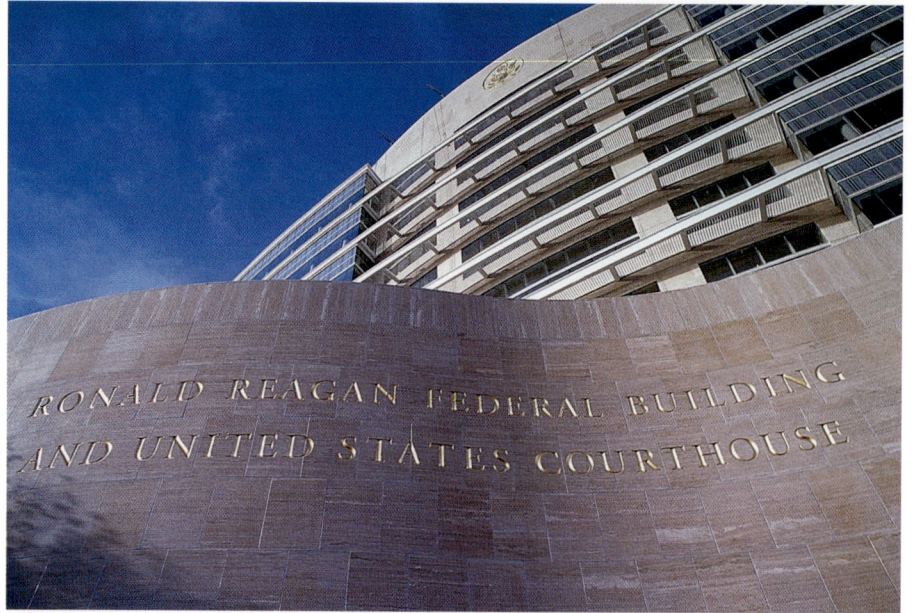

1

2

3

1 - 4. Ronald Reagan Federal Building
and United States Courthouse

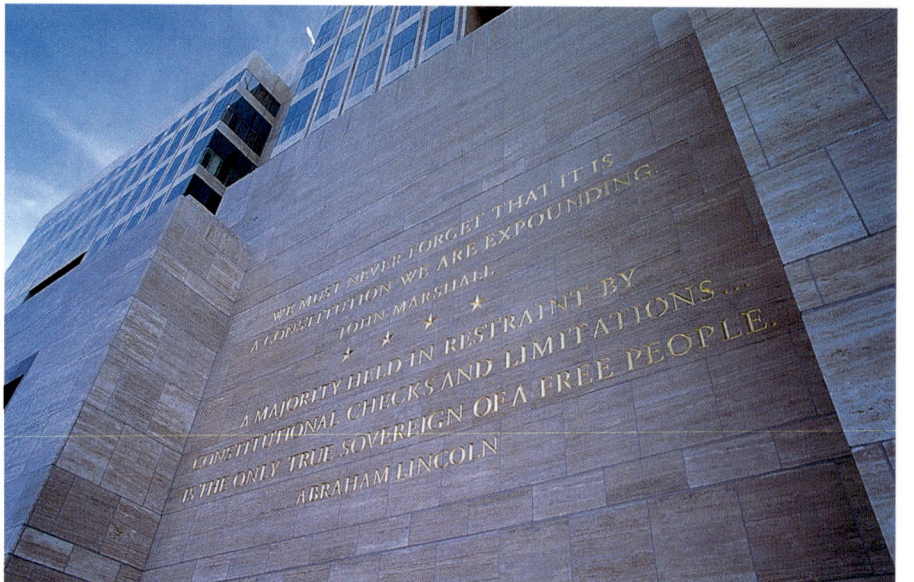

4

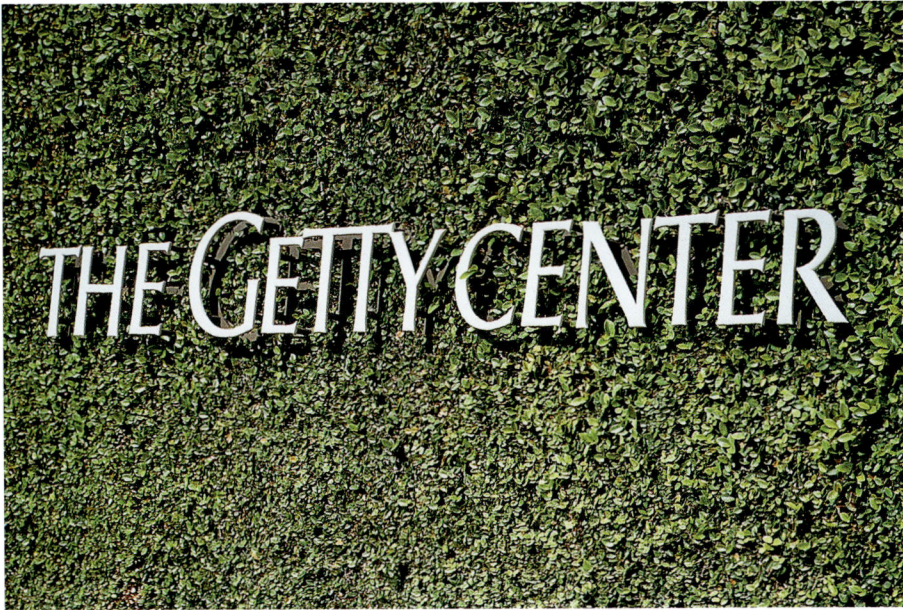

1

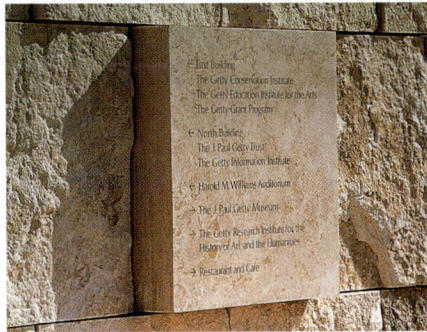

2

3

4

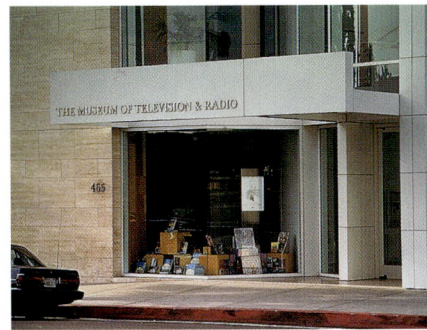

5

6

1 - 4. The Getty Center, in collaboration with
Saul Bass, Bass Yager & Associates
5. Museum of Television and Radio, CA
6. Gagosian Gallery, CA

1

1 - 3. Long Beach Memorial Medical Center
4.   Rose Hills Memorial Park & Mortuary

2

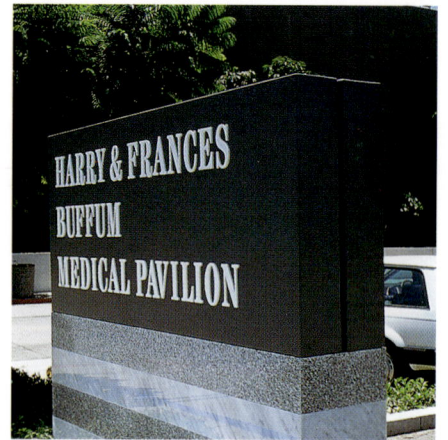

3

4

1

2

3

1.   Los Angeles Convention Center
2 - 3. Supermarine, Santa Monica Airport
4 - 5. Queen of the Valley Hospital

4

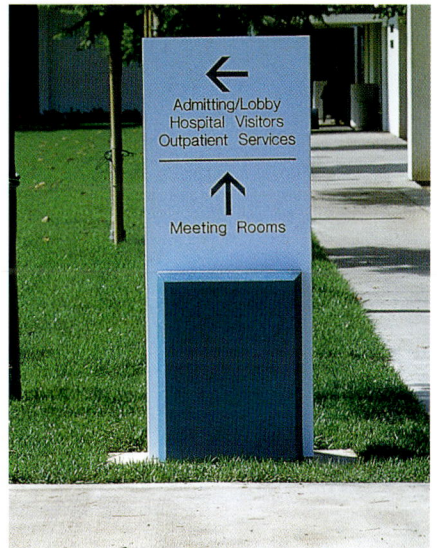

5

1 - 3. Natural History Museum, Los Angeles
4 - 5. Nestle Corporate Dining Room

1

2

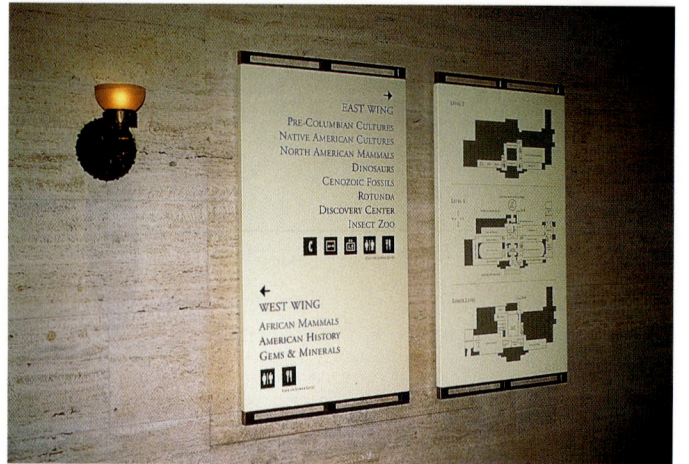

3

4

5

1

1 - 4. Ontario Convention Center, CA

2

3

4

1

2

3

4

5

1. Supermarine, Santa Monica Airport
2 - 4. Downtown Manhattan Beach, CA
5. Curtis School
6. Ahamonson Training Center,
    Los Angeles Police Department

6